How To Grow Up When You're Grown Up

Achieving Balance in Adulthood

Also by Nancy O 'Connor

Letting Go With Love: The Grieving Process

HOW TO GROW UP WHEN YOU'RE GROWN UP

Achieving Balance in Adulthood

NANCY O'CONNOR Ph.D.

La Mariposa Press
Tucson, Arizona

Cover designed by David Fisher

LA MARIPOSA PRESS
P.O. BOX 13221 TUCSON, ARIZONA 85732-3221
TELEPHONE (602)326-9292 FAX (602)326-3305

First Edition
First Printing May, 1994

Library of Congress Cataloging-in-Publication Data
O'Connor, Nancy, 1933-
How to grow up when you're grown up:
achieving balance in adulthood / Nancy O'Connor
p. cm.
Includes Index.
Preassigned LCCN: 94-075168.
ISBN 0-9613714-5-5 (pbk.)
ISBN 0-9613714-6-3 (hard.)

1. Self-actualization (Psychology)   1. Title
BF697. 036 1994   158'.1
                                    QB194-343
           10-9-8-7-6-5-4-3-2-
Printed in the United States of America

Dedication

This book is for my three
wonderful sons, Timothy, Daniel,
and Joseph who are the loves of
my life. They have been constant
and accepting in their love and
support of me even though I
was still growing up while I
was raising them. And to my
healthy and loved grandchildren
Caitlin, Colin, Garrett, and Keegan.

CONTENTS

Foreward

Forward

There is a Hebrew word that embraces the value of this book: **Shalom.** There is no adequate English translation of this all-encompassing all-embracing human experience of wholeness. Perhaps Shalom is realized by *Growing-Up*, by becoming our best and highest self.

That is what this book is all about. It addresses the process of growing into mature, wise human beings whose lives can be expressions of joy, balance and peace. It shows you how to reach beyond the fears and obstacles in living life that we all experience into wholeness , not just personal wholeness, but planetary wholeness.

This is not just a book you read, it is a book you do, a participatory interaction between body, spirit, emotions, and intellect. The result?...Balance.....within and without. Such balance creates a new you and a new world.....a world of adults who have *Grown Up.*

Dr. P. David Wilkinson Rel. D

Tucson, Arizona

February , 1994

Acknowledgments

So many people have been teachers for me and contributed to my personal growth and knowledge, including family, friends, and clients. Some of the lessons have been learned kicking and screaming and others joyfully, like the births of two new grandchildren in this past year.

I am appreciative and grateful to those writers who have gone before me and shared their wisdom in their own works. I humbly stand on their shoulders, and hopefully go a little beyond.

I am blessed with three loving surrogate mothers who have adopted me and give me unconditional love, something my own Mother could not do. They are Cruz Murietta, Myra Miller-Smith, and Beatrice Archer.

My efforts in writing and publishing this book span seven years of writing, research, and work squeezed into a very busy private practice. Any reference to clients are composite of several people rolled into one. There are so many stories to tell. So much healing and growth to rejoice over. Thank you all for the contributions you have made to my growth.

I appreciate and especially want to thank and acknowledge those people who have made a direct contribution to this book. They are: Carol Sowell for her editorial work, Nicole Miller and David Fisher for the cover design, Jan Ripberger and Dennis O'Neil for computer assistance above and beyond the call of duty, Jody O'Connor and Jessica Christian for reading the manuscript in great detail, and finally to David Wilkinson for his example, support and encouragement. Without their unselfish and heroic efforts this book would still be a dusty manuscript.

I also want to acknowledge Sigo Press for their interest and support.

PART ONE

GROWTH AND GROWING UP

To Dare

To laugh is to risk appearing the fool

To weep is to risk appearing sentimental

To reach for another is to risk involvement

To expose your ideas, your dreams, before a crowd is to risk their loss

To love is to risk not being loved in return

To live is to risk dying

To believe is to risk failure

But risks must be taken, because the greatest hazard in life is to risk nothing

The people who risk nothing, do nothing, have nothing, are nothing

They may avoid suffering and sorrow, but they cannot learn, feel, grow, love, live

Chained by their attitudes, they are slaves: they have forfeited their freedom.

Only a person who risks is free.

Anonymous

CHAPTER ONE

WHAT DOES GROWING UP MEAN?

Eight-year-old Carin held the black crayon tightly in her clutched fist and made firm bold lines on the paper I had just given her to draw on. She looked at me defiantly and said ,"I'll never grow up I don't want to grow up and you can't make me!" "Okay " I said, "You don't have to grow up until you are ready to. Can you tell me what is so bad about growing up?" I gently prodded her. She exchanged her black crayon for a red one signaling me that her sadness had changed to anger. She surrounded the black center lines with bold red circles, drawing circle after circle before she answered me. "Because it hurts too much", she said quietly with her head down and eyes averted. I waited to see if she would say more, "And I don't like the things grown ups do", defiant again, eyes flashing, "especially the things they do to kids". "Did a grownup hurt you Carin?" She hesitated then slowly said "Yes". "Would you like to tell me about it?" I said in a soothing voice. She put the paper and crayons down, hung her head and said, "You will think I am a bad girl and you won't like me any more if I tell you". I said, "Carin, I know that you are not a bad girl. You are a very good girl. Sometimes bad things happen to children, but that doesn't mean that the child is bad. There is nothing that you can tell me that will cause me to not like you, so now you can tell me what happened."

She closed her eyes and silent tears began to stream down her cheeks as she told me what her stepfather did the first time he molested her in the barn in a stack of newly mowed hay. She remembered and relived that painful event, healing herself in the process. That was 37 years ago. It was the first sexual assault and it lasted for six years on a weekly basis until she ran away from home at age 14. After all those years the emotional wounds were still raw and painful and needed to be healed before she could ever grow up.

Carin was the youngest of eight personalities who were fragmented parts of one of the clients that I have been treating. After 15 months of therapy Carin was refusing to fuse with the other parts. The others had worked through the painful memories and traumatic events that caused them to split apart into separate personality ego states. Carin needed to remember and to feel the pain of her helplessness, fear, and rage she had to repress when her stepfather raped her.

Her fear of remembering and telling someone about this was locked behind walls of shame and guilt. The grief and sadness at the core of her being were revealed in the bold black lines in her drawing. The red circles told me that we needed to deal with the rage she felt before we could get to the grief issues. Until she grieved for her stolen childhood innocence, her lack of choice, her helplessness, and the betrayal of her by the adults in her life, she could never grow up, and the 45-year-old woman who was sitting in my cozy office week after week would never grow up either.

Growing up is a process. It is something that we are engaged in for our entire lives. It is a process that sometimes finds us bouncing back and forth between responsible, mature behavior and irresponsible, childish behavior.

Like any other process human growth is always changing. Sometimes the change is subtle and slow, even feels stalled. Other times it hits us like a tornado, creating turmoil in every part of our life, challenging all our reserve and resources to survive.

At times we are confidant, calm and together. Other times we lose our cool and fly into an immature rage over some small affront and feel ashamed of our loss-of-control and childishness. The anger that is triggered by some person or event is our clue that we need to look inside and to work on something within because at that moment we are not grown up.

HOW DO YOU KNOW IF YOU'RE GROWN UP?

Are you grown up when you've reached your full height? Pass your 21st, 40th or maybe your 65th birthday? Or, when you pay bills, hold down a job, have children to raise? What does being grown-up mean to you? Doing things because you have to even if you don't want to? Paying taxes and helping kids with their homework? Fixing things around the house, facing a never-ending mountain of dirty clothes and dirty dishes? Rushing here and there to satisfy the needs and demands of others? Reluctantly adjusting to more and more stress in a busy life?

Yes, those are all things that grownups do. But just because you do all those adult things doesn't mean that you --the person you carry around inside you -- are completely grown-up all the time.

You have moments, or days, when you remember more carefree times from your childhood without all of the demands and deadlines to meet. You long for enough time for yourself to rest and regenerate.

There are times when you check that face in the mirror for new wrinkles or the latest gray hairs and ask yourself, "What am I doing. How did I get all this responsibility. I can't handle it all. And how did it happen so fast. I'm not ready for this. I want to be a kid again. Free and having fun."

These thoughts make us want to run away from being grown up. It isn't as much fun as we had hoped. Sometimes that little kid inside you feels resentful or afraid. Perhaps the new boss at work makes you unaccountably nervous, and you realize he looks or sounds a little like your father. Or you are supposed to make an important decision or presentation or take a test, and you find yourself chewing your nails, watching television mindlessly or drinking too much to avoid the dreaded task.

A crisis may trigger a realization that you don't feel grown up enough to cope. The child who still lives within you and always will, is frightened, bored or mad. In fact you may have several little kids within you, or one little kid with many moods different ages and faces. You may have kids that like to play and have fun all of the time, you may have one who is sad, wants to cry a lot and does so at sad movies, especially when people show genuine love for each other, another who is suicidal and hurts himself, another that is a joker and hides anger behind jokes and thinly veiled sarcasm, one who eats or drinks too much or uses drugs to escape internal pain, another one who is sexually promiscuous and gets you involved in relationships that are doomed to failure and pain. There may be others that continue to surface and sabotage your adult life.

This book is written to show how getting to recognize, know, nurture and heal these little kids within us can facilitate becoming a mature adult, feeling happy and joyful, fulfilled, balanced and peaceful within. It gives us a chance to make important strides toward growing up.

Just as Carin had to remember, express and feel the feelings she couldn't feel at the time of her rapes. You may have to dig into your past life, however painful, to heal your old pain and put it behind you, and to allow you to grow up and to liberate your adult.

When you occasionally explode from built-up stress and attack your children or your spouse, your best friend, or your pet, you can hurt the ones you love most by displacing your anger on them and then feeling guilty later after you calm down.

And how long have you been trying to find the courage to tell your parents to get their noses out of your business? Sometimes they still treat you like a child. Or you still feel like a child in their presence even though they try to treat you like an adult.

How grown up do you feel at times like those? Do they remind you of a familiar little kid who found the world a scary place?

Then how about the times when you forget you're a grownup now and act like a kid just for the joy of it? You leap into a big pile of leaves, or yell like crazy about a football game on TV, or spend an hour giggling over a silly movie. You feel like a kid again, just for a little while. And it feels good.

If you have times like these, are you really grown up? Does growing up mean you can't play or have fun any more? Not at all. Being grown up doesn't mean that you are serious all of the time. You can balance your life between work and play.

GROWTH IS FOR GROWNUPS TOO

When I was young I believed the myth that I would be all grown up when I reached the age of 21. I also thought that adults automatically had all the right feelings, thoughts, and ideas, and always made the right decisions. I believed that from that magic time on I would always have grown-up thoughts and feelings, make correct decisions, and know all the answers.

But, you and I both know by now that it doesn't happen that way. Not when you're 18 or 21 -- or even 35, 58, or 75, we don't know all the right answers, in fact we often don't even know the right questions. And more often than not, when we make the right decision it's just a lucky guess. The best that any of us can do is to take life as it comes, using what we've learned through the years to answer each new question and problem as it arises.

Grownups start being smart when they realize there isn't always one right answer. Rather we have options and choices to be made from these options. Sometimes it becomes the "lessor of the evils" type of choices. Other times we have to make hard choices about good things, like two wonderful job offers that come in on the same day.

Growing up is something that you do all your life, no matter how long that life turns out to be. The journey is full of paradoxes. You reach the end of your journey only when you die. And like many people, you may make the entire trip without ever growing up.

On this journey of life, there will be times when you want to run away. Especially on those days when you feel overwhelmed by all the responsibilities of the family, neighborhood, job and so on. You are bound to have moments of fear and insecurity about your ability to cope and at times you may want to run away, to escape.

Here's the good news! Being grown up doesn't mean you have to do everything right all the time. Being a grownup just means you have to do the best you can for as much of the time as you can. All of us have areas of our lives in which we can do better. Facing these challenges leads to true growth and change.

The process of growing up means that you leave behind the worst parts of childhood -- the dependency, fears, and lack of self-control, not having choices but, you keep the best parts -- like being spontaneous, laughing, loving, giving, playing, and having fun.

This book will help you identify how grown up you are: in what ways you are less mature than you could be; what patterns are keeping you from growing up; and what techniques you can apply to move yourself along the pathway to adulthood. You can finish the job that your parents and teachers started, in fact, you have to finish it -- that is the basic task of living. In the long run, you're the one responsible for your own maturity, parents and teachers were only in charge of you for a few years. Don't let all this adult responsibility depress you. Being grown up is not all duties and hard work. Growing up is what gives life meaning. As you take on real responsibility for all your decisions and actions, you become your Self; the best Self you can be. As a grownup, you have choices and opportunities to achieve, to contribute, to serve others, to create, to save the world and to say, "This is who I am. I like myself. If you don't like me, it doesn't matter much, because I am becoming the best person I can be."

As a grownup, you know who you are, and you have learned to accept yourself with all your warts, fears, and failings, and to take pride in the things that you do well. You give up expecting everyone else to like and approve of you and to accept you because you know that you are okay just the way you are right now.

THE ABILITY TO RESPOND APPROPRIATELY

I have used the word Responsibility often in painting this picture of a grownup. *Responsibility is* the key concept in understanding what it is to be grown up. It essentially means *the ability to respond appropriately to whatever happens in your life.*

Grownups take responsibility for what happens in their lives. Grownups know you can't always control events, or other people, but you do have choices in how you respond to situations. You don't avoid this responsibility to change, to learn, to adapt, to accept.

Grownups know that the time comes to give up childhood fantasies and expectations. If your spouse, your job, your children, your life aren't perfect, they are nonetheless yours, and full of rich possibilities for joy and love. Grownups know when to hang in there and work out solvable problems, and they know when to leave, grieve, and start over.

Grownups have confidence in themselves. They acknowledge their errors and accept their limitations and weaknesses. They take credit for their accomplishments and pride in their strengths. They improve what is worth the effort of changing, and don't agonize over things that are impossible or unimportant to change.

THE CHILDREN WITHIN

Remember those little kids that I talked about before? Inside every adult are little children, at times insecure, frightened, uncertain, needy. These younger parts of you always look for the same things -- love, approval, acceptance, safety, security. Your inner child wants to be taken care of. The child in you struggles between dependence and independence and sometimes wants to escape from responsibility. These old needs surface most often in stressful situations, conflicts, and crises.

Being grown up is largely a process of keeping the little children in check, and at the same time nurturing them. These children are more of your responsibilities, just like the children you are raising. If any child within you is indulged and allowed to make all the decisions, it may not always choose wisely. Your adult part has to choose for your inner child's best interests. You have to control that child -- its wants, fears, impulses, needs, and drives -- with love, patience, understanding. You need to become to yourself the wise loving parent that you didn't have. You have to support and encourage your inner children to grow up.

Why does this little child keep interfering with your growing up process? Shouldn't we, at some point, put all that childhood foolishness behind us and get on with the serious business of life? Clients frequently tell me that the past is over and should be forgotten. When I hear this I know that they are in one form of denial or another and are looking for a quick fix to relieve them of a temporary misery.

Forgetting the past may be a great approach in theory, but it simply isn't in human nature to cut ourselves off from our past. We spend most of our adult lives dealing with the myths, illusions, disappointments, hurts, neglect, abuses, and separations of our childhoods. Even with the most sensitive parents, children experience trauma. Well-meaning parents can't protect their children from every hurt in life. The nature of protecting and socializing your children can lead to unrealistic expectations about what is available in life, especially when children are over-protected. It is a fine line that parents walk between allowing children to deal with life's disappointments and protecting them from abusive situations.

What is also sad but true is that most of us were raised by parents who were damaged and hurt in their own childhoods and they had no clue how to raise happy, healthy children.

Adulthood is the time to set aside the grim tales of childhood along with the fairy-tale fantasies. You learn that things aren't as perfect as those bedtime stories promised or as horrible as your early traumas warned. Life's events are interesting and worthwhile. You must say good night to Dr. Seuss and Mother Goose, stop dwelling on whatever monsters and wicked witches were present in your childhood. It's time to write your own happy endings.

The best news about growing up is that, because it is a process, you can see yourself making progress all the time. Every step you take in the direction of emotional maturity, self-sufficiency, and accepting responsibility for your actions brings you closer to a more rewarding and fulfilling life. If you're committed to becoming more grown up, your life will just keep getting better and better.

The bad news is that you will never get there and stay there all the time. Issues based on that little child's fears and needs will continue to surface and make things complicated. For instance, the grown-up you wants to do the responsible thing and reduce expenses so you can pay bills, while the child in you wants to have fun and go on an expensive vacation using charge accounts. The grown-up you knows that staying with a husband who frequently beats you is painful and wrong while the helpless child in you keeps saying maybe you deserve his abuse or it's easier just to stay and hope that, magically, one day he'll change.

Even though you'll never reach perfection as a grownup, there is a bright side to the ongoing struggle. Each of these conflicts or issues presents you with a new, challenging opportunity to learn, another chance to face the problem areas in your life, resolve old conflicts, and change cast-in-concrete behavior patterns. Another chance to become more grown up.

STRIVING FOR BALANCE

Growing up is not really a matter of reaching a certain place in life that can be labeled as adult, and then you've arrived. Growing up is a question of balance -- taking care of the various parts of yourself so that they stay in balance with each other. When you feel your life is out of whack, when it's not working effectively, it's a signal that you need some adjustment in your balance. We get out of balance when one of four aspects of being human is taking over the other parts of our lives or is being seriously neglected.

These four aspects are: physical, emotional, intellectual, and spiritual. You can be mature or immature in any one or more of these areas. Even when you feel things are working well in two or three of those areas, if the other is lacking, you'll be out of balance.

Staying in balance can be quite a challenge. Sometimes an enjoyable and rewarding challenge, because losing your balance now and then isn't a disaster. It can be a sign that you need to do some more inner work and that you are ready to do more growing.

You've probably seen jugglers at a fair or circus, you were thrilled at that breathtaking moment when they got all the plates spinning at once. But how long did it last. A few seconds, maybe a whole minute at the most. The juggler inevitably drops something, or his legs or arms get tired, or the plates lose their built-up energy and stop spinning. Does the juggler retreat in disgrace? No, he simply accepts the applause of the crowd, picks up his plates, and starts them spinning again.

Trying to live the way you feel is best for you. You'll drop your plates now and then because the balancing act of being a grownup is difficult. But every time you notice yourself falling out of balance gives you another opportunity to improve your skills. Every difficult moment in your life offers you another chance to grow up a little more. As children, we call it growing up. As adults, we call it growth.

FEAR INTERFERES WITH GROWING UP

When you do things that don't make sense, things you know better than, things that keep you from growing up, things that don't fit your image of yourself -- they're usually motivated by some childhood fear. Fear is the bottom line element that holds us back. It's at the basis of all crippling emotions, like anger, depression, anxiety, shame, blame, self-pity, guilt, and despair.

Unexamined and unresolved irrational fears from childhood can be triggered by crises such as divorce, death of a loved one, being unemployed for a while, moving to a new town, or starting a new relationship. They can also be triggered by more subtle and simple things hidden from your awareness like the color pink, a baby crying, an article in the newspaper, hearing people yell at each other.

During such times we feel painfully vulnerable, easily hurt. But at the same time, the events that trigger fear also make us more open and receptive to making significant life changes that mean progress toward the growing-up goal. These triggers offer us an opportunity to explore and face our fears. Finding a good therapist to help you do this will speed up the process in a safe, accepting environment.

Remember crisis is an opportunity to learn, to grow, to face and cope with your fears. Rather than something to be afraid of, it's a chance to recognize, own, understand, and then let go of that fear.

LEARNING SELF-LOVE AND ACCEPTANCE

What happens when you start to give up your fears? If you learn how to travel along the pathway of growth and leave your fears behind one at a time, where will you wind up? Where are you going?

The place where the growth journey takes you is Love or Selfhood. Love--the place we'd all like to be, is the opposite of Fear. Love is a state of being where you feel at home, you are unafraid, safe, secure, and self-sufficient because you love yourself and believe in your ability to survive and take care of yourself.

You stop taking affronts from others personally. You realize they have problems too and can respond with compassion and understanding, rather than with defensiveness. You can listen without fixing and can share without fear of being judged.

Self acceptance means that you know from deep within yourself that you will continue to become the best person you can be, and that you like yourself.

CHAPTER TWO

GROWING IN ALL DIRECTIONS

Four inseparable parts of your Self -- physical, emotional, intellectual, and spiritual -- contribute to the balance and harmony of every human being. Any one of these can get out of balance with the others by being neglected, misused, overemphasized, or affected by an unexpected accident. At the same time, each can be a strength, giving us skills and resources to apply to solving problems in other areas.

Each of these aspects demands special attention at different times in our lives. For example, recently my friend lifted a heavy tool box and strained his lower back. He was immediately thrown out of balance. The severe pain he was suffering demanded that he focus all his energy and attention on his physical condition. Visiting a doctor, taking medication, and bed rest replaced his plans to paint the kitchen.

The painful muscle spasms he experienced called all his attention to his body. His emotions were heightened also as he felt frustration at having to change his plans. He became depressed as he felt helpless to change the situation rapidly. And he felt fear at a possible negative outcome, such as surgery to correct the problem.

He tried to use his mental abilities to read and study, but couldn't concentrate. He involved his spiritual self in his healing through meditation, relaxation against the pain, and visualizing his back as healed.

A week later he was back in commission. He painted the kitchen and was able to carry on in his usual responsible way -- once again in balance.

When a grownup is in harmony, all these elements merge and work together so smoothly you are not even aware of them as separate. You are in balance, you are whole. This harmony enables you to be the best you can be in every respect. You live with a sense of well-being and you know that you are moving forward with your life.

After we look at what being grown up means in each of these four dimensions of the Self, we'll look in more detail at how the four work together, and how you can learn to keep them in balance. For now, here are some of the concepts of growing up, and the things that interfere with the process, that we will be examining throughout the book.

SPIRITUAL GROWTH

Spirituality is the glue that holds all parts of the Self together. As human beings we all have an eternal essence, a spark that ignites life in our bodies and leaves when the body dies. Our life experiences move us to believe in something greater than ourselves. Modern and primitive people alike have had the same urges throughout all of recorded history to look beyond observable reality for answers to questions about meaning, life, and death.

Picture a hand with a glove on it. The glove is your physical body, and the hand is your essence or spirit. When the glove is removed, the hand remains. Most people on this planet believe that the soul or spirit lives on in another dimension after physical death.

Being spiritual doesn't necessarily mean being religious. Each of us has different beliefs about God and eternity, and some people say they have very few beliefs at all about life beyond everyday existence. Being grownup spiritually means learning to appreciate the spiritual dimensions of your *being* -- your creativity, intuition, and consciousness. This dimension leads us in the search for meaning and truth, the truth beyond the facts of everyday living.

The spiritual path leads you to cultivating your capacity for love and for positive, constructive experiences. Spiritual maturity can help the individual turn negative or painful events into opportunities to learn and grow, and to develop higher levels of compassion and empathy for the suffering of others.

We've all experienced the conflicting impulses of good versus evil, and felt the clean, strong sense of peace that comes from doing what is morally right, even at a cost to ourselves. Becoming spiritually mature is a process of learning to listen to the best voices from within.

The threatened, frightened part of yourself is small and egotistical, the devil on your shoulder whispering, "Go ahead and do it. Just don't get caught." Your positive impulses to do the generous, unselfish thing come from your higher spiritual side, the angel whispering in your ear to do good and to act in love toward yourself and others.

Growing up spiritually is necessary to your full development as a human being. The other three aspects of the self are just clothing and jewelry on the spiritual hand. The hand is the real substance. In terms of growing up we need to develop a sense of selfhood to help us stay on the positive path. Selfhood means being "full of your self". Accepting and loving yourself is essential before you can truly love another.

Selflessness is different, that is the position of giving to others at the sacrifice of your own needs. If this is your guiding principle, resentment eventually will build in you, and you will stay stuck in spiritual and emotional infancy.

The selfish person gives only to get something back. If your gifts carry a price tag, you are not giving in the highest spiritual sense. If you are easily threatened and frequently defensive you're reacting to life's challenges and to other people selfishly, from your negative, fearful side -- like a child.

When you learn to love and accept yourself you can become strong and generous enough to accept others at their level of development, openly and unconditionally, and without judgment.

Do you want to develop your Selfhood, to open yourself to spiritual growth? If so are you willing to:

♦ Allow the spiritual side of your being to guide you in integrating your physical, intellectual, and emotional aspects?

♦ Gain power in your own life, no matter what goes on in the world you live in?

♦ Tap inner resources you didn't know existed through the use of intuition?

♦ Be receptive to the insights available from religious observance, prayer, meditation, nature?

♦ Develop more flexibility in your attitudes?

♦ Find the courage to take risks and try new things?

♦ Learn how to enjoy being alone?

♦ Forgive yourself and others for old offenses?

♦ Convey a spirit of peace, love, and acceptance to others?

♦ Face tragedy, loss, and death with courage and serenity?

♦ Believe that everything in your life has meaning and purpose?

♦ Conduct your life according to the way that works for you, regardless of what others think?

♦ Overcome selfishness, pettiness, and being judgmental?

♦ Know that you are always in the process of growth and learning?

♦ Live in the here and now, and in faith that things will work out for the best?

Selfhood is a position of personal maturity that allows you to meet your own wants and the needs of others without sacrificing your own integrity. Growing up spiritually is the way to reach this place of inner peace.

PHYSICAL GROWTH

It's tempting to think that growing up physically ends when our adult bodies have developed. But even after the rapid changes of childhood and adolescence, our bodies continue to change. They require on-going care and maintenance throughout adulthood. As you move past mid-life, your body will need even more intense care.

Since you only get one body you need to take the best possible care of it. You may live to be 80 or 100 years old or more. If you wear your body out in the first 20 or 40 years, you will spend a long time walking around in a worn-out body.

These days we can't escape the constant media messages about taking care of our physical condition. The emphasis on health and fitness has been a great boon to many people. If you need to eat better, exercise more, reduce stress, or quit some destructive habit like smoking, drinking in excess, or abusing drugs, you have no excuse for not getting with it now. Grownups take responsibility for their personal physical behavior, they don't need Mama to tell them to take better care of themselves.

Even if you're physically fit you still run a risk of getting out of balance. As with any good thing, physical fitness can be carried too far. If you focus so strongly on perfecting yourself physically that you neglect other aspects of your being, you will eventually pay the price, like the young athletes who abuse steroids without considering the negative long-term effects on their bodies.

You can lose your balance when you let stress damage your body. Our lives are loaded with stressors. A moderate amount of stress is stimulating, but too much is deadly. Excessive stress not only exhausts the mind and frays the emotions, it powerfully affects the immune system and reduces the body's ability to fight off disease.

Grownups don't use alcohol or other drugs to relax and reduce tension. They learn to employ meditation, physical exercise, or an enjoyable hobby to regulate the stress levels in their lives. We all need to use relaxation, self-hypnosis, and other healthy strategies to keep the stress in our lives under control.

Do you want to grow up physically? Would you like to:

♦ Be able to monitor and control your stress level?

♦ Use physical exercise to reduce depression, and meditation to stop pain?

♦ Find the will power to end your bad habits with food, drugs, tobacco, or alcohol?

♦ Stop worrying about what your genes didn't provide and take pride in your own inherent beauty?

♦ Quit searching for that ultimate exercise or vitamin to make your body perfect?

♦ Find out why reliance on the pleasures of sex, drugs, sports, or other forms of stimulation which ultimately leaves you unsatisfied?

♦ Get past the traumas and inhibitions that interfere with sexual fulfillment?

♦ Enjoy all aspects of life despite physical disability or illness, including a healthy and fulfilling sex life?

Getting your physical self integrated in balance with the other aspects of yourself will present you with these discoveries. Growing up physically doesn't stop with the body's natural growth out of childhood. Growing up physically means acquiring a valuable knowledge of your body, its needs, and its joys.

EMOTIONAL GROWTH

The key to being grown up emotionally is to learn to acknowledge, express, control, and manage your feelings. This isn't an easy task and few people are trained for it while they're young.

Our society is *feeling-phobic*. We are afraid to examine and change our emotional responses because we fear the discomfort of emotional pain. That simply means we are afraid of a part of ourselves --our feelings. Most of us were taught very early, by first and primary teachers, our parents, not to show our emotions, to hide them, and to numb them out, resulting in emotionally immature adults.

Of course parents need to teach their children to control their impulses and to use appropriate behavior to get their needs met. But these lessons can be taught without punishing the child's expression of feelings. We are just now learning to validate children's emotions. To comfort them when they are hurt, or sad. To allow anger to be expressed and taught ways to handle it, rather demeaning them by ridicule, punishment or shaming.

Unfortunately, most parents are adults who also had their feelings denied as children. They learned to fear and repress their emotions, and now they pass those fears on to their children. They pass on to their children the same punishing messages that they got as kids.

Impatient and frustrated parents told us not to cry, not to get angry -- or at least not to show if you were hurt or angry. As a child, how many times were you told, "Stop crying!"... "Don't be a baby"... "Be a big boy"... "Be a nice girl".

The unspoken part of those messages is, don't feel fear or pain or hurt or anger. Hide those feelings. Or when you show that emotion, you're a bad person. A healthier message is learn to express and understand your feelings in a safe, appropriate time and place.

In order to get the adults in our lives to love and accept us, we learned to deny and hold back our emotions. Some of us were physically or verbally abused when we didn't. We learned to make ourselves numb when we had strong feelings, especially negative ones like anger, pain, fear, or sadness. As a result we have a serious problem in this country with childhood depression that we are just beginning to address.

Those old messages were cast in concrete in our minds, and you may spend most of your adult life chiseling away at them.

Often the behavior that we learned to use to survive as children does not serve us well as adults. If your emotions were punished or ridiculed instead of being validated and acknowledged, growing up emotionally will be a lifetime struggle. Most people in the *civilized* world are not emotionally grown up. Cultural anthropologists tell us about tribes that nurture the emotional development of their children like the Bushmen in Africa and the Senoi Indians, who attend to the dream messages of both children and adults every morning. It is interesting to note that in these *primitive* societies there is no crime or mental illness. Instead of resisting, denying, fighting, and avoiding pain, grownups must learn to admit it, feel it, and report it. No matter how hard you resist pain, resistance doesn't make it go away, it only causes more hurt. All emotions get stronger when you fight them. Denial and defenses take away your power to deal with your feelings, and just make the painful feelings stronger.

At the other extreme, people who are learning to acknowledge their emotions may go around constantly talking about everything they feel. That's a temporary, adolescent phase in the growing-up process.

Grownups learn to determine which feelings to express, and the appropriate ways to share them, and safe people to share them with. Grownups also learn how to recognize when a feeling is a simple, visceral reaction to an old message or fear, and when it indicates a need to work out a problem with someone or to change something in their lives that creates emotions that are too difficult to live with.

Would you like to become grown-up emotionally? Do you want to:

♦ Learn to face your fears and stop living in
    a state of anxiety?

♦ Develop some strategies for managing
    your anger?

♦ Turn negative feelings into positive
    experiences?

♦ Stop depression before it takes hold of

you, and turn it around?

◆ Let go of guilt and shame?

◆ Recognize mild feelings like disappointment
    and frustration before they turn into
    overpowering depression and anger?

◆ Forgive your parents and others, including
    yourself, for not being perfect?

◆ Communicate your feelings in an assertive,
    non -threatening way?

◆ Learn that real control comes from inside-
    out, not outside-in?

◆ Finish the job of parenting yourself where
    your parents left off?

◆ Feel and express love and caring for others
    in your life?

◆ Use your thoughts to create positive emotions?

◆ Be more joyful and happy than you have
    ever been in your life?

Growing up emotionally promises freedom from all these
forms of pain. You don't have to let them rule your life any more.

INTELLECTUAL GROWTH

Another aspect of growing up is to develop successful
problem-solving techniques that you can call on when you need
them. Grownups use their intelligence and reasoning capacities
to create an ability to analyze, rationalize, and project the
outcomes of several possibilities. When faced with a crisis or
challenge, they survey the options available for the situation and
make the best possible choice from the information they have.

Researchers in cognitive development believe that the
ability to think begins at age 7. At that time, the brain can be

trained, and memory begins to be based on learning rather than on instincts and conditioning. Conditioning is the way we train animals by changing their behavior using rewards and punishments. This isn't the best way for humans who are beginning to grow up to learn.

The ability to think and solve problems is what separates humans from animals, and being able to use these capacities well is a characteristic of growing up. Throughout our lives, we expand and refine our abilities to think, conceptualize, analyze, and predict. To be fully human is to use your brain in balance with your other capacities.

Of course, we all know people who rely almost entirely on their intellectual capacities and become overly rational. They analyze their feelings away, discount the importance of the body, say they don't need a spiritual belief. Others who aren't grownup intellectually don't think enough, they just react emotionally or physically, or operate on blind faith, instead of deciding and taking action after considering the facts and the consequences of their choice.

Real intellectual maturity has nothing to do with the amount or type of formal education one has. Growing up intellectually takes place inside you, not in a classroom. It means appreciating the joys of learning, applying creativity and imagination, remembering things that matter instead of cluttering the mind with trivia, and using the gifts of the brain to make your life run smoother.

Do you want to be an intellectual grownup, no matter what your I.Q. or educational history? Are you willing to:

♦ Use your thoughts to change your feelings or your physical habits?

♦ Discover intellectual capacities you didn't realize you had?

♦ Improve your memory?

♦ Gather the facts you need to make better
   decisions?

♦ Develop new problem-solving techniques?

♦ Recognize how and when to use the right or
   left brain?

♦ Understand how language affects your
   attitudes?

♦ Set your imagination and creative abilities
   free?

♦ Lose your fear of learning new skills and
   ideas?

♦ Feel you can hold your own in any
   conversation?

♦ Make up for any gaps in your formal education,
   no matter how old you are?

♦ Learn to stop your busy, bombarded mind so
   you can relax or focus on a specific issue?

A grownup has all these skills, and learns to balance the intellectual gifts with the other aspects of the self. Grownups remain curious learners all their lives, never thinking they "know it all", but continuing to nurture and challenge the mind by building on their knowledge and sharpening their thought processes.

GROWN-UP BEHAVIOR: BALANCE AND RESPONSIBILITY

How do grownups behave? What happens when someone becomes mature in all four aspects of the Self and keeps them in balance most of the time?

People are grown up when they make responsible

decisions and follow through with responsible actions, when they respond appropriately to any given set of circumstances or issues, negative, positive, or indifferent, good news or bad. *Grownups have the ability to discriminate among responses and to recognize the appropriate ones.* They can find several options available to them, examine how each will affect them emotionally, spiritually, intellectually, and physically, then make the best decision for themselves at the time. When you are grown up this process is usually fast and automatic for simple decisions, and more deliberate and careful when a decision has a major impact on your life.

Grownups don't always make the right decision, but they try to make the best decision -- depending on the timing, alternatives, people affected, and other circumstances. *Grownups also know that whatever they decide, it will be all right.*

Grownups are open to learning from every experience.

Grownups attempt to create win-win situations in all their relationships and interactions with others.

Grownups take reasonably good care of their bodies.

Grownups are willing and able to face and release old fears that keep them locked behind self-imposed barriers, instead of acting out in response to childish emotions.

Grownups replace condemnation, judgments, blame and hatred with compassion, tolerance, forgiveness, and love.

Grownups are receptive to listening to their inner voices.

Grownups strive to maintain a balance of body, emotions, mind, and spirit. They know that this is a lifelong struggle, and they welcome it. For it is only in being engaged in, and responsible for, those struggles in your own life, that you become the best self you can be.

Taking responsibility for what happens in your life sets you free from the judgments of others and the fears of childhood.

Taking responsibility offers freedom from conflicts that you can't win, and challenges you to a life from which you can learn and grow.

THE WHOLE YOU

If growing up sounds like a lot of work, and you are concerned about how you can ever keep all those things in balance, control all those children and learn all these new things -- don't worry.

You can be a grownup without doing everything right all the time. Remember, the goal is to find and maintain balance among the four aspects. The frequent struggles with those inner children who are stuck in the old, frightened ways, are what will keep throwing you off balance. Your job is to get to know them, their games, cons, manipulations, resistances, pain, defenses and denial and to nurture, love and support their growth. If they don't grow up neither will you.

When you finish this book, you won't be a 100 percent, walking, talking adult, but you will be farther along the path. Just remember, it's the discoveries along the way -- not just arriving at the end -- that makes your trip worthwhile.

An important discovery on your journey is that growing up means looking at yourself wholistically -- as a whole human being. You're not just a body, or just a mind. The whole you is something greater than the sum of the four parts. We all have the potential to be so much more, but we fall short because our parts sometimes get out of balance, or when one or more part is much weaker and less mature than the rest.

I invite you to join me on this journey within yourself. It's time to take an honest look inside and see where your life is working and where it is not working. With some insight and courage you will be able to do whatever is necessary to reach your potential. Your only limits are the ones you set for yourself.

THE FIRST STEP

Examining the way you respond to things that occur in your life will give you some clues as to how grown up you are, and what parts of yourself you'd like to work on. Most of your responses to life's events fall into patterns that are determined by early childhood fears and needs. Sometimes these response patterns become automatic and you don't realize they're holding you back from being all you can become. Since being grown up means making appropriate responses. Here's some homework.

Below are some questions that will start you thinking about how you respond to or cope with the questions, problems, emotions, needs, and wishes in your life, and how well the four aspects of your life are balanced. There aren't really any correct answers or scores here. The purpose of these questions are to start you thinking and exploring what your attitudes are, what is important to you, and how you would like to be.

Just read through the questions and rank the given choices according to your usual ways of responding--- 1. For the response you have most frequently, 2. For the next most frequent, 3.,4. and so on. Rank the whole list for each question

Notice how you feel as you answer each question: Are you ashamed of your answer? Afraid to tell the truth? Wish to avoid the question? Confused? Never thought about this before?

After you have marked your answers, examine them for old patterns. Do your answers reflect physical, emotional, intellectual, and spiritual maturity or immaturity? Are the answers consistent with what you know about yourself?

THE GROWN-UP QUESTIONNAIRE

1. People are attracted to me because of:

My physical appearance

My achievements in life

My warm and friendly personality

My self-confidence and self-assurance

My stimulating conversation

My financial resources

My charisma

2. When I consider a potential mate, I am most interested in his or her:

   Physical appearance

   Achievements in life

   Warm and friendly personality

   Self-confidence

   Stimulating conversation

   Money, professional position, and social status

   Intelligence

3. When I failed at something, I tell myself:

   You're a dummy -- you're stupid

   Everybody makes a mistake sometimes

   You ought to be ashamed

   What can I learn from this?

   I should have let somebody else do this

   I know my friends and family love me, no matter what I've done

   I want to hide from everyone

4. I would like to have more money because:

   I want to buy new things to impress the neighbors

   I can give more to people who need it

   I can feel more secure in my old age

   No one can tell me what to do

> *I can be free to devote myself to*
> *creative pursuits*
>
> *My family's future would be secure*
>
> *It would take a lot of pressure off me*
>
> *I don't have any desire for more money*

5. My attitude about formal education is:

   > *It's for kids*
   >
   > *College is a good place to meet the right*
   > *kind of people*
   >
   > *College graduates can train for high-*
   > *paying careers*
   >
   > *The intellectual stimulation is valuable in*
   > *itself*
   >
   > *I want to spend my whole life learning,*
   > *in school and outside*
   >
   > *What's important is learning about myself*
   >
   > *Whether I use all my talents matters more*
   > *than what degrees I have*

6. When I have to make a decision, I:

   > *Study all my options and try to figure*
   > *out the best answer*
   >
   > *Panic and fall apart under the pressure*
   >
   > *Try to get someone else to decide*
   >
   > *Pray for guidance*
   >
   > *Avoid it as long as possible*
   >
   > *Know that whatever I decide will work*
   > *out - in the long run*

7. What makes me happiest is:

   > *Winning in business or competition or*
   > *sports*

Being in love and being loved

Achieving a goal

*Being immersed in a worthwhile
    project*

*When someone gives me a nice gift or
    surprise*

Forgetting all my troubles for a while

Partying with friends

Being close to my family

*Giving of my time to someone who
    needs it*

Feeling connected with God or nature

8. When I feel afraid I:

*Whistle a happy tune and pretend
    nothing is wrong*

*Keep it a secret because I'm
    embarrassed at my weakness*

Feel panic in my body

Take it out in anger at someone else

*Imagine the worst things that can
    happen*

Fortify myself with liquor or drugs

*Confront the situation immediately to
    show I'm in control*

Look for someone to take care of me

Relax and stay with the feeling

*Realize I am in control and I have
    choices*

9. My body is:

A machine that must be carefully

> *maintained*
>
> *Ugly*
>
> *A sex object, a way to get what I want*
>
> *A burden that has let me down*
>
> *A source of pleasure*
>
> *A chore that requires too much of my
>   time*
>
> *A shell for my soul or real self*
>
> *My pride and joy*
>
> *The temple of my soul*
>
> *An outer projection of my inner self*
>
> *My best asset*
>
> *A fun challenge to make look and
>   feel as good as I can*

10. Death is:

> *Frightening and painful*
>
> *Final, the end of everything*
>
> *A peaceful end to one's problems on
>   earth*
>
> *Sad and depressing to think about*
>
> *Sadness at leaving my loved ones behind*
>
> *An unfair, meaningless loss*
>
> *Something to prepare for and face*
>
> *A   mystery*
>
> *The end of physical existence and the
>   start of a spiritual life*
>
> *A reminder of how precious every day is*
>
> *A new beginning, the start of something
>   wonderful*

Now that you have answered these thought-provoking questions, and considered what they may tell you, here's another, special tool to rate yourself on the four types of development on a scale of 1-10. One is the lowest and 10 is the highest. Answer honestly about where you think you are now, not where you'd like to be. Add up your total score. Look at the distribution.

PLACE A + ON THE LINE CLOSEST TO YOUR LEVEL OF DEVELOPMENT

1   2   3   4   5   6   7   8   9   10

PHYSICAL   1------------------------------------10

Score___

INTELLECTUAL   1------------------------------------10

Score___

EMOTIONAL   1------------------------------------10

Score___

SPIRITUAL   1------------------------------------10

Score___

TOTAL SCORE_____

We will deal with the results in a later chapter. Now I invite you to travel along the path with me, and learn how to turn life's fears and crises into opportunities to grow.

PART TWO

GROWING UP
SPIRITUALLY

CHAPTER THREE

WHAT DOES IT MEAN TO BE SPIRITUALLY GROWN UP?

"The most fundamental human desire is
longing for transcendence and unity."
Erich Fromm, *The Art Of Loving*

Being grown up spiritually means being able and willing to hear the inner voice that tells us what really matters in life and points us to the truths that we intuitively know. Being grown up spiritually means going deep *within* ourselves without fear to discover capacities and knowledge that we'll never find by looking outward.

Spirituality is available to everyone, whether you follow an organized religion or not. Your spiritual growth is the key to healing your body, mind, and emotions of all the things that are keeping them from healthy growth. Spiritual development is the fuel that makes growing up happen.

Spirituality means accepting, even if we don't understand intellectually, that life will always contain mysteries. It is being willing to live with unknowns, relying on faith that there is meaning and truth and reason beyond what is apparent. As with all the other levels of maturity, spiritual growth is an ongoing, lifelong process.

People find various means of guidance and support in this quest -- from organized churches, from inspired leaders, through shared ritual, by prayer or meditation, by reading and discussion of the literature of spirituality from all the corners of the earth. Some are guided by their own inner voices, which they may hear more clearly with the aid of music and art, sexual or emotional connection with others, closeness to nature, or meditation.

Whatever your method of reaching within and beyond, your way is the right way for you. If you are committed to growing up spiritually, you can use your method for finding your answers to your questions. Most of us start with the same basic questions about the meaning of life, death, suffering, love, right and wrong. But we each encounter and question these experiences in different ways. Thus we find our answers in ways that speak to us individually.

The important thing is to acknowledge that the questions exist and that the answers are worth seeking. It's the search for the answers that creates growth, through struggling and suffering.

The willingness to wonder, to admit confusion, to accept on faith, makes us receptive to learning. As the New Testament says "Blessed are they that have not seen, and yet have believed". John 20:29. Remember all of those crackpots that we read about in the 1400's who believed the world was round? They had no proof before the voyages of Christopher Columbus, only their intuition to guide them. And they were considered weirdos by most of the people of their day. Ultimately, experience proved them right.

Science may never verify the spiritual truths you believe,

but your heart can tell you that the knowledge in your soul is as valid as the "facts" of outward *reality*. The act of belief in this inner wisdom is called *faith*.

Spiritual growth can fill the seeker with confusion, because the more you learn about the greater truths, the more you wonder. You often find that the truths are paradoxes, that one lesson seems to contradict another. The real lesson is often that both opposing insights are true. The ability to accept dichotomies, knowing that truth is greater than logic, enables us to go on, to feel happy, to find meaning in a world full of confusion and pain.

Spiritual maturity is important to growing up because it provides strength and endurance, an anchor in the larger sea of life. This strength helps us deal with whatever problems and challenges arise in our physical, emotional , and intellectual experiences. A sense of spiritual understanding connects and holds the other three aspects together to keep us in balance. It is this higher wisdom that makes the struggle worthwhile.

SEPARATION AND UNITY

While we consider spiritual growth as one of the four aspects of the Self, it is the most important one for growing up. Spiritual growth encompasses the other three levels of the Self. Spiritual growth is essential to achieving the selfhood of being grown up. When a person is integrated and in balance, the result is inner peace and tranquility.

Not only does the spiritual aspect of ourselves connect and integrate our internal parts, it also connects us as individuals with each other.

The ultimate misery of the human condition is our sense of separateness from each other. We all feel lonely sometimes, even in a crowd, or with loved ones. In times of crisis, you may feel that the torment of your suffering is personal; no one else could understand or know how you feel. If there is a Hell, it is this stark isolation, this painful, lonely journey of living, struggling, and suffering alone.

Spirituality can help breach that gap between yourself and others. When you reach out, share, touch, help and serve others, you become connected and united again. It's one of the paradoxes that signals great truth, the deeper inward you go in your search for self-knowledge, the more you become connected to others in the world around you.

SPIRITUAL OPENNESS

Perhaps you are an intelligent and ethical person, and you have avoided spiritual challenges or just never particularly thought about the role of the spirit in your life. Factors in your life may have kept you from developing this particular aspect of yourself. Perhaps no one has ever shown you the way to start the journey.

Maybe all the spiritual talk you've ever heard sounds like mumbo jumbo, and you can't find anything to identify with in the belief systems you know. Perhaps you've suffered pain and disappointments in life that interfere with your willingness to believe in a higher order or purpose.

Maybe your early experiences in traditional religions re-vealed hypocrisy, judgments, and cruelty among the so-called enlightened or left you feeling guilty over things that made sense to you. So you've decided all beliefs in things outside of observable reality are false, inconsistent, or unbelievable.

Being spiritually immature or disinterested in spiritual matters doesn't mean you're bad, any more than emotional prob-lems or lack of education make you bad. Yet if you ignore your spiritual development, you are missing something. You're suffering from our old nemesis, imbalance. You may be very responsible physically, intellectually, and emotionally, but without the element of the spiritual, it's easy to forget why. Faith in something larger helps make the other struggles easier and gives you the willingness to take the risks that these struggles require.

Spiritual maturity is a rock to lean on when being grownup is just too hard. It not only provides rewards for doing your best, it also is the source of the strength to do it.

The body, the mind, the feelings, all get frustrated and tired at times. The spirit feeds and nurtures all aspects of the Self, and holds you up when you falter. The spirit is greater than all your parts, greater than we can know, at least while we are in a physical body.

AWAKENING -- SOUL MANIFESTATION

Each of us is at a different level of development and awareness on our spiritual paths. Some people are born with uncanny natural talents, like Mozart who could play three musical instruments at four years old and compose music at seven years.

I think of our spiritual development as being like a dimmer switch or rheostat on a light. At the earlier stages the light is very dim, difficult to see. Gradually over a long period of time the light gets lighter and brighter: based on learning the lessons of life; amending hurt and pain you have inflicted on others; and serving others without expecting material rewards.

Many of us know things without any idea of how we acquired the knowledge. We know because we learned it before and our soul remembers. The famous Swiss Psychiatrist Carl Jung believed that we all can tap into a wealth of universal knowledge, he called it the *collective unconscious.*

Every lifetime is a mini version of our whole spiritual path. We start out as infants, dependent and innocent. Next we are babies, self-centered and demanding for our needs to be met. Then we are young souls gratifying ourselves in material ways, satisfying ego needs, wanting recognition and approval from our peers.

Later in life we are mature; we are able to evaluate what we have learned and to discard outmoded or useless values. Finally, we are old souls and wise in many ways, more openly receptive to love, more flexible, spontaneous, tolerant, and patient.

LIFE CRISES

Within every lifetime, there are three major developmental life crises that bring on intense questioning about the meaning of life; with those questions come the greatest opportunities for renewal and growth. During each of these three times -- adolescence, middle age, and retirement -- it is a universal experience to undergo a prolonged period of inner searching for a sense of identity apart from your everyday life and for meaning in your life.

The task of adolescence is to make a bridge between childhood and adulthood. It is a time to establish personal values and break away from parental values. The adolescent experiences vacillation and tension between wanting to be independent and still needing parents.

When my oldest son was 15 years of age, he woke up one morning feeling upset and frightened. He had dreamed about a mother hen sitting on a nest. One little chick who was restless and curious strayed from the nest. The chick had a good time exploring the world for a while, then became frightened and tried to find his way home. He looked everywhere and finally, after a frantic search, found his way back to the nest and dived in to sleep safely again under his mother's feathers. Of course, my adolescent son was the little chick trying to find his way in the world, but not quite ready to make the complete break and face life's challenges on his own.

Adolescence is a necessary and critical time to confront fears and explore different behaviors, integrating some into the personality, rejecting others. Peers are important during this time to use as a sounding board while searching for new values, attitudes, and beliefs. It is a time of rapid physical change, intense intellectual development, and sensitive and deep emotional growth.

The busy and demanding years of the twenties and thirties leave little time for soul-searching. Most people at this age are fully absorbed with the practical challenges of college, career, finding a mate, and starting a family.

Middle age presents us with a different set of tasks. It is a time to search for meaning in our lives. Questions surface like, "Why am I here?", "Who am I?", "What do I want?", "What is truth?", "What is good and what is bad in my life?", "Where do I go from here?", and others.

There is no set time for midlife, but it generally occurs with major changes in a life situation. A number of factors can bring on a mid-life reassessment, and this crisis may occur more than once between the mid 30s and the 60s.

Whatever the trigger, midlife is a time to take stock of progress so far in your life, to come to terms with and accept certain limitations, to recommit to relationships or end them.

In your work life, you may realize that you will never become head of the department or of the company. Parents say good-bye to their children and adjust to an empty nest. Time takes on a different meaning; you start thinking about how much time remains until your death instead of how long you've lived since birth. You read the obituaries in the daily newspaper regularly and notice the age of death.

At midlife we begin to recognize our essential aloneness. And the search begins for inner peace, harmony, and balance. For some of us this is very painful. We must admit our failures and our part in them. Failed marriages finally end. The second highest rate of divorce occurs in unions of 20 to 30 years. The pain and confusion of severance and separation are fertile ground for introspection and a reordering of personal priorities. This search may also create a renewal of joy and recommitment in a long marriage.

The frantic busyness of life, of raising a family and

earning a living, eases a little and most middle-aged people have more time and money to enjoy life. In times of introspection a reconnection with your essence re-emerges. Your soul manifests as you explore your inner mandates to *being,* instead of *doing.* It is another phase of growing up, growing into new knowledge of yourself.

Once more you are confronted with relinquishing some of your childish myths. You get another shot at learning what you didn't learn well at adolescence.

By this time you are satisfied with your work and you appreciate learning for its own sake. You value taking care of your body and you've given up bad habits. You have left behind most of your childish emotions and now look for joy in what you do. You finally acknowledge there's no use in crying "It isn't fair!" and fairness isn't the issue anyway. Integrity is the issue. Living each moment for the most you can glean out of it, treating yourself and others gently, kindly, and with respect are what really count.

By middle age, we've acquired enough wisdom to know that life is unpredictable, and we've become somewhat resigned to its unexpectedness. Just when things seem to be going well, a problem develops. Fame, fortune, failure, defeat, disease, death , divorce, love and separation, appear in your life to challenge you once again. These events seem to come unexpectedly and unsolicited. But in fact, we draw them to us, to teach us what we need to learn, so we can continue to grow and to grow up.

The spiritual path is awakened during the middle of life. If you live creatively and openly, receptive to your opportunities to grow and learn, then as you get older life becomes enriched as you learn to accept what you cannot change and change what you can.

Welcome each struggle because it is also your resurrection. Just as Christ arose three days after his death, you too will rise after each life crisis. Death is symbolic of any type of ending -- of a behavior, a job, a place to live, a friendship, and love. After the grief and pain comes a new beginning. Confusion clears, vision returns, and you integrate your new knowledge into your new vision of what your life can become. This process is called *awakening.*

Every one of us gets repeated opportunities to accept the challenges life presents to us, or we can reject these lessons. We always have choice, since free will is a part of human makeup. We can choose to live with periods of confusion, doubt, ambiguity, fear, or failure, or we can avoid them.

Many people retreat into mindless behaviors like using drugs or alcohol, soap operas and romance novels, illness, numbness of feelings, rigidity, chronic depression and despair. If you take one of these avoidance methods, you will continue to be presented with opportunities to learn. However, if you choose avoidance, and you won't accept the lessons your life offers, you'll stay stuck, a spiritual child, without the joy of growth.

The third crisis time in life is retirement, which can occur at any age but for most people happens after age 60. When active work life ends, it is again a time to search for identity, meaning, and the value of your life.

Many people identify the purpose and usefulness of their lives with their work. Have you become the job you perform? Do you say, "I am a doctor, a lawyer, Indian Chief,?" or "I am a secretary, an accountant, a wife and mother?" These are social roles they are not who you are. Not the essence of your unique Self.

The tragedy of defining your identity so narrowly is that when the role ends, so does the meaningfulness in life.

When this happens people feel useless and unneeded. Think of the high rate of death among men shortly after their retirement, and the high suicide rate among the elderly, especially older men. It is the highest rate of suicide for any age group.

One of the issues of this third transition time is coming to terms with your personal death. Old age is the time to check the score card for victories and defeats, to let go of old resentments and disappointments, to clean up unfinished business in relationships. I have worked for many years with the elderly and have listened to endless stories of unresolved offenses and hurts. Many of the people involved are dead now, but the pain lives on in the hearts of the offended. When a person carries the unnecessary burden of unresolved grief, anger, love, or other feelings for years, it takes a toll on the individual. In the last years of life, it's time to be done with it, once and for all.

If one has successfully met the earlier tests along the path, and continued to grow and learn, then this transition is relatively easy. Your process for handling times of self-doubt and soul-searching is established. Painful events will still surface as they will at any time in life, but you can meet them with courage and resolve them.

For the person who reaches old age spiritually grown-up, personal death is not feared and dreaded but welcomed as the just reward for living a long and full life. It is viewed as a natural part of the life cycle. You make amends, forgive yourself and others, take care of the unfinished business of living, and use your energy in living each day to the fullest in love and service to yourself and others.

Death ,the final stage of growth and of life as we know it is viewed differently throughout the life span. This is explained in detail in my book *Letting Go With Love: The Grieving Process.* Time during the life span is a gift given to you to learn lessons leading to self-awareness and self-consciousness. If your time here is used well, then death becomes a triumph not a tragedy.

SPIRITUAL GROWTH

Life is a never-ending process of making mistakes and then growing and learning from them. My father used to tell me that if I would only listen to him I could learn from his mistakes. Often his advice was right, but not in that particular case; life doesn't work that way. We learn best from living with the pain and consequences of our own mistakes and decisions, not from someone else's advice.

The only genuine experience we have in life is with ourselves. We are the creators of our life scripts and of our destiny. Every event and relationship in your life is an opportunity to learn and to grow. You learn to cope, to survive, to take care of yourself, to be authentic and honest in your dealings with others. Coupled with learning lessons, is wisdom, a knowing with all of your heart and soul. Striving for and reaching this deep knowledge is the process of spiritual growth, and it is essential to becoming a balanced adult.

To learn and to hold the pearl of true wisdom, you must surrender control to your higher Self. The essence of who you are is much more than the body you wear to drape your spirit. When you relinquish control to a power higher and more profound than the physical, emotional, or intellectual self, you give up fear and negative thinking, self-destructive habits, anger, and guilt.

Your spiritual or religious beliefs, to enhance your spiritual growth, they should take you deeper within yourself. Spiritual growth doesn't happen when you follow certain rituals or attend services. It happens when, through those practices or services, you become aware of new insights and strengths in yourself and convert your beliefs into positive action.

The process is, you look outward to spiritual leaders, a church, to shared participation in ritual, to a set of beliefs about the larger questions. As you explore these paths to spiritual truth, the answers take you inward to the intuitive understanding and acceptance of what you find -- the experience of faith.

As your spirit grows stronger, you believe more in yourself -- the spark that connects you with the ongoing life of the universe, as well as the higher Self that gives you the strength to meet problems that come your way. In the process, you grow to care more about the world you live in and the people who share it with you. Your awareness takes you outward again, outside yourself, to give back, help, and serve others in a way that produces even more growth, happiness, and satisfaction for you.

CHAPTER FOUR

ISSUES OF SPIRITUAL GROWTH

The events of our lives, particularly the ones we think of as crises, raise many issues about how we've lived in this limited time we have on earth, and how we're going to live out the rest of that time. We make decisions about morality, values, the kind of person we want to be. We discover things about ourselves that we don't like--and things we do like. If we're committed to growing up as a lifelong process, we decide to change some things--to become better, to be truer to our inner sense of right and wrong, to get along with others better, to tolerate things we don't like.

Some of the issues that may arise and indicate an opportunity for spiritual growth have to do with how flexible you are -- can you handle change, the planned kind and the unwanted kind? Crisis also makes you face the question of whether you take risks. The ability to let go of things that aren't important to control is another issue, along with gaining the kind of inner-directed self-control that helps you grow. Yet another spiritual growth opportunity comes when you face being alone and learn how to appreciate that solitude as an opportunity, rather than to dread loneliness as something miserable and frightening.

Finally, the most important spiritual issue you'll deal with throughout your life is love -- love of yourself, of mankind, and of life itself.

FLEXIBILITY VERSUS RIGIDITY

The spiritual grownup is flexible. He is not afraid of changing his mind or discovering he's wrong; in fact, he finds it exciting because change means he is learning and growing. Rigidity in beliefs or behavior limits us and makes it impossible to grow. Rigidity emphasizes structure, rules, deadlines, and very specific goals. It also requires institutions to make and enforce the laws and rules. Sure, we need organization in our lives and institutions in our society, otherwise we would have chaos. But we also need some leeway for flexibility, for creativity, for looking at old things in new ways. This is how we make appropriate changes.

Rules are sometimes ways to escape self-responsibility. When people don't want to do something, they look for a rule to hide behind. If *they* or the rules won't let you do something, then you're not responsible; you don't have take the risk or make a decision. How many times have you been told (or told yourself) that some simple thing could not be done because "it's against the rules"? And how did you feel about that? Probably frustrated because your needs and opportunities were thwarted by some rigid, outwardly imposed rules.

Recently, I went into a store to buy a battery for a quartz watch for a friend. I had the watch with me and asked the store clerk to open the back of the watch to see what kind of battery I needed. She refused and pointed to a hand-lettered sign that said that the store personnel would not assist in changing the batteries in watches. I had batteries changed there before with no problems.

Now, I was in a real dilemma. I didn't know how to take the back off the watch, nor did I have any tools to do so. I asked to speak to the manager and after a lengthy discussion, he loaned me the tools and told me how to get the battery out. The manager explained that the reason for the rule against helping customers change batteries was that a customer had been unhappy with the store's service and the store had to furnish him with a new watch. So now everyone has to be inconvenienced because of one person.

That is the way most rules are made -- not to enhance growth and creativity, but to prevent future problems, even though the probability of the same problem happening again is very low. Rules are made to protect one party's interest, not to enhance everyone's opportunity to learn and grow.

The rigid person has an authoritarian personality, one who must have rules for everything and insists that everyone adhere to them. Wayne Dyer in *The Sky's The Limit*, tells us that the authoritarian personality can't tolerate ambiguity, thinks dichotomously (everything is either/or, good/bad, black/white), is rigid in thought, anti-intellectual, anti-introspective, a conformist who submits without question to any authority. Shades of Nazi Germany and modern-day cults. Dyer continues stating that the rigid person, at the extreme, is also sexually repressed, ethnocentric, frequently paranoid, abhors weakness in any form, worships power, and is often a superpatriot.

Doesn't sound like any fun at all. It is fearful and sad to go through life with such rigidity. It is a frozen position, with little room for growth, learning, or progress on your spiritual path. It also has an unfortunate effect on those in relationship with you. Communication is never direct and clear; it is confused, full of double and mixed messages.

Rigidity allows no room for honesty, feedback, for another point of view. Children of rigid parents become confused and alienated when they hear and see other ways of being in the world from television, teachers, or families of friends.

Flexibility is essential to successfully growing up and coping with life, because much of the time life refuses to follow the rules. There aren't any guarantees, so we have to be able to adapt to whatever changes and surprises come along. The rigid person exists in a state of _being._ _The flexible person exists in a state of becoming._

The flexible person knows that she has choices and that, no matter what surfaces, she can handle it. Instead of clinging to a canned, prepared way of reacting to change, she approaches each new situation in a creative way. The flexible person is open, warm, enthusiastic -- and she listens. She weighs the pros and cons before making a decision. She strives for win-win solutions, which often involve compromise.

In order to advance spiritually you must allow yourself to experience problems, doubts, ambiguity, and indecision. You must roll with the punches. If you live by a set of rules about what is true, what is right, and how people should behave, look at those rules. Examine each rule carefully to see if it serves your growth at this time; if so, follow it -- if not, reject it.

RISK TAKING

You can't grow without taking risks. The old saying "Nothing ventured, nothing gained" comes to mind. Every aspect of growth and maturity requires risk. We sometimes resist growth because it involves risk, and we're scared we might lose. Such fear is a normal part of facing new situations.

Remember climbing up to a high diving board as a kid and standing there deciding whether to jump? What were you thinking? Were you afraid? What did you do? Did you consider it a challenge and approach it as something to conquer? Did you run with glee and jump in just for the thrill of it? Did you stop and consider the pros and cons of jumping? Were you so concerned with what your friends would think of you if you didn't jump that you ignored your fear and plunged in?

Or did fear overpower you to such an extent that you turned around and climbed down the ladder, trembling all the way? Or maybe you calmly looked over the situation and decided that the risk was too great at that time and just walked down the ladder without concern for what anyone else thought or said.

My guess is that you take risks the same way today. Take a few minutes to look inside and examine honestly your willingness to take risks. Since growing up is a matter of continuing to learn lessons, we must all take risks in order to learn. Sometimes we choose cautiously and the risk factor is minimal. Other times we stretch and reach beyond what is safe and comfortable.

Fear of the unknown is what usually stops us from taking risks. When you want or think you need guarantees about the outcome, you limit yourself.

There are no guarantees in life, only opportunities. Sometimes the risk factors work in your favor. Sometimes they don't. Without trying you will never know. I have a sign in my office that says, "A person who wants to do something will find a way. The other person finds an excuse."

What we call *lack of opportunity* is usually nothing more than refusing to take advantage of a situation when it presents itself; the opportunity is there, all right, but you've ignored or run from it. When you do try, sometimes you fall on your face. Then you get up again, evaluate the lesson, and try again with the benefit of what you learned from your mistake.

Joe, 33, had a steady job, his own house, and a new pickup truck, but no one to share his life with. He had dated only once in high school, and it was such a disaster that he hadn't had the courage to ask another woman for a date since.

When he came to see me, Joe had dreams of getting married and having a family. But his shyness and fear paralyzed him when he even thought of asking someone out. Thinking about the type of woman he liked, Joe decided he wanted to face his fears and meet someone to date. He asked himself, "What is the worst thing that can happen if I ask someone to go to the movies with me?" The answer, "She could say no". And what was so awful about that?

Joe realized he had been terrified of rejection, but after imagining concretely what it would feel like if someone said no to him he decided it wouldn't be so terrible. He could live with it, and then he could ask someone else out.

Joe and I role-played several situations -- things to talk about on a first date, ways to strike up a conversation with someone he'd like to meet, the type of evening he would be most comfortable with at first. We also rehearsed some telephone calls in which Joe got "no" for an answer, and some in which he got "yes". Joe grew more comfortable with the idea of each step toward his goal, meeting someone, asking for a date, going out, making conversation.

By this time, he was excited about the possibility of finding a mate; the search itself sounded pretty interesting. He had waited long enough, and he was tired of being afraid. His thoughts and self-talk were changing, and reality was beginning to look more inviting.

He ran an ad in a singles newspaper and got 27 responses. By calling all of them, he got a chance to practice his social skills some more. Joe found someone he liked, and they dated for several months. At each stage of the relationship, Joe felt a little more self-confident, and enjoyed himself. By allowing himself to trust his girl friend and himself, he left his old fears far behind him. Now he believes in himself, and knows he can find love. I am listening for the faint tinkling of wedding bells for Joe.

NEED TO CONTROL VERSUS SELF-CONTROL

Rigid people and fear- based people have a strong need to be in control at all times -- in control of themselves and of others. They are afraid to cry, to expose their vulnerability, to be spontaneous. Because they are unsure of themselves, they dread being exposed or criticized. This fixation on being in control is a real barrier to emotional and spiritual growing up

People who need to be in control are afraid to give up control to someone else. Those who truly are in control are secure and self-confident -- and they can give up control when it's appropriate.

Giving up control doesn't mean giving away your freedom or your self-determination. It means that you determine what is important to control, and trust yourself to judge when it's okay to let someone else be in charge. You let the sales staff represent the product you've designed, let your teenager go out on a date, trust the trained pilot to fly the plane. When you are secure and trust yourself, you will not have a childlike need to control yourself or others.

The difference is that you will have positive self-control directed from the inside, not external events rendering you helpless and powerless because you can't control them. There is a big difference between being afraid to lose control and having self-control. The desperate needs to control others and to stay in control at all times are destructive. They are based on distrust of yourself and others. Sometimes they develop into phobias, which we'll explore in Part III.

Positive self-control is quite different. It is an adult response and an adaptation to the realities of life. The key to having self-control -- or *selfhood* or self-discipline -- is becoming inner-directed. Inner-directed people feel personal power because they know they can make choices that are life-enhancing. Inner-directed grownups have traits like high morale, good coping skills, flexibility, and social involvement. They are self-assured and tolerant, use their intellects well, and have high energy levels. They take responsibility for their behavior, admit mistakes, and don't blame others for what goes wrong in their lives. They are resilient in handling emotional crises.

At the other end of the spectrum, someone who feels

that his life is controlled by outside forces, luck, or other people, feels powerless, is prone toward depression, and believes that there is little he or she can do to make life better. This person is fearful, rigid, intolerant, immature, and has poor social and coping skills.

Being inner-directed means being grown up, making decisions and taking charge of all the aspects of your life; determining what you can't change and accepting it; deciding what to change and doing what it takes to make those changes.

Inner-directed people live happier, more effective lives. Even under limitations such as severe disability, living in an institutional setting, or financial sacrifice, the inner-directed person maintains control over whether he allows events around him to affect his sense of identity and selfhood. Researchers believe that most people become more inner-directed as they age. I don't think this is true for everyone. Without positive intervention, we all become more of what we always were. That is, if you were shy and withdrawn as a child, you will become more so as you get older -- unless you make the determination to grow up and do the work it takes to change that trait.

ALONENESS VERSUS LONELINESS

Henry David Thoreau said, "The mass of men live their lives in quiet desperation." If this is true it is because we allow ourselves to become accustomed to boredom, monotony, routine, to security and comfort. We live by the clock, an *alarm* to warn us we will be late to work or to tell us when to sleep, tired or not.

We trap ourselves in habits and routine and relationships, thinking we are rewarded by comfort and security. But in so doing we dull ourselves to any chance for new interests and opportunities to emerge. We sell out to group norms and society's mandates rather than listening to an inner voice. Clark Moustakas, in his enlightening book, *Individuality and Encounter* says, "Once a fixed pattern of living is established, the person only dimly perceives his own inner response to experience, his own real thoughts and feelings."

What stops most of us from becoming all that we can be is a fear of being alone. We look outward to others for our values and approval, rather than inward for truth. It's true that spiritual growth is a private experience, as are all the other types of growing up. We often equate being alone with loneliness, so we fear not only taking these steps into the unknown, but having to do it all alone.

But aloneness and loneliness are not the same. We must have times of aloneness in order to know ourselves and hear our inner voices. Solitude is a nourishing, fulfilling experience for the grownup. Loneliness is a sad feeling, most often experienced in relation to a loss through personal tragedies like death, separation, or illness. It is also connected with feelings of rejection and guilt for not living up to one's potential. You don't have to be alone to feel lonely. I have been in a crowd of 5,000 people and felt terribly lonely.

Marriage can be one of the loneliest states of existence, if the relationship leaves you feeling rejected, isolated, misunderstood, and unappreciated. Have you ever watched an older couple in a restaurant who barely speak or communicate nonverbally with each other? There is no joy, no spontaneity in their relationship. They are trapped by the routine and familiarity of having lived together for many years, dulled by knowing what to expect from the other person, waiting for one of them to die and free the other from this terrible boredom. They have togetherness, but they are two lonely souls occupying adjacent space, caught in a web of mutual dependence while yearning for joy and meaning and love.

Helen Keller wrote about how her great teacher, Anne Mansfield Sullivan, taught Helen about love. She said, "You cannot touch love either but you feel the sweetness that it pours into everything. Without love you would not be happy or want to play." When I watch people locked in loneliness and boredom I feel sad because they have forgotten how to play and how to love. They are like robots waiting for their lives to end. Sad as they may be, however, your feelings of loneliness are a gift; they warn you that all is not well in your life. Something is missing. As with any gift, you may fail to appreciate its value and reject it, *or* you can really appreciate it and use it to your best advantage.

The truth is that we are always alone, like it or not. We are born alone and we die alone. No one comes with us. We may be in relationships with several people in the course of our lives, but we are essentially alone. Our experiences, choices and feelings are uniquely ours. Self-understanding and growing up come from learning to convert loneliness into solitude.

Aloneness is a positive experience, when it's associated with solitude, reconnecting with nature, tapping your inner resources. Being alone enables you to become aware of yourself as part of the beauty of the natural order and uniqueness of every living thing, to appreciate the inter-relatedness of wind and sea, air and sky, and earth, the warmth of the sun, and the mystery of the moon and stars.

Being alone, especially in a place of nature, helps you to put your life into perspective. An ocean, a forest, a mountain top, is a place apart from the day-to-day demands of the world. There you are confronted with the pettiness of your problems and recognize how much time and energy you give to trivial issues in your life.

Being alone and silent gives you a chance to listen and talk to someone very important to your growth and happiness -- you. It is only when you give yourself the gift of aloneness that you are whole, at one with yourself. This is when you are connected most directly with your essence, your spirit. Most of us, when overloaded by stress, turn to escapes like a drink or a ball game on TV to forget our troubles. But that's only half the answer because we're filling our minds with more distraction; you have to clear your mind and go within to see whether your behavior creates too much stress in your life and whether you should change.

The great writers and philosophers know the value of taking time for self-reflection through solitude. Creative productivity can't take place in a crowd. Herman Hesse addresses this issue in *Demian,* "Each man has only one genuine vocation -- to find the way to himself. He might end up as a poet or madman, as prophet or criminal -- that was not his affair, ultimately it was of no concern. His task was to discover his own destiny -- not an arbitrary one -- and live it out wholly and resolutely within himself."

When you spend time alone exploring new dimensions of yourself, awakening new areas of your being, sensing new awareness, the expanding self may come to realize that for your life to become authentic some changes must take place. Moustakas says, "When the lonely spirit awakens, the individual questions all the dimensions of his life."

In solitude, without your everyday petty distractions, you can face what your inner Self knows about relationships, work, the direction of your life, your ambitions and needs and hopes. Then you can begin to decide whether to put new energy into what's going on in your life now, or to abandon an unfruitful path and go on to something new.

In your private moments with yourself, you can call on your spirit to provide the nourishment that you will need to do what you have determined to do to make your life work again. Solitude is necessary for a periodic checkup, a rest from excess stress, a recharging of all your systems. In order to keep on functioning well and growing up in the world of other people, you must stop and check with yourself now and then, to see how you're doing, who you are, what you want.

AGAPE -- UNCONDITIONAL LOVE

Every religion in the world teaches love as the ultimate good. In life we should leave only footprints and teach only love. Effective teaching is not preaching, but teaching by example as well as by words.

If someone says "I love you" but treats you badly by making demands, abusing you, or setting limits to his love, he (or she) really does not love you, nor does he love himself. He is using you to get what he wants and needs in life. True love has no limits and no conditions. It is never expressed by words or actions as, "I will love you *if....*".

Unconditional love doesn't mean that you need to allow abusive people into your life. You can love the essence of someone even when you dislike the person's behavior. You can affirm such a person and love him or her from afar. In fact, people who are violent, abusive, irresponsible, and insecure need your unconditional love very much.

We all have the capacity for limitless love. *Love is infinite.* You can give it away and share it and never runs out. In fact you are enriched by loving because sometimes you get it back.

Love is sweet when you have a reunion with another after feeling apart or separate. Since the human condition is one of separation and aloneness, true love, not narcissistic love, gives us that opportunity for union and transcendence, which Erich Fromm has defined as "the most fundamental human desire."

In a spiritual sense the experience of loving gives us the chance to reconnect with the God within each one of us. Loving another allows me to know the secrets of the universe. I am reunited with my essence, my soul. Love brings us together; fear drives us apart.

Erich Fromm, in his classic book on love, *The Art Of Loving* says, "Love is not primarily a relationship to a specific person; it is an attitude, an orientation of character which determines the relatedness of a person to the world as a whole, not toward one object of love. If a person loves only one other person and is indifferent to the rest of his fellow men, his love is not love but a symbiotic attachment, or enlarged egotism."

The components of mature love, according to Fromm, are *care, responsibility, respect, and knowledge.* There are differences among the types of love we feel for different people, the love of parents and children, brotherly love, erotic love, self-love, and love of God. Each is an opportunity to bring to the surface different aspects of our selves, to experience the connectedness among all beings.

We are all *at-one-with* each other, struggling the same struggles, suffering the same insecurities, crying the same tears, learning the same lessons. When we realize this and put it into action in our lives we reach *atonement* (at-one-ment) -- the ability to really love our neighbors as ourselves. This is *agape,* unconditional love -- the highest form of love that mankind can achieve.

If we can recognize that everyone is at a different level of growing up and that others are working on their own lessons in their spiritual development, perhaps we can be more sensitive and patient with them. This is the position of being *nonjudgmental.*

As a psychotherapist, I am not in the position to judge or evaluate the relationships and circumstances of another life. I can only love and accept someone where he or she is right now. If she is stuck or miserable, I can help her to move forward, perhaps to reduce her confusion, explore options, and support her choices.

I remember learning to put this concept into practice a few years ago when I worked for a community mental health agency. Women would come to see me who had been emotionally and physically abused by their husbands. After listening to the stories of the women, I formed an image in my mind of the monster husband. But each time a husband came in to see me, I could only feel compassion for the tragedy of his life. I realized that forming a judgment of him even before I met him made me ineffectual in any intervention or therapy with that family. As I dropped my judgments I was able to work with the men in resolving their problems and making their relationships with their families healthier.

In order to make progress on our spiritual paths we must rid ourselves of negative feelings and thoughts. We cannot live in love and light while harboring hatred in our hearts or carrying around a sack full of unresolved feelings of resentment, rage, repressed anger, disappointments, hurt, and guilt.

You may have gone through life building on old hurts and expecting them to happen to you again, erecting emotional barriers to protect yourself. And guess what happens! You get exactly what you expected. You draw to yourself the very thing that you fear, because you have put all your energy into expecting it. This is a good illustration of how life gives us repeated opportunities to learn the same lesson until we *get it*.

Forgiveness is one way to let go and to stop burdening yourself with garbage from the past. You may think someone has treated you unfairly for no apparent reason. In your hurt and resentment you may brood and obsess over the offense. I have heard people say, "Okay, I will forgive him, but I will never forget" or "I don't get mad, I get even." Cancel the debt! Let go!

Both these attitudes imply that you have to protect yourself because the world is out to get you -- the world is a dangerous place --everyone is a potential enemy. If your mind and spirit are filled with these beliefs, and you can only see danger, you cut yourself off from your fellow human beings, and from being loved.

We have all been offended and hurt by other people's words or actions. Their cruelty may have been deliberate, out of insensitivity, or from their need for something that conflicted with what you wanted or needed. And you felt pain from the unkind thing they said or did as a result.

So what! Your feelings of hurt, guilt, anger, and

resentment are yours. You can wallow in them or use them to learn. Pain is a warning and a chance for you to look inside yourself and see where these feelings are coming from. Welcome them! Bless them! Use them to learn more about yourself. *Forgiveness is for you.* Forgive yourself. Forgive the other person so you can go on with your life. *Let the negative feelings go;* they are excess baggage that you do not need. Holding on to them hurts only you.

William Shakespeare said, "To err is human, to forgive divine." To forgive is critical for your growth and happiness. You are only responsible for your own thoughts, actions, and reactions. You are not responsible for what others say or do. Looking at a hurt as the other person's problem frees you to be nonjudgmental and to feel compassion. By releasing feelings of injury you free your energy to focus on the more creative and happier aspects of your life. You may even recognize your hurt as a blessing in disguise, because you can also forgive yourself for real or imagined offenses and begin to feel more love and compassion for yourself. And this is an important step in your growing up spiritually.

CHAPTER FIVE

TECHNIQUES FOR BECOMING SPIRITUALLY GROWN UP

Aldous Huxley said, "Life is not just what happens to you. It is what you do with what happens to you." If you do not bring to a conscious level what you have learned, you may make the same mistakes over and over again, as many times as it takes until you really learn the lesson and recognize it as learned.

Awareness means bringing the lesson to a conscious level, and letting experience become your best teacher. You have many lessons churning beneath your awareness but until you become conscious of them you can do little with them. Awareness allows you to explore your options and to take action. You can move to a resolution of each crisis or question, followed by a knowingness that assures you that you will not make that particular mistake again.

It may take a crisis to bring your wisdom to the surface. You may have to reach rock bottom with abuse or addiction or self-destruction or failure or fear, coming to the point where you will lose it all -- your freedom, your family, your very life -- before you are willing to learn and grow.

HEARING YOUR OWN WISDOM

How can you get to all those lessons churning beneath your conscious awareness before your problems reach a crisis point? First, you can develop a habit of looking inward. When something important is happening, something that has a strong emotional effect, causes physical discomfort, or poses a difficult question, ask yourself: "What does my inner being know about this question? What do I already know, deep in my soul?"

Then listen. Someone has said prayer is asking for help, and meditation is listening for the answers. Both are ways to invite your unconscious wisdom into your consciousness. There are other ways too: hypnotism, therapy, emotional breakdown, inspirational examples of others, intuition.

The great psychiatrist Carl Jung believed that we all have all of the answers within ourselves to live positive, happy, and productive lives. Think of that! You already have all the answers to any possible question. When you learn to tap into this storehouse of wisdom made up of all the experiences and all the knowledge acquired by the human race throughout history you will have a resource that is free and always available.

After you have gone through a difficult or an exciting experience, do you usually think it's time to move on to something else? If it has been painful, you're glad it's over and your primary interest is to find relief from the pain. But you will be so much better prepared for the next challenge life dishes up if you take some time to review that experience, and see as honestly as you can what it can teach you.

A good way to be able to learn from every opportunity

is to develop the habit of staying with the experience in your mind for a while. Explore the thoughts and feelings and insights and sensations it stimulates. If you prefer a different outcome, mentally rehearse the result or outcome you would like.

Ask yourself, What did I learn from this? What could I have done differently? What would I have preferred the outcome to be? Be creative, and be honest. If you don't get to the answers right away, don't worry. Relax and wait. Your subconscious will be working on the questions in unseen ways. To learn these important truths, you are tapping into the inner resources, of your higher Self.

When you are willing to listen to yourself, you will get the answers. They may come to you unexpectedly in a dream, a flash of insight, in reverie, or at some odd time, such as while you're driving or washing dishes or thinking about something completely different. You can learn from these revelations by recognizing these messages as a sign that your subconscious has something to tell you.

You can improve your ability to hear the subconscious speak from its inner wisdom to the conscious mind by developing your understanding and use of intuition, dreams, meditation, visual imagery, humor, nature, music, and creativity. You can learn which of these work best for you and begin to apply them to any thorny problem or change you decide will help you grow up.

Sometimes the inner "voice" is called intuition. It reveals messages in different ways. On occasion we get flashes of insight, and suddenly we get the answer to a perplexing problem. Many significant scientific, artistic, political, or intellectual breakthroughs have been intuitively sensed. Albert Einstein discovered the Theory of Relativity in an intuitive "flash." But in order to reach that insight, he had to be receptive and he had prepared his intellectual understanding of physics through years of working on solving this problem.

Every person has the capacity to be intuitive, but some of

us trust and are more receptive to our intuitive minds than others. How do you feel about your own intuition? If you use it on a regular basis, great! If not, come to terms with your resistance and begin to tap into this wonderful resource. All you have to do is listen!

It's like having have inner guidance. Have you ever told yourself as you were falling asleep that you wanted to wake up at a certain time, and you did, without using an alarm clock? Have you ever been driving through a busy parking lot looking for a parking space -- with no luck? Then you say to yourself, I want a parking place close to the door of the store. And immediately someone pulls out right in front of you. Have you ever thought about someone for no apparent reason and ten minutes later you receive a phone call or a letter from that person?

We have all had these experiences. Maybe they are coincidences and maybe not. Maybe they are the work of our personal angels or spirit guides, maybe not. Maybe some presently unknown inner mechanism is responding, maybe not. I think of solving problems in terms of guidance, which may be either inner or outer guidance. I trust this guidance, and I get personal help every time I ask for it, including parking spaces whenever I need them. Try for yourself and let me know how well it works for you.

In order to hear your inner voice you must learn to quiet your busybody mind. In Part V, I'll describe a thought-stopping technique to help you quiet yourself, which begins with relaxing the body. Relaxing the body will automatically extend into relaxing the mind and the emotions. You approach these two systems through the body; the body carries around your emotional tension, so relaxing one will help ease the other.

MEDITATION AND PRAYER

While you're relaxed is the time that you can listen to your inner voice. Meditation helps. Meditation is the practice of tuning into your inner Self. It's a systematic way to get in touch with your intuition. In meditation, your body, mind, and emotions are receding from your attention, and you are tuned into the deeper place within yourself.

Praying is a way to ask for help, guidance, understanding, or healing, from whatever source works for you. Be patient. Praying regularly will help you slow down and find inner peace and answers to implement the changes and goals that you want most, as well as reduce the stress and tension produced by your everyday life. Be sure to listen for the answers.

Meditation is easy, but like any other skill it takes practice to master it. Here's how to start. Stretch out on a sofa or bed or comfortable chair. Remove any visual distractions. Take off your shoes and jewelry and loosen any tight clothes like belts or brassieres. Do not cross your arms or legs. Turn off the radio and television, unplug the telephone, and shut out any distracting noises or lights.

Now take a deep breath and focus all your attention on your breathing for the next few minutes. Breathe in through your nose, then exhale slowly through your mouth. Concentrate on inhaling clean air and pure energy, and exhaling all the tension and toxins accumulated in your body. Fill your lungs full and hold your breath in to a slow count of 8. Then slowly exhale through your mouth to a count of 8. Stay still before inhaling again to another count of 8. Repeat the cycle, but exhale more slowly to a count of 16, then to 24, then 32.

After only four or five breath cycles using this technique, you will be very relaxed and in a state of mind and body ready to tune in to your inner wisdom. You will be amazed at what only 10 or 15 minutes of meditation can do to change your state of mind and relax your body. It is helpful to focus on one word to keep unwanted thoughts and unresolved problems from disturbing you. Visualize the word RELAX written on the inside of your forehead, and regulate your breathing to match it. *RE--* inhale *LAX--*exhale and breathe from your belly as you do when you are asleep. Meditation can be directed or nondirected. The technique just described is used primarily to relax you and is not directed toward any purpose. It will help reduce tension, anger, frustration, or intrusive thoughts.

Directive meditation is similar to prayer and used for healing and problem-solving. After you have relaxed, you can focus on the part of your body you want to heal and imagine a green or white light penetrating and vibrating in that part of your body. Visualize that part healed and healthy.

To solve a specific problem -- at work, in the family, about the future, regarding money, in any aspect of your life -- examine mentally and systematically all of the issues involved, and ask your inner guidance for a solution. Then let it go. Release thoughts about the problem and wait for the solution to occur. It will come, but be patient. The more complex and difficult the problem the longer it takes to be solved. Sometimes the solution is a decision you make within you to take some positive action on your own behalf.

RIGHT BRAIN AND CREATIVITY

Now that you have learned to relax your body and quiet your mind, you are ready to tune into your inner Self through other intuitive processes. When you switch over to your right brain (the imaginative, emotional, nonlogical part of your mind), you will discover creative solutions to the perplexing problems in your life. Often the solutions are revealed to you in the language of the right brain -- symbols, not words. These symbols reveal connections with events in the past -- your personal past or the universal human experience -- to help you understand what is happening in your life in the present.

The right brain may return an answer to you during meditation or prayer, or it may deliver its message at unexpected times when you're busy with everyday things. The media for the right brain's symbolic language include dreams, flashes of insight, words that pop unexpectedly out of your mouth, a powerful attraction to a person or place, "gut feelings" that warn you away from a person or situation, a song or TV image that you can't tear your attention away from.

The messages conveyed in right-brain language come from the *superconscious*. This is different from your *subconscious*. The subconscious works like a computer; it stores all of your sensory data: sights, sounds, smells, thoughts, memories, and experiences. When called upon or during traumatic situations it can retrieve information and impressions in the form of memories. Sometimes however, only fragments surface and you may need to work with a professional to recover a broader and more detailed memory.

The superconscious, on the other hand, contains the memory of all you are; and the wisdom of all the knowledge in the universe. The superconscious is the home of Jung's collective unconscious. It is your inner or higher Self, your soul or spirit.

DREAMS

Let's look more closely at dreams as an example of how the super conscious talks to us. Our brains do not stop activity when we sleep. Everyone has four or five dreams during a night's sleep, though you probably only consciously remember the last one you had before awakening. When you dream, your right brain expresses the content of your superconscious in its symbolic language. You can learn from this storehouse of spiritual knowledge by developing techniques to help you recall more of your dreams and interpret their meaning as it applies to the current events in your life.

Keeping a dream journal will help you to recognize repeated themes in your dreams. If you are interested in pursuing dream interpretation at a deeper level, look for a dream group led by a Jungian therapist. Some dream symbols have universal meanings, water represents emotions; a house or tree represents yourself or your our body or your life. Most symbols are uniquely yours, they are drawn from the experiences of your life. For example, a spider may be a friendly pet to one person and a ghastly monster to someone else. How the right brain uses spiders in your dreams depends on your actual past experience with them.

Working with your dream content is a fascinating and fun way to unlock the mysteries within you. It can speed up your understanding of your responses to events in your life, and give you insights into self-defeating patterns of behavior. With that knowledge, you can make better decisions about how to get your life on track and continue growing up.

Marsha is a 34-year-old social worker who came to see me after the breakup of her marriage of seven years. It was her second divorce, and she felt like a miserable failure -- not because she wasn't a good person but because she kept getting involved with men she regarded as losers. After our third session, she had a dream that helped her to unravel her problems.

During her dream, she kept seeing and hearing one word shouted and whispered and flashed before her, "Rescuer -- Rescuer -- Rescuer." She was in a park where there were many birds in the trees and on the ground. In the morning she looked up the term "rescuer" in a book on transactional analysis, conveniently waiting in her bookcase. Marsha realized that the men in her life were inevitably childish, needy, dependent, and passive-aggressive. They were attracted to her strength and nurturing. She saw them as "birds with broken wings" that she could take home and fix up.

With this new insight, Marsha was able to see that her broken birds didn't appreciate her rescuing. They only wanted to lean on her and sap her strength. They didn't get any stronger, but she got weaker and more disillusioned. Marsha began to define more clearly what she wanted in a man. She was able to watch out for and avoid the rescuer role, and search for a man who was responsible and grown up and had his own strength.

Dreams can teach you similar things about your life --
from that well of all wisdom that lives deep in your soul when
you take the time to pay attention to them. Working with your
dream symbols to unravel the messages can help you understand
your present fears or personal problems. *Gestalt Therapy
Verbatim*, by Fritz Perls, describes several dream work techniques.

However, I believe it is best to do dream work with a
therapist or in a group that allows you to get support and
feedback in a safe environment.

LOOSENING UP

It isn't easy to get past rigidity, especially if you've lived
by a code of rules for many years. But if you need to become more
flexible so you can learn the lessons of growing up, you can do it.

Start slowly with something simple, like wearing a
different color dress or ordering a meal you've never tried.
Consciously listen to other people's points of view. When you
find yourself giving a ready answer, stop and think of other
possibilities. You don't have to like them all or change your
opinion; just acknowledge that there are other answers. Try to
imagine how another person's rules or viewpoints might work as
well for him as yours do for you.

Allow yourself to enjoy new situations, even those in
which you don't know what the outcome *should* be. Your inner
Self can handle new approaches and new situations. It is
marvelously adaptable. It is your frightened ego that says, "No,
I must do it this way. I can't take a risk." But your inner Self is
so much stronger than your ego. Put your faith there, and it will
guide you safely through new territory.

BECOMING INNER-DIRECTED

If you think you are affected too much by outside events

and want to become more inner-directed, you will have to work at it. You can choose one of the techniques described throughout this book, or some type of therapy or self-help group to help you. Inner direction is one of the major parts of being grown up. Any change requires inner direction and strengthens it. You can apply these general steps in increasing healthy self-control in a number of situations, whatever strategy you use:

1. *Recognize that life is a series of separations and losses* that lead to temporary disorganization of your body, mind and emotions. You lose balance for a while. Changes especially ones involving loss can cause temporary confusion, sadness, and imbalance. After the cycle of grief or adjustment to loss is completed, you will restructure your life at a higher level of development. It's too bad this doesn't happen without pain, but few of us change without a crisis forcing us to.

2. *Be willing to examine, re-experience, complete, then release old painful experiences.* You can gradually empty that burdensome sack full of old hurts, resentments, disappointments, anger, and eventually leave it behind instead of dragging it along wherever you go. A support group, a good friend, or a therapist is important, because in telling your story to someone else you bring old issues to the surface. Then you can grieve, rage, allow yourself to feel the pain. Only then can you release it, so you can heal.

3. *Take risks! Dare to do something new and different.* Look around your life and decide what you want to change. Where do you feel happy, trapped, stuck, or undernourished? Is it in your love life? Take some risks to work things out with a friend, lover, mate, or find a new one. Is it in your job? Ask for a promotion, raise, new responsibilities, or start reading the help-wanted ads, polish your resume, go take classes to prepare for a new career.

If your marriage is in trouble, go to marriage counseling, attend a couples marriage encounter workshop together, go on a vacation, talk out your problems honestly, or get a divorce. Use wise problem-solving skills to examine the needed information   about your options and choices; then listen to the voice inside that tells you what you really need to make you happy and follow that voice. No one else can or will take responsibility for your life. It is up to you!

4. *Overcome your fears! Don't let them keep you rigid and inflexible.* Start by making a list of your fears. Brainstorm, write down everything that pops into your head no matter how silly it is. You may end up with several pages. Now group them together into major areas like fear of the unknown, fear of abandonment, fear of rejection, fear of not being able to take care of yourself. This will help you to pinpoint the areas of your worst fears so you can work to overcome them.

Spiritually you can let your subconscious mind assist you in recognizing your fears and discovering their sources. What do your dreams, fantasies, and flashes of insight tell you about your fears? Remember most fears are based on frightening or traumatic experiences in your past and are irrational and dysfunctional in your present every day life. They are smoke, fog, castles in the sand, and can be swept away with a wave of self-confidence. When they are gone you will quickly forget the paralyzing effect they once had on you. Then you will be free to grow up and get on with your life.

5. *Start to play again! Get to know that fun loving playful kid inside of you.* The one who loves adventure, a good joke, laughs, loves to play games, go to movies, watch a ball game. That kid sometimes fell down, got bruised and cut, but got up and tried again. Even as a grownup you will be hurt sometimes, but don't let that stop you, get up and keep going. This is how to learn and grow. Don't forget to laugh along the way!

APPRECIATING SOLITUDE

Solitude is necessary to listen to your inner wisdom.

Regular times of introspection will strengthen the connection between your unconscious and conscious awareness, and allow the messages to come forth so you can apply them to the situations you are presently learning about in your life.

Find your own best time and place to be alone. If you have a family and a busy life, like most of us do, it may take some creative planning. Try a few minutes for a morning walk, or some time on your lunch hour, a weekend at the ocean, or in the woods, a religious retreat, maybe keeping a journal will work for you. Trade off private time with your spouse or partner so you both can enjoy your "space".

Maybe you enjoy listening to music, playing an instrument, painting, gardening, taking photographs, or writing poetry. Make solitude a priority. A little time each day will keep you balanced. You deserve it. Remember you are as important as the other people in your life who make demands on you.

REACHING OUT

If your life is in turmoil ask for help. Find a person or group to talk to. There is comfort in knowing you are not alone, that others are in the same boat. Self-help groups are everywhere. The Alcoholics Anonymous model has expanded to many areas. There are groups for adult children of alcoholics, (and dysfunctional families of origin in general), co-dependency, emotions anonymous, sex and love addicts anonymous, sex abuse groups, gamblers anonymous, and others starting daily as new needs are identified. These groups are free, except for a voluntary donation. They are in every town. They are not a substitute for therapy, but are an adjunct to it.

For grief and loss there are *therapy groups,* for which you are charged a fee to pay for a professionally trained therapist who facilitates the group. And there are *self-help groups* at many churches, funeral homes, and community centers. There are also speciality groups dealing with specific losses; like Mothers

Against Drunk Driving, for deaths and injuries involving drugs or alcohol; Compassionate Friends, for parents and siblings who have lost a child (no matter how old the child was); Children to Children for children who have lost a parent; and Parents of Murdered Children.

Most cities have chapters of these or other similar groups. The support in being able to share your grief and pain is valuable in helping you to heal from your immediate crisis. Reach out to help others when you can, and ask for help when you need it.

LOVING UNCONDITIONALLY

Sometimes another person's faults interfere with our desire to be loving. When you think of him or her you can't seem to help feeling resentful, being critical or making assumptions and judgements about their behavior. On occasion you have to associate with someone you just plain don't like.

In such cases I use an affirmation that frees me from the negative charge I get when I am with, or even think of that person. Using the person's name I say,

"I love you, John.

I bless you, John.

I forgive you, John.

I release you to your highest good in the Universe".

Practice looking for the good in each person. Every time a negative thought arises, replace it with a positive one. Sometimes we see and focus on things about another person that we don't like about ourself. This is called projection; we *project* on another some trait we haven't acknowledged about us.

Negativity only hurts you. It drains your energy, and keeps you disconnected from your soul. If you begin to focus on more positive aspects of people and events you will start to become more lovable yourself. And you'll like yourself better too.

PART THREE

GROWING UP
EMOTIONALLY

WINNERS AND LOSERS

How do you account for the difference between those who "make it" and those who "bomb out" in any effort in life? Talent isn't the whole answer. Nor is luck. There is another element that separates winners from losers.

When a winner makes a mistake she says,
"I was wrong."
When a loser makes a mistake she says,
"It wasn't my fault."
A winner goes through a problem.
A loser goes around and never gets past it.
A winner says, "I'm good, and I can be better."
A loser says, "I'm not as bad as a lot of people."
A winner says, " I'll be glad to do it."
A loser says, "That's not my job."
A winner listens.
A loser just waits for his time to talk.
A winner takes responsibility for his actions.
A loser blames others for his problems.

Author Unknown

CHAPTER SIX

WHAT DOES IT MEAN TO BE EMOTIONALLY GROWN UP?

"Growth in self-fulfilling persons can come through struggle, agony, and conflict, as well as through joy, and love --or through any other emotion"

Clark Mostakas

Emotional development is the most complex of the four aspects of growing up and getting in balance. There is more information to cover in this section because this is the area in which most adults are the most childish and need the most work.

We humans are just now evolving to the stage of being able to handle our emotions. Recent progress in knowledge of human psychology, has given us new and better understanding and strategies for parenting our children and of validating, instead of punishing, shaming or belittling, their emotions. And as adults we need to learn to quit doing the same to ourselves.

Most people today are not so fortunate. For adults

whose childhood feelings were not validated or respected the process of growing up emotionally is like being lost in the woods without a map -- stumbling, struggling, and suffering in isolation and confusion -- taking many wrong paths, then finally, with a little luck and a lot of hard work, you may find your way out.

People are most often motivated to understand and change their emotions during a personal crisis. Emotions warn you when you are in danger, when your basic needs are not being met, moving you to make changes. You will benefit most from your emotions when you realize that you have options leading to choice. Choice is empowering, it puts you in control of your life.

Most people stay focused on what they know, and what feels familiar to them even if it doesn't work. There are many ways of "being". In order to become better we must be willing to expand beyond the set limits and learn to be open and receptive to something new. In order to grow we must be willing to see, hear and feel things in new and different ways.

Some people, however, are so out of touch with their emotions that they are in serious trouble before they begin to deal with life's problems. Jerry came to see me mandated by the court, he was on probation, after being convicted of pulling a gun on his wife, threatening to kill her or himself. He told me that his only problem was that he didn't have enough time to get everything done that he needed to do. At first he wasn't interested in counseling except to help him manage his time better.

When I asked about his relationship with his wife, tears came to his eyes and he said that if he didn't do more at home she was going to leave him. When we broke down his daily schedule I saw that he was already working 14 hours every day. There was no more time to do the extra things she demanded from him.

When I asked about his family of origin he told me , again tearfully, that his mother had died when he was 18 years old. He never finished grieving for her. Now 54 years old, with a Ph.D. in

Engineering this man was extremely depressed, anxious, and very out of touch with his emotions. They were so much on the surface that he cried in every session we had for three months. He had ignored his own feelings and emotional needs for so long that now they were all crowding to the surface for attention. His strong defenses were crumbling and letting him down. His feelings were all coming up at once and he felt confused and out of control. He considered suicide as a way out.

An important key to growing up emotionally is learning to recognize and identify your emotions -- not ignore or control them in a rigid or repressive way, but using each emotion to let you know whether you are on track or not. Every strong reaction comes from within you and is a signal that something is wrong and requires special attention from you. Even negative feelings have a helpful aspect.

Your feelings are a part of you. Honor them! They will not be ignored forever. They must be acknowledged and expressed in order to enhance your growth and for you to have good *mental health*.

We human beings have a wide variety of emotions available to us. Being grownup emotionally means that you are able to *identify* your feelings, *experience* and *express* them, *choose* an emotion appropriate to the situation, use them to learn and grow, and then *release* them appropriately.

You can learn to convert your negative emotions to positive, appropriate ones to aid in your growth. Emotional maturity also means that you can monitor and identify your emotional responses and change them to work to your advantage.

IDENTIFYING YOUR EMOTIONS

Emotions make up much of what we experience in life as human beings. Yet formal education has neglected to help us develop appropriate emotional maturity. There is little taught on what to feel, when to feel, or how to feel. A shocking number of people are numb when it comes to describing or even naming their feelings at a given moment. Most of us go through life reacting to our emotions in a kneejerk fashion -- acting on them but not understanding or even being able to identify them.

Emotions are not as easy to identify and define as the physical organs and functions of the body. When something goes wrong with the body it is relatively easy to detect and correct the problem. Emotions, on the other hand, are fuzzier and more subtle. They are intermittent, they pile up on top of each other, they progress and change unpredictably, and their boundaries are undefined. Often you feel more than one emotion at a time. Sometimes mild feelings escalate into powerful ones.

For example, concern may become panic, frustration may erupt into an angry outburst or a violent rage. Happiness may become bliss with the right timing and circumstances. We often experience mixed emotions, such as feelings of sadness at the loss involved in change, along with an equally strong excitement about new opportunities.

In counseling sessions I frequently ask clients, "What are you feeling right now?" A common answer is, "I feel that we should look into this in more depth." The word *that* when combined with "I feel" always changes the feeling to an idea or a thought. Or the answer is "I feel bad" or "I feel fine" or "I feel good". Feeling "bad," "good", or "fine" is not one feeling but a composite of several possibly negative or positive feelings, which need to be sorted out if you are to understand your emotions in a grown-up way. We call these *mixed emotions*.

The average person experiences ten to fifteen emotions per day, ranging from feeling anxious about being late for work, frustrated by slow traffic, impatient at a long-winded person on the telephone, loving toward your spouse, friendly toward a neighbor, playful with your cat, disappointed at not getting a raise, and on and on with every event of the day.

The real purpose of emotions is to send you messages about how an event affects your total self, and to act as a barometer for how well you are doing in keeping your life in balance. Whether you listen to the message or not is up to you. Think of your emotions as caring friends who are there to help you learn about yourself, to assist you in taking control of your life, and to advise you to make the necessary changes when you get off track.

Say that you dread going to work, or you are forgetful. Perhaps you often feel hopeless, you get irritated over small things, and frequently argue with your spouse. Your emotions tell you that something is wrong in your life. There could be something wrong in your job or your marriage. Or the problem could be your perception of and response to those situations, based on old fears that play over and over like tape messages in your head.

Instead of feeling victimized or trapped, let the uncomfortable emotions warn you that it would be wise to take some time to evaluate what you are feeling about some areas of your life that need your attention. Because your emotions come from within you, you must look within to recognize what you are feeling at any given moment.

Many people believe that they are victims of their emotions and they respond as if they have no control over these feelings. The truth is, you not only can control your own emotions but, with a little information and practice, you can choose appropriate emotions for any situation.

When you control your emotions, you control your life. So powerful is this part of you that without control you are ever at the mercy of an unexpected bombardment of elusive and poorly recognized moods and feelings. Without control, spontaneous emotional responses rule your life, with control your feelings can enhance your sensitivity, compassion, and sense of well-being. Healthy, grown-up emotional control is awareness and selection, not rigid and repressive control that stops emotions before they are felt and fully experienced.

YOUR UNIQUE PERSONALITY

All members of our species share common basic emotional responses to the events in their lives. We all feel sorrow and grief when a loved one dies. We are all afraid when threatened. We all feel guilty when we hurt someone else without provocation. We all get angry when our loved ones are wronged. We feel joyful when a baby is born healthy. We celebrate weddings, mourn at funerals, enjoy sex.

Different cultures and individuals may show these emotions in different ways, and individually we all learn different patterns of expressing or repressing various feelings as we grow up. But at heart, as human animals, we all start with the same basic emotional equipment before we learn through experience what to do with it.

Our survival emotions of fight or flight are regulated by our limbic system, the primitive part of the human physical brain, an evolutionary remnant from times when we were competing with lions and tigers for food and shelter. Just as our wisdom teeth once served the important function of tearing off and chewing raw meat, the limbic part of the brain still responds to danger with a burst of adrenaline which provides us with super strength to cope with an immediate crisis.

All emotions grow from this simple animal base. Our feelings are far more complicated today because we have much more complex situations to respond to. Just as in more primitive times, strong emotions make demands on, and add stress to, the body.

While you are 95 percent the same as your fellow human beings you are also unique. Each of us is an individual in personality. Among all the personalities in this world, there are no exact duplicates, not even twins. Nowhere in the universe is there an exact duplicate of you.

One of my favorite exercises with students demonstrates this point. I give each one a walnut (or a lemon or an apple). They are instructed to get to know their object intimately. After about five minutes I collect the walnuts and put all of them into one bowl. The students are asked to come forward and to find their own walnuts in the bowl.

They can always do it. In just a few minutes, each has gotten to know the uniqueness of his or her walnut -- its shape, feel, appearance, texture, little wrinkles and bumps. Sure, it is only a walnut, but it is special and different from any other walnut in the world -- just as you are!

Your uniqueness -- your personality -- is a combination of your genetic makeup, your social environment, your intellectual capacity, and your level of spiritual development. You feel this difference emotionally, you may feel proud, special, misunderstood, inadequate, uncomfortable, or some other way about what makes you different. Grownups learn to appreciate their uniqueness, because they understand that those differences are what make up their individual identities.

EMOTIONAL DEVELOPMENT

Emotional development begins with the raw material from the genes and is tempered by relationships with the primary people in a child's life. Children who are treated with respect and love, and taught to believe in themselves and made to feel good about who they are, will grow into secure and positive adults. If your parents gave you a healthy, stable emotional foundation, you'll be able to establish positive and trusting relationships and have confidence in yourself throughout life.

Conversely, a child whose early years have been loaded

with punishment, threats, frustration, abuse, neglect, death of a parent, parental divorce, exposure to violence and fighting, war, witnessing or being involved in sadistic religious practices will have difficult relationships and a damaged self-image throughout life. She or he may grow up into a suspicious, accusative, jealous, unfriendly, withdrawn, and uncooperative person, who may spend adulthood trying to avoid or sort out these confusing and conflicting feelings.

Frequently the traumatic memories are suppressed, repressed, and buried deep within the subconscious mind. Good therapeutic intervention is necessary to heal the old wounds. In a safe environment the person needs to remember and to relive with appropriate feelings the traumatic events. It is like healing an open, bleeding, pus-infected wound. After it is healed it becomes like scar tissue, still there as a reminder, but no longer having power to hurt.

When abuse is early, severe, and ongoing, the adult may have become psychotic or develop a personality disorder as a way to cope with childhood traumas. Sometimes they never recover.

The emotionally abused adult/child may desperately want love but not know how to recognize and accept it. This person will carry scars, just as the victim of physical abuse bears.

Most of us got a combination of healthy and abusive messages during our childhood, as our parents simply conveyed their emotions to us, not always appropriately. This combination of messages from your childhood makes up much of your emotional identity today.

Your individual emotional nature also draws on the emotional responses you learned from other adults in your life, and from the role models you saw around you. You observed the responses of your parents, neighbors, and teachers to events, and you picked up feelings from song lyrics, peer reactions, shows, and movies.

If your adult role models weren't perfect, and didn't

always respond to your mistakes and questions with patience and loving care, you will have a little repair work to do. It's not too late to offer tenderness to that child that was you. The child is still around, inside you. You can begin to re-parent yourself and to complete the growing-up process by giving yourself the love and acceptance everyone needs. Then you can get your emotions in better order -- and grow up.

LEARNING YOUR EMOTIONS

Because of our vulnerability at birth we humans are physically and emotionally dependent on our parents to feed and nurture us for many years. This dependence is absolute. Without their support we would die. Human infants cannot be left alone because they cannot take care of themselves.

Even as adults, sometimes we still have dependency needs. When we are vulnerable we feel weak, soft, scared and believe that we can't take care of ourself. We want to be held, fed, touched, listened to, nurtured and reassured. If these dependency needs were not adequately met during infancy and early childhood we will always be looking for someone to take care of us to meet these needs.

This is why some people look for the loving parent in adult relationships that they never had in childhood. The young woman draped on the arm of a man her father's age, or the young man involved with a woman as old as his mother are the more obvious examples. These unconscious needs continue until we learn to meet our own needs or to ask for what we want and need in healthier, more appropriate ways.

ADDICTIVE BEHAVIOR

Other people try to get their needs met using addictive behaviors. Recent work by twelve-step advocates have revealed many different addictions including substances like food, alcohol, drugs, nicotine, or anything we ingest or sniff or inject into our body. Other addictions include action or behavior addictions like gambling, shoplifting, work, extreme physical activity and so on. Another form of addictive behavior deals with relationships, romance addicts, sex addicts, people who are emotionally numb, and are unable to make a permanent commitment.

An addiction gives you a temporary mood lift or "high", then after a little while you dip down to where you were before or even lower, which stimulates the desire to do the addicted substance or action again. One signal of addictive behavior is obsessing about it when it (including a perceived love object) is not present. To crave *it* or a *person* is to become a slave to it and temporary relief comes when you use it or see the person.

People use addictive behaviors when they feel disconnected from other people, their spiritual Self, their family, and friends. To break out of this trap we must reconnect with these resources. Recovery is the process of being able to recognize when we are vulnerable, afraid, sad, and hurt, and to figure out what we want and need to feel okay. Then we must ask for it, preferably from someone who is capable and willing to give it. It may only be a hug, or someone to listen without trying to "fix it".

Our external emotional needs are met by connecting with others. Our internal needs are met by reconnecting with our own spirit which seeks once again balance and harmony.

SEPARATION ANXIETY

One of the major emotional stressors for infants and young children is learning to accept the absence of the mother, father, or primary caretaker. Separation anxiety, which can surface at any age, and carries over into adulthood, is the undefined, pervasive fear of being abandoned or deserted. For infants, every time the primary caretaker leaves it is like a mini death. Children gradually adjust to the parent's absence as they become old enough to understand that the parent always comes back. This fear often resurfaces for adults when they find themselves alone after a death or divorce, or when children leave home.

Sometimes parents are physically present, but emotionally absent to the child, especially parents who abuse drugs and alcohol or use other escapist behavior to avoid responsibility for the child. Or parents who were emotionally abandoned themselves as children and don't have the capacity to provide emotional love, support and nurturing to their child.

This child will also develop an underlying fear of not being able to take care of himself. He believes that any demands for having his needs met will be received with anger, blame, and fault-finding or punishment. Very early this child will learn that to be safe means repressing needs, wants and worst of all, feelings. He will become an adult that is not emotionally available to himself, nor to others, feeling frozen in an infant's unmet needs, at a time that was pre-verbal. And as he tries to understand and sort out why his life isn't working he will be frustrated over and over at knowing he feels bad but can't tell anyone why. He is a prime candidate for addictive escape.

Imagine an infant in a crib, crying from hunger or dirty diapers, neglected. Or a two-year-old who falls and scrapes his knees, runs to his mother for comfort. She tells him, "Stop being such a baby," or " Shut up. I'm busy watching television (or talking on the telephone). Just stop crying! " The mother who doesn't want to be bothered to comfort her child inflicts wounds that go much deeper than the skin. When neglect of a child's needs is constant, the skin on his knee will heal, but the other wounds will remain painfully present. When a human child's physical and emotional needs are not met, the seeds of problems (weeds) are planted, to be harvested again and again in adulthood.

In adulthood, when the fear of not being able to take care of ourselves is triggered, it re-emerges as anxiety or undefined fear. As you get older, life events force you to grow up, rely on your own resources, nurture and save yourself. And most people do this very well under normal circumstances.

But, during a crisis like a death of a loved one, divorce or ending a relationship with a significant other, a serious illness, surgery or an accident the emotions that surface can be very frightening, especially if the crisis involves some type of a separation.

The reason many people stay in dead or destructive relationships and avoid the pain of separation is the fear of being left alone and not being able to take care of themselves, even though they are able to dress, bath, shop, cook, drive a car, hold a job, make friends and function in every other way. They still feel inadequate in meeting their own emotional needs.

That old separation fear is re-triggered and you once again become a helpless emotional infant or little kid. A little later I will discuss what you can do to help your infant to feel safe, secure, loved and taken care of.

Conscience, which is related to the emotions of guilt and shame is also learned early. The child feels guilty for not doing what mother wants. As guilt develops so does the controlling mechanism of moral development, that elusive inner device called human conscience. In its earliest form, this is the angel on one shoulder and the devil on the other giving conflicting directives about our choices in behavior. Conscience -- the preference for the angel -- is generally well established by age five. With proper parental guidance the child learns to make correct choices, though later the moral dilemmas become more complicated.

Moral maturity means determining your own standards of behavior. The standards you apply throughout life will be based on early childhood teachings, religious training, and the lessons you learn in the lifelong process of growing up. Your emotions will act as a barometer to warn you when something is wrong inside, when you are out of balance.

NEGATIVE FEELINGS

Mistrust, shame, and guilt are all learned by age five. When the feelings a child expresses are not validated or are ridiculed or ignored or punished the child learns that his or her feelings are trouble. The safest thing to do and survive is to stop feeling. Feelings are dangerous. The child is taught or pressured by this disapproval to deny his or her true feelings, thus learning that those feelings are wrong or "bad."

And because little children cannot distinguish between themselves and their feelings, they begin to believe that *they* are bad. Their parents may even call them a "bad boy" or "bad girl". So they quickly learn that in order to get their parents love and approval and to be taken care of, they must hide their true feelings, to feel ashamed of them, to deny them.

Thus begin self-doubt, feelings of worthlessness, poor self-esteem, and all the negative feelings that live within the individual throughout life, and are passed on from generation to generation in our shame-based society. With each new affront the child internalizes more fears.

By the time a child is 3 or 4 years old he has an unhealthy shame bank, buried and readily accessed with each new event that creates self-doubt, anger, or sadness. When a person is hard on himself or is overly controlled, rigid, or aggressive, it is a sign that he has an overabundance of negative feelings.

Aggressive behavior begins very early in life. By age 2, a child has developed a sense of "thine and mine" about toys, clothes, and other possessions; this sense of ownership is part of the child's process of realizing that he is a separate being from all that is in his environment. When toddlers are encouraged to share their toys with friends, they usually do so reluctantly, then after a short period they snatch back the toy, leaving a bewildered playmate.

Physical aggression, directed against siblings and age-mates, begins about the same time. If a parent doesn't protect the child from such attacks, and doesn't make it clear to the offender that such behavior will not be tolerated, the child may integrate physical aggressiveness into his personality. If your parents hit you as a punishment for aggressive behavior, they taught you that using aggression is the way to stop aggression -- just the opposite from their intent. Children learn from what adults *do* more than from what they *say*.

When a young child is frustrated, he or she is unable to identify and verbalize disappointment or fears. Sometimes the first reaction is to attack another physically by hitting, kicking, punching, biting, or throwing an object. Parents must help the child to talk about the problem and to find another way to deal with it.

Aggressive behavior and uncontrolled anger may emerge strongly at adolescence. When you're grown up, if your first impulse is still to strike out or make threats, you've got to begin teaching yourself new ways of responding to frustration.

This culture allows our sons to express anger, but not our daughters. We are more tolerant of outbursts of anger or temper tantrums in little boys and encourage them to play sports, where the "kill the enemy/competitor" theme prevails. They learn to see women as weak and helpless, vulnerable and easily victimized.

It's not so common to see girls and women expressing anger. Angry women are frightening to most men, calling up visions of being reduced to little boys, feeling helpless as they often did at their mother's anger. In our culture, angry women aren't "nice". They are seen as bitches, nagging, castrating, destructive women.

Just as little boys are encouraged to express their anger, little girls are forbidden to express theirs. They learn to repress it and to "stuff" it inside. They are made to feel guilty for such feelings so they freeze them behind shame, guilt, and self-doubt. They become confused about their own feelings, limits, and rights.

Instead the young woman learns to be a *nice* girl so people will like her, especially mom and dad upon whom she is dependent for her very survival. Even when a woman has achieved some status in her business or profession, her assertiveness is misinterpreted as aggressiveness and is seen as unfeminine, while the same behavior by a man is manly, competent, and successful.

Depression is the biggest mental health problem of the elderly in this country. It is a major part of the grieving process. You go through a period of depression before you accept the reality of a change or loss in your life. The longer you live, the more separations and losses you will experience, and you can expect to feel depressed at such times.

By the time you're elderly, you probably will have buried parents, siblings, friends, and maybe even your children. Losses in early years give a child a chance to learn how to manage sadness and depression. If each loss is not handled emotionally and grieved for as it happens, the sadness will build and depression can become chronic. See my book *Letting Go With Love: The Grieving Process* for grieving for different relationships.

HAPPINESS

Happiness is a feeling of well-being and satisfaction. We can experience it alone while watching a sunset, hiking in the wilderness, or soaking in a bubble bath, or with others while dancing, singing, laughing, playing a sport or game, walking together, talking intimately, or sharing a tender moment.

Happiness is experienced during the present, in the here and now and is not connected with events or thoughts of the past or future. It is a positive, involved feeling that fills you up with feeling good. Happiness also involves the absence of stress and depression, at least for the moment. Unfortunately most people find happiness as fleeting as leaves falling from a tree, after a special event ends, or when a relationship is in trouble.

You can learn to stay happier longer by having positive, loving thoughts. It is easier to be happy when you are feeling loving toward yourself and others.

LOVE

The most complicated emotion to learn -- and the one we most need to feel and understand is love.

When and where do we learn to love or not love ourselves? Some theorists in human development believe that feelings of trust, worth, happiness, and love are learned very early in our socialization process. The basic way you now relate to the world was written pretty early, beginning in your crib. If, as an infant, you were made to feel secure, nurtured, fed, cuddled, and played with, you are probably a loving positive adult, in general.

On the other hand, when infants and young children are neglected, emotionally abandoned, abused, or mistreated they may grow up feeling insecure, fearful, and doubting their self-worth. They will have a hard time trusting themselves or others, let alone accepting love. Their lives will be dominated by insecurity and fear, not love. When a child gets negative messages about his worth he will begin a lifetime search to find out who he is inside.

He will always be initially suspicious of any other person who loves him, and will often try his best to sabotage the relationship, thereby proving what he feared all along -- that he really isn't lovable after all.

Growing up emotionally is a process of learning to minimize your fears and increase your capacity for love.

CHAPTER SEVEN

ISSUES OF EMOTIONAL GROWTH

Your emotions are part of your basic nature. They serve the important purposes of warning you when you are in danger, telling you that you have a basic need that isn't being met, allowing you to recognize harmony and happiness, notifying you that you have violated a personal value, and alerting you to negative patterns that interfere with creativity and having loving relationships that work.

Emotions have both helpful and defeating messages for each of us. For example, sadness lets you know that you have had a loss and that to heal and recover you must grieve, express your feelings, reevaluate your new life situation, and then get on with your life. The danger in sadness is getting stuck at some stage of the grief and wasting your time living in the past, dwelling on circumstances that cannot be changed and over which you have no control.

We all have emotional issues that need resolution in adulthood. These issues stem from our childhood experiences, even from events we no longer remember. Earliest memories are from three to four years old. A lot of damage can be done to children before that age.

Powerful emotional over-reactions can be triggered by events that cause you to reexperience an important event from your childhood. Crises in particular bring old emotional pains, especially unresolved ones, to consciousness. These moments of reliving old emotions may cause you to realize that there are behaviors and feelings that have been with you all your life but that have kept you from being grown up and happy. The time to make some changes in those old patterns is now.

The primary emotions that most people need to work on, in order to grow up, are: trust, shame, guilt, anger, depression, fear and anxiety.

When you are able to attain some control over the negative aspects of those powerful emotions, you will be able to experience more happiness and joy in your daily life.

To attain emotional maturity you need to understand the source of your emotions, then learn to discriminate and identify them, and then to remember and feel, and express them in an appropriate way that causes no harm to yourself or others. Finally, with some practice you will be able to change negative, growth-inhibiting emotional responses to positive feelings that can help you grow up and move you toward much more happiness and joy in your life.

CONNECTING WITH YOUR EMOTIONS

If it is often difficult to know exactly what you are feeling, you may need to turn inward and stay with an uncomfortable feeling until you can identify it. Remember, you often feel several emotions at once.

Sandra had a powerful negative reaction whenever she entered her study. She had been avoiding finishing her master's thesis in geography. Papers and books used in her research were scattered throughout the room, but she had been unable to work on her thesis for over a year. The more time that passed, the more depressed she got. Her life was on hold. And finally the university was ready to drop her from her graduate program.

I suggested that Sandra go into the room and force herself to stay there and to allow whatever feelings that surfaced to have expression. The following week, after trying this exercise in staying with her feelings, Sandra reported that, while standing in her study, she became aware that she was very angry at her ex-husband because she felt he had forced her to take the graduate program. If she finished her thesis it was like letting him have his way, and she didn't want him to win anything else from her. After she was able to see how irrational and self-defeating this anger was, she let it go and finished her thesis for her own satisfaction.

When you look inward to identify your feelings, you discover that surface emotions may cover deeper feelings that are quite different. For example, beneath anger you may find hurt. For some people anger is easier to admit and to express than hurt is because showing your anger generally puts you in the controlling or attack position and puts the other person on the defensive. To admit hurt makes you more vulnerable. Yet to admit and talk about your pain and vulnerability is much more growth-producing and leads to true intimacy between people.

Our feelings are often layers of several emotions, connected and overlapping. For example, layered emotions may look like this, one rising to the surface but burying others beneath.

FOR MEN	FOR WOMEN
ANGER	*SADNESS*
SADNESS	*ANGER*
FEAR	*FEAR*

While stereotypical, it is generally true because of the way this culture socializes boys and girls. Displays of anger are more tolerated in boys, and crying is more acceptable for girls. These responses are learned in childhood and most people continue to use them as the first line of defense as adults. Of course when little boys cried and it got them the needed attention, or when little girls got angry and it worked, they automatically keep using these strategies as adults.

EMOTIONS APPROPRIATE TO THE SITUATION

When you have a problem that triggers a strong emotional reaction, you can use your intellect to try to analyze what the trigger is. Sometimes you can change the trigger and the problem is solved. If this won't work you can try to change the circumstances or situation. If the risk of seeking change is not worthwhile emotionally, physically, or practically, then you can choose to change your emotion or leave.

Perhaps your emotion is not appropriate for the situation. Maybe you're taking it too seriously or not seriously enough. Inappropriate emotions often get you into trouble, like flying into a rage over a small incident.

Let's say your daughter left her bicycle in the driveway again. Or it is raining one Saturday when you planned to play golf.

Rage is inappropriate for either of these occurrences. Disappointment is an inappropriate response to the bicycle in the driveway, and frustration at the weather is also not appropriate. None of these emotions will help you produce what you really want to happen. They will use up your energy and get you nowhere and perhaps cause harm.

When you feel frustrated you realize that you will not get your way this time, but you keep trying. When you are disappointed, you realize that the situation is beyond your control and you let go of it and go on to other things.

If you feel disappointed with your daughter and give up on her, you will tell yourself, "She'll never learn to put that bike away, no matter how many times I tell her". Then you'll accept her thoughtless behavior and perhaps not take the necessary steps to tell her why she must not leave her bicycle in the driveway. The result is you abdicate your duty as a parent to teach her.

Frustration at your daughter's behavior is appropriate because you want your daughter to change that behavior. You hope she will learn to be more considerate and responsible in the future. You realize that, again, you must communicate that message to her. It's frustrating to have to tell her the same thing over and over, but that's part of being a parent. Feel frustrated. Let it pass. Then talk to your child.

On the other hand, if you feel frustrated when it rains on your golf day, your feeling is inappropriate because you can't change the weather, no matter how much you want to. The rain is not within your control, it will not stop until the cloud is empty or moves on to another place. But feeling disappointed allows you to accept what you cannot control and to go on to something else -- a very good way to handle a rainy day.

DISPLACING EMOTIONS

The danger of inappropriate emotions is that you often express them by displacing your feelings onto another person or animal, usually someone near and dear and undeserving of what you project. I have seen animals severely beaten and abused to satisfy a rage attack.

Perhaps you feel powerless or frustrated with your supervisor at work. You don't get your way on something important to you, and you are angry. You get home from work and that bicycle is in the driveway again. You have to get out of the car and move the bicycle before you can put your car in the garage. You are now furious. You go looking for your daughter with clenched jaws, and when you find her, you yell at her and spank her in front of her friends, then angrily send her to her room.

Obviously this is not an appropriate response to your day. It isn't your daughter's fault that your boss was a pain. You really aren't that angry at her, but you take your anger or frustration at your boss out on her -- thus *displacing your emotions* from one situation to another, safer (for you) one.

Unfortunately, displacement is common behavior for a majority of us, and it's not very grownup. Letting things go in one part of your life without assigning them the appropriate emotion has a profound effect on another part. You were passive with your boss, so you went home and became overly aggressive with your daughter. Learning to be assertive with your boss is what is needed here.

FEEL YOUR FEELINGS

Feeling is part of being human. To grow up, you must be able to experience or feel your emotions in positive, nondestructive ways.

If you are not willing to do your emotional homework now, you may be forced to do it when you have a life crisis. Crises force you to get in touch with your emotions and to make some changes for better or for worse. But the good side of a crisis is that it is an opportunity to do your emotional homework, and change old behaviors and feelings that no longer serve your best interests.

Now let's look at some of the debilitating emotions that keep us trapped in old dysfunctional patterns.

FEARS

Growing up emotionally is a process of transforming fears into love and intimacy. Intimacy means being emotionally available to others and to yourself when in need.

Fear is the bottom-line emotion, lurking at the root of all negative emotions. Stripped down, all pride is fear, all guilt is fear, all shame is fear, all jealousy is fear, all hurt is fear, all worry is fear. These negative feelings can keep you trapped in self-doubt, cloud your creativity, confuse and inhibit your spiritual growth, and interfere with your ability to think clearly, to concentrate, to remember and to live a life of happiness, freedom, inner peace, balance, and harmony.

When fears rule your life most of your experiences become negative and pessimistic. You look for evidence to support your own personal "Murphy's Law." If anything can go wrong it will, by your expectations and by the way you see events and people around you. Remember, you always create your own reality and superstitions fueled by fears. You stop yourself from seeing events objectively, and from seeing the positive, loving possibilities around you.

Sometimes fear helps to protect you. It warns us of danger by engaging our fight or flight response, just as pain and illness are warning signs that the body needs attention. Adrenaline pumps through our veins to allow us to take the necessary action to be safe. We all know about the mother who, after her child was run over by a car, single-handedly lifted the car off her child's body.

Of course, some fears are healthy. Fear acts as a warning signal that something needs to be attended to, just as pain and illness are warning signs that something in the body needs attention. If you allow these fears to rule your life you are delaying your growth and cheating yourself out of the joy and happiness you were born to have.

Some people fear fear. They think that if something awful happened once it will happen again in similar circumstances. Because you had one negative experience don't put your life on hold. The only way to conquer fear is to face it. The sooner you do the sooner you will be free of it.

BEHAVIORS BASED ON FEAR

If you hate, blame, manipulate, con, steal, make excuses, and lie, you live in fear. If you are afraid of losing control of power, money, strength, your emotions, or the behavior of others, you live in fear. If you believe that you are not lovable, and will never have the love, support, caring, and affection of another, you live in fear.

If you pretend that you are strong when you are not, if you pretend that you are happy when you are not, if you pretend that you love someone when you do not, if you smile when you are in pain, you are living a lie because you're protecting yourself from the knowledge of your fears. Worse--you are cheating yourself of your chance to face your fears and become truly free. True liberation is freedom from fear.

Here are seven basic emotional traits that are based in fear, though it may not seem obvious at first. You probably will recognize one or more of these as patterns in your emotional response to life.

Stubbornness is the fear of dealing with new situations. Do you avoid change at all cost, despite valid reasons to change? Do you invent ways to avoid new situations? You may call yourself determined, but is your determination born of fear? Stubbornness is very hard for others to live with because you offer no flexibility.

Self-destruction is basically the fear of loss of control. If you are a disciplined perfectionist or a political or religious fanatic, your effort to maintain control at all costs may be masking a fear of intimacy that might reveal your feelings of worthlessness. Operating from a need to control creates barriers between yourself and those who love you. Feelings of worthlessness can lead to slow self-destruction by abusing drugs, alcohol, food, sex, or other escapist behaviors.

Self-deprecation comes from the fear of inadequacy. Do you feel humble or insignificant in many situations? If you are forever putting yourself down and warning others that you will let them down, you probably often do. If you get caught up in meaningless projects and rarely finish anything, or if you heap compliments on others in hopes that something positive will be returned, you may be living from this fear.

Martyrdom is the fear of being worthless. If you're a martyr, you wallow in manipulative self-sacrifice, hoping that someone will pay tribute to your worth. While constantly pointing out your personal sacrifices for others, you're making unreasonable demands on these loved ones for their appreciation. Martyrdom can sabotage careers, destroy personal relationships, and bring on debilitating illness.

Greed comes from being afraid of loss or want. The greedy person never has enough of anything -- love, fame, money, material objects. They can be voracious and ruthless in getting what they want, and never look back to see who or what they trampled in the process. If you're vain, with a tendency to brag, you may be functioning from greed.

Arrogance has an underlying fear of vulnerability. You are shy but you appear conceited and haughty to keep others away. Others find it difficult to establish an intimate relationship with you because you won't let them close enough. You must protect your vulnerability. You may discover that underneath your vanity and pride is emptiness.

Impatience is a fear of missing something, in the belief that whatever is around the corner is better than what is going on here and now. Someone who is impatient may start many things and finish few of them. Do you constantly feel restless and dissatisfied, want things done quickly, and have trouble waiting? The impatient person makes those around her feel neglected because she'd rather be doing something new than nurturing and appreciating what is at hand.

We all display each of these traits at some moments, but one is usually predominant. If you can identify your major fear trait, you can work to overcome it and manage your emotions in a more mature way.

SEPARATION ANXIETY, ACUTE ANXIETY, AND PHOBIA

Unresolved fears may escalate into anxiety or phobia. Acute anxiety is basically a fear of the unknown, of what may happen. Usually it is connected to the immediate future and is often related to a specific situation, like needing to leave a relationship or a job or an upcoming move to a new town.

Anxiety ranges from mild feelings of dread, aggravation, or worry to stronger feelings like fear, agitation, or terror. People complain of physical symptoms like sweating, heart palpitations, hyperventilation, blurred vision, tingling in hands and feet, and inability to think clearly or to concentrate. The symptoms are frightening. The more conscious attention they get the worse they become. For a person in the middle of an anxiety attack, serious illness or death may seem imminent. At its most extreme, anxiety leads to panic attacks.

For some people the seeds of later anxiety associated with separation and loss are planted in childhood. Their greatest fear has come true, their parents are not there when they're needed. It is especially traumatic for children who lose a parent through death or divorce. They are indeed abandoned, and all later love relationships carry an element of the fear of being left or abandoned again.

Ray, a 23-year-old client, used drugs for many years to cover the pain and guilt he felt over his parents divorce when he was 8 years old. Just before he came to see me, he and his girlfriend, Pat, had visited her parents, and Pat left for a few hours to see some other friends.

Though Ray had not objected to her absence, when she returned he was furious. "You left me!" He yelled over and over, pounding on the walls in complete anguish. Nothing Pat could do or say calmed him down. She realized that what was going on inside him was more powerful than his response to her short absence. As he continued crying, "You left me!", she asked him who left, and he said, "My Dad left me when he and my mother got divorced." Ray collapsed, sobbing with the old pain of feeling abandoned.

Pat had the insight to stay and hold this suffering young man who had been reduced to an eight-year-old experiencing the pain of abandonment by his father. And Ray had the courage to stay with his pain until the hurt surfaced to be released. If he had not dealt with this old buried emotion by allowing himself to feel, describe, and express his pain, he would have subconsciously expected to be abandoned in all of his intimate relationships throughout his life. Without realizing he was doing so, he would have created situations to sabotage any relationship so that he could experience the pain of being abandoned again and again, until he allowed the hurt to surface and then to heal.

A phobia is an exaggerated emotional reaction of extreme fear in the present based on a traumatic incident from the past, which is often but not always related to a loss.

Jack had a phobia of stairs that stemmed from an incident in his childhood. When he was seven years old he was sent to the root cellar to get some potatoes for supper. On the stairway a big rat jumped on him and he screamed in terror. Now all stairways represent a potential and unexpected danger deeply embedded in Jack's subconscious mind. After the incident was long forgotten, the anxiety -- blown into a phobia -- remained to haunt him every time he was confronted with a stairway.

Any stairway became a trigger to tap into the old fear without the conscious memory of the incident. We worked for several sessions before we got the memory back. After we got it and he relived the trauma, the fear of stairways went away.

A phobia includes a very strong component of anxiety. You may be anxious without being phobic but you are never phobic without being anxious. In phobias you are reacting in a present situation to an incident from the past (often long forgotten), and projecting the fear into the future. Anxiety involves fear of the unknown outcome of a future event.

One in five adults experiences phobias in the United States today. They are sometimes accompanied with emotionally crippling panic attacks, which we have labeled panic disorder.

The irrational and overwhelming fear experienced during a panic attack taps back to some very early, serious threat to security and survival. If you experience anxiety or a phobia, get professional help. These problems are relatively easy to treat in therapy.

GUILT

Guilt is the emotion that keeps us locked in the past. You ruminate about what a bad person you are because of something you did or didn't do, said or didn't say, felt or didn't feel. Guilt is evident when you tell someone or yourself what you *should or ought* to have done or said or felt.

You feel guilty when you violate a personal value or belief. Guilt appears when you fall short of your internal measure of accountability for right and wrong, good and bad. Guilt is a legitimate, useful feeling for a grownup who has really wronged or hurt another person. In such a case you need to make amends the best way that you can, by paying back if you took something that belonged to another, by apologizing and asking forgiveness, or whatever remedy is appropriate to the offense.

A little guilt can serve as a helpful checkpoint, allowing you to check up on yourself from time to time to see if you are being fair and honest and living within your value system. If you are not you may want to make some changes.

If you are living with outdated values, old messages from your upbringing that no longer work for your present life, you may want to discard or modify them. What was important to protect you or to teach you a lesson at age five or ten may not be important or work for you as an adult. Revising your values and beliefs to meet your present needs is important for grownups to do.

There are no specific physical signs that signal guilt. A guilty person may want to sink within herself or hide, or feel vulnerable. You can recognize that guilt is becoming powerful when you hear yourself starting to beat yourself up with your critical thoughts, or calling yourself names like dummy, stupid, fool, etc.

The destructive side of guilt is seen in someone who believes that he is defective and is to blame for anything and everything that goes wrong, whether it is his fault or not. Extreme cases of guilt may create self-destructive behaviors like eating disorders of anorexia, bulimia, and compulsive overeating, as well as substance abuse of drugs and alcohol.

The guilt-ridden person tries to be perfect, but never feels quite good enough. By taking on responsibility for everyone else's problems he feels powerful in a powerless system.

This person follows a rigid inner mandate that he must never make an error, which means he can never be human. The guilt-ridden person is constantly very hard and judgmental on himself for every small mistake, and often jumps on others for their errors. He believes he's not good enough in the eyes of others, even though at least some of his burden may rightfully belong to someone else.

The guilty person isn't able to distinguish the difference between responsible adult behavior based on inner directives of right and wrong, and mandates from outside authority figures such as parents, teachers, law-enforcement figures, work superiors, and religious leaders.

Guilt is tied to the past. You've learned a whole list of things you can be guilty about from your parents, at church, in school, from lovers and spouses, from strangers in public interactions such as sales clerks and waitresses, and from your children -- in short, from anyone who ever gave you a dirty look or let you know that you should have done something differently.

One buzzword that can often induce guilt is "caring". Did you ever hear this one? "If you really cared you would take me with you", or "If you cared for me you wouldn't work all of the time", or "Never mind, I will do it myself, just forget I asked".

These kinds of messages give struggling grownups plenty of prompts to beat themselves up verbally and emotionally. They feel hurt because they believe you have let someone else or themselves down.

Grownups are able to distinguish for themselves the moral boundaries that allow them to live with and like themselves, to be able to look in the mirror and say, "I like you, you are a good person." Guilt is counterproductive to this grown-up goal. Establishing moral values for yourself, according to your own choice, is a part of spiritual and emotional growing up.

The most prevalent issue that raises guilt in grownups is sex. We all got early messages that stopped the toddler's natural childish curiosity about his or her body, childhood sexual play with age mates like "playing doctor", and adolescent masturbation.

For many adults this old guilt acts as an inhibitor for normal healthy sexual intimacy.

Remember that guilt is over some event in the past, and nothing you can do can change the past. You can't go back and do it over again, but what you can learn from the past can begin a positive process of change and growth. You always have the choice to change. You can change your guilt from feces to fertilizer in the grown-up garden of your life.

TRUST

Trust and mistrust are the earliest stages of development in an infant. A newborn is totally dependent on its mother and father or other caretaker to provide all of its basic needs. It needs to be fed, bathed, clothed, diapers changed, kept warm, touched and cuddled if it is to thrive and grow. The mother mirrors to the child that she is precious, wanted and loved.

If these needs are neglected or delayed, the baby quickly learns that the world is not a safe place and she begins to mistrust. If, in addition, she is abused by being hit or stuck with a pin, or worse, she will carry this mistrust into adulthood and her emotional development will be arrested. She will carry fears that cannot be described because these abuses happened when her development was pre-verbal.

In adulthood, trust issues may manifest in being paranoid and not trusting anyone, or being naive and trusting too much at the risk of not sensibly protecting herself. This lack of self-protection sets her up to be taken advantage of, used, and confirms fears that nobody can be trusted to provide her with love or care. This behavior repeats the same infant patterns over and over until she comes to the realization that she can survive and take care of herself very well.

When an adult has an overreaction to being alone, a wound of neglect or abuse can usually be traced to very early development.

LYING AND DISHONESTY

Another issue related to trust is telling lies. For some people this is such a severe problem that professional help is needed. I have seen lying ruin marriages and other relationships. Eventually the liar gets caught in his own web, one lie leads to another and another until even the liar himself is confused about the truth. Inevitably everything is exposed and the severe breach of trust destroys the bond between people. It is very difficult to re-establish trust once it is violated.

Trust is not a gift it must be earned, and when it is destroyed it is very hard to rebuild and restore. The wronged person is forced to be vigilant for future lies and is in the uncomfortable position of constant suspicion and doubt about things that are said and done by the liar.

Basically there are three types of lies. The protective lie, the aggressive lie, and the fantasy lie. The *protective lie* is the kind of lie that seeks to protect the liar from being detected in a wrong doing. Often called the little white lie, sometimes it is justified by saying that you are just trying to protect the other person's feelings. What you are really doing is protecting yourself from a confrontation, from shame, from being accountable for what you did or didn't do, or say. The bottom line is lying is dishonest.

The second type of lie is the *aggressive lie*. In this case the liar deliberately attempts to shift blame or bring punishment upon another person. This behavior is common among young siblings. People who cling to vendettas against others haven't outgrown the need to lie like this. Blaming another by saying, "It is her fault not mine," is a childish evasion of responsibility. This is also a vengeful way to get even by getting someone else in trouble. It is a passive aggressive way to deal with anger felt toward another.

The third type of a lie is a *fantasy lie,* which is an exaggeration or concoction of the imagination that helps to embellish the prestige of the person telling the tale. Lies may be overt (open) and deliberate, or covert (hidden) by withholding information. Either is an act of dishonesty and a breach of further confidence. Often passive or passive-aggressive people find it easier to tell a lie than to be assertive, honest and deal with the truth and consequences of their actions.

Pathological lying is a symptom of mental illness. In this case there is a compulsive drive to lie, even about insignificant things. Basically, this extreme way of lying is a combination of the three types of lies described above. It is often used to cover up of feelings of worthlessness, shame and guilt. In time the lies are traps that destroy relationships by destroying trust. Professional help is necessary to resolve the underlying issues that lead to this self-destructive behavior.

SHAME

Until recently shame has been confused with guilt. In the past few years psychologists have come to realize the devastating effects that negative shame has on the human spirit and psyche. Shame goes to the very core of the individual's self-concept, self-esteem, and self-confidence. It is one of the most important underlying issues for most forms of mental distress and mental illness.

Developmentally, shame is instilled in children between the ages of 18 months to about three years. However, in a toxic shame-based environment shaming messages may be given throughout an entire lifetime. Early shame messages come about potty training time, when parents begin to expect and demand some self control and self responsibility from their child. When the child fails to comply to parental expectations shaming messages are given, like "Shame on you", or in public, "Don't make me ashamed of you".

Thus the seeds of self-doubt, self-depreciation and personal failure are planted. And this happens even before children have words to express themselves, before the brain is developed enough to recall memories, and before emotions are formed. So adults who have both trust and shame issues suffer from pre-verbal confusion about themselves when strong feelings are triggered.

There is a positive side to shame. It helps us to know boundaries and limitations, both personally and culturally. When children begin to explore the world they are taught boundaries about physical safety and danger. They test these limits in the process or learning by experimenting with new things and behaviors, and they learn that there are consequences for crossing the boundaries set by parents. For example, they learn to wear clothes when they go outside to play. Then later as adults they know they cannot run to the supermarket naked. This healthy function of shame allows us to act within a framework proscribed by society.

Unfortunately the negative effects of shame lead to much unhappiness for most people. In his pioneering book, *Shame: The Power of Caring,* Gershen Kaufman writes, "Shame is the affect (feeling) which is the source of many complex and disturbing inner states: depression, alienation, self doubt, isolation, loneliness, paranoid and schizoid phenomena, compulsive disorders, splitting of the self, perfectionism, a deep sense of inferiority, inadequacy or failure, the so-called borderline conditions and disorders of narcissism". (My parentheses).

Most of us equate shame with embarrassment, feeling foolish, shyness, and blushing. Shame in a psychological sense goes much deeper. It relates to humiliation and emotional trauma that can lead to inner alienation, feelings of worthlessness, and withdrawal for normal living, even to agoraphobia the ultimate isolation.

John Bradshaw, in his insightful book, *Healing the Shame That Binds You,* focuses on the destructive side of shame, which he calls toxic shame. He says, "Toxic shame gives you a sense of worthlessness, a sense of failing and falling apart as a human being. Toxic shame is like internal bleeding. Exposure to oneself lies at the heart of toxic shame."

Children internalize toxic shame when they are neglected, abused, overlooked, or pushed aside as in large families. Shame-based children have been abandoned either emotionally and/or physically, or raised by shame-bound parents who were themselves shamed as children.

Unfortunately, this description covers the majority of adults today. We are an entire population of insecure people with poor self-concepts, unsure of ourselves in many situations, often trying to figure out why we feel isolated and lonely and why our lives and relationships don't work. Shame-based people frequently try to take care of other people's needs, hoping that somehow they will get the attention, love and validation they need in return. This behavior is called co-dependency.

If your emotional growth was impeded during those early years by a trauma like the death or abandonment of a parent, or by on-going neglect or abuse, chances are great that your normal emotional development was inhibited or stopped at that time. So when you experience a serious emotional upheaval, especially one involving grieving and loss, you are likely to be thrown back to an early emotional age. Maybe even one that is pre-verbal, so that you know you hurt, but you cannot sort out exactly what is wrong, or how you really feel.

Martha, a fifty-two-year old woman, came to me for therapy after her mother died. Martha was in the hospital with her mother when she died at three in the morning. Even though Martha knew she was dying, when Martha was told that mom had died she ran out of the hospital and ran and ran until she was exhausted and out of breath. She was trying to run away from her own feelings, something we all do when an event so terribly threatening feelings, something we all do when an event so terribly threatening happens to us. We resort to our primitive fight or flight instincts.

If emotional growth was slowed or stopped we regress back to the age when we were damaged. So you may feel like a helpless three year old at times, no matter what your chronological age is. In one way or another we defend against pain.

One of the biggest issues that adults try to cover up is shameful and frightening dependency needs--fearing that you cannot take care of yourself emotionally, like Martha feeling like a little child who indeed could not meet her own emotional survival needs when her mother died. She felt frightened, helpless, dependent, and confused all at the same time.

Probably the biggest fear of shame-based people is exposure. Shame lies hidden deep within the recesses of our psyche or subconscious mind, and is carefully guarded by secrets. We were set up for shaming responses before we can remember, so we developed emotional survival strategies to cover up this sense of inadequacy at a very young age. Some of these cover ups include machismo, grandiosity and bragging, denial which takes many forms and will be discussed at greater length later, hysteria, hypochondria (using physical symptoms to deflect underlying feelings), anxiety and depression.

Toxic shame is a sense of defect or flaw within the Self, of not being good enough as a person. It goes unrecognized on the surface, but manifests as feelings of inadequacy, self-rejection, self-doubt and being unlovable. Because shame is so painful it gets buried deep within the shame-bound person.

Adults who constantly worry about what others think of her or him, try to keep up a front so people won't know the *real me* have problems with shame. Shame robs you of being able to have a genuine loving and intimate relationship with yourself or anyone else.

The deeper the shame is buried the more difficult it is to

bring to the surface, to reveal the source, to examine old shame inducing events, and to heal the wounds.

"Exposure fear", says Kaufman, "then operates to further encapsulate shame, hide it from view, and finally mask shame from consciousness. All too frequently, only the fear remains consciously accessible".

Once shame is internalized any event can cause spasms of stored shame to surface and torment you. Criticism, a look on someone's face, a rebuff, feedback, will be interpreted as rejection or disapproval and a sign of your inadequacy. Events such as the end of a relationship, getting fired, getting a traffic ticket, or any abandonment will trigger profound feelings of worthlessness, shame and failure as a person.

Kaufman calls this the "snowball effect". Every new occurrence of shame is added to the old accumulated shame and sparks a re-experiencing of all the old shame as well as the latest shameful event. The resulting effect is solidifying and deepening the internalized shame. It is like an internalized downward shame spiral.

The problem that internalized shame poses to growth and to growing up emotionally lies in the powerful defenses people develop to protect themselves from exposing their pain both to themselves and to others. Shame then is compensated for by approval seeking or co-dependent behaviors, or is transferred to someone else through blame or inducing shame in others, especially someone near and dear.

Because our culture is shame-based we pass on shame from one generation to the next through reactive bad parenting and by keeping hidden shameful family closet issues in the form of *secrets*. Secrets about who was homosexual, who committed suicide, who was mentally ill, about sexual and other abuse issues. Secrets are like mushrooms: they thrive in the dark and feed on manure.

In order to stop the familial shame you must open the

closet doors and tell the secrets. Many people confuse family shame with personal shame. You are not responsible for what someone else did, only for your own actions. Don't be slimed with shame that belongs to someone else. By telling the secrets to one other person you begin the healing process.

Deal with it and heal it!

CHAPTER EIGHT

MORE ISSUES ON EMOTIONS

ANGER

Most people believe that anger is not only part of the human condition, but that we have a right to express our anger. It is true that expressing your anger is better than repressing it, but only if it's done appropriately. Let's define it first.

There is a whole group of behaviors that can be interpreted as anger. They range from nonverbal messages that we give to others like a "dirty" look, slamming a door, leaving in the middle of a conversation, boredom, leaning forward with bared teeth, finger pointing, to verbal expressions including name calling, shouting, sarcasm, and criticism, and barbed humor.

There are also many emotions related to anger. Think of a line, a continuum, and along this line place milder feelings at one end and stronger feelings at the other end. At the milder end let's start with frustration and work our way toward the stronger end.

Next, in order of power, might be annoyance, irritation disappointment, resentment, impatience, aggravation, hatefulness, anger, rage, loss of control, craziness. Your line might look a little different. The point is that all of these feelings are considered as angry reactions by some people.

The value of these anger-related emotions is that they let you know when your needs are not being met, when you are being used or taken advantage of, your rights are being violated, or that you are being hurt in some way. The milder emotions on the continuum warn you that you need to stand up for yourself and something needs to change. Remember change is possible, but it requires commitment, hard work, and time.

There is a very fine line between slipping from one feeling to a stronger, more destructive one. For example from irritation to aggravation to rage. The difference in most cases is caused by your thoughts, your self-talk.

Anger may spark a physical impulse to be destructive toward something or someone. Crimes of violence occur when people have allowed their anger to build to the far end of the continuum and are feeling enraged, out of control, or "crazy". Most rapes, murders, battering, and other incidents of physical abuse occur when the perpetrator is in one of those states. In courts of law these feelings are often called temporary insanity, which is really loss of control of your emotions.

If you are really out of touch with your anger emotionally, you may recognize the physical symptoms associated with it. They are the same as those for stress-induced illnesses: tension, sleeping disorders, colitis, diverticulitis, sexual dysfunctions such as premature ejaculation (believed to be repressed anger at women), ulcers, asthma, rashes, heart palpitations, accident proneness.

Anger is a reactive emotion, safer to express than the underlying, more painful feelings. Like an onion, emotions are often layered. You peel off one layer at a time and sometimes you weep. Under the outside layer of anger lies hurt, shame, guilt, fear, and helplessness.

A battering husband, under his rage and violence, is most likely a frightened little boy who was abused himself and is terrified of losing his only close intimate relationship. Instead of dealing with his childhood issues of fear, abandonment, shame, and hurt he tries to use his anger to control, bully, scare, and manipulate his mate. By these self-defeating methods he destroys the very thing he wants most -- to be loved for himself, to be validated, to be taken care of and nurtured.

Too many women have felt trapped in violent relationships with men who were obsessed with their suspicions of the woman's infidelity. Despite the woman's denial, and the lack of evidence, the man works himself into a frenzy of rage and becomes violent toward the woman and the children.

The woman lives in fear and terror of his unpredictable moods and rage, especially when the man has cut her off from her family, friends, and other support systems. (Recent statistics indicate that about three percent of batterers are women, and 97 percent are men.)

A person who allows his anger to reach these shocking limits has a clinical thought disorder problem, and probably more serious psychological personality disorder problems, stemming from the problems in his own childhood. Unfortunately, this type of person rarely seeks help. He blames others for his problems, remains in denial, and doesn't take responsibility for his behavior by seeking psychotherapy. There is little hope of recovery or change.

Anger is a learned behavior. Babies aren't born angry. People keep showing anger because it pays off for them. It gets them attention, it can be used to frighten and control others, they get their own way, they can manipulate others, and they can avoid intimacy and closeness. It is also addictive.

The more it pays off the more it is used, and becomes a source of power, and can lead to violent outbursts against someone weaker and more vulnerable.

Even if you are not abusive to others in your family, you may have a temper that goes out of control too often, and which can contribute to the emotional abuse of others. Childish possessiveness about property and persons can be modified to a healthy sense of self-protection and ability to share, as a child grows up. When you're grown-up, if your first impulse when angry is to strike out, you've got to teach yourself new ways of responding to the events that trigger your anger.

The emotions on the far end of the anger continuum are destructive and dangerous to yourself and others. Healthy expression of the feelings related to anger occurs when the feelings are in the safer range, before the expression could become harmful.

It's important to express anger appropriately and safely because repressed anger leaks out. Unexpressed anger surfaces in the forms of sarcasm, thinly disguised humor and jokes, "I was only kidding!"

Depression often defined as anger turned inward, helplessness and immobility in making positive choices, running away, both physically and emotionally, and displaced anger, i.e. taking your anger at one person out on someone weaker and more vulnerable, as a bully or batterer does.

Anger tends to build up. For passive people, small affronts, criticism, resentments, frustrations, when not dealt with assertively, accumulate like single drops of gasoline falling into a quart jar. Individually they seem harmless enough, but what happens when the jar is full? The latest event sparks an explosion.

Anger erupts into a rage and the usually passive person becomes aggressive. Nasty things are said, people get hurt, violence may occur. Then the guilt, the regrets, the apologies, the promises to never say or do such terrible things again. Slowly the jar begins to fill again and the cycle repeats itself.

In therapy, anger management consists of emptying out the reservoir of stored up old anger by doing *anger work*. This often deals with digging into the past, remembering and feeling the rage and anger that you weren't able to feel or express when you were a powerless little kid. When the old hurts have been reduced to scar tissue, there is a lot more room to deal with new anger.

When you learn to be assertive in your daily interactions, no more anger will accumulate. One of the best favors you can do for yourself is to take an assertiveness training class at your local community college, church or community center.

Mature adults talk about angry feelings when it is still safe, before it reaches the explosion stage. By becoming aware of emotions and assertively stating your feelings of frustration, disappointment, resentment, or irritation to another, you can find a solution to the problem before deep anger has developed. Stop that drop of gasoline from falling into your jar. No accumulation, no explosion.

Explosive anger or extreme aggressiveness is the opposite of healthy assertiveness. Another unassertive, immature response is being passive-aggressive, or expressing your anger indirectly. For instance, a friend asks you to pick up an item for her since you are going shopping anyway. You agree to do it, although you resent this friend for making these requests often. Instead of telling her you don't want to do her shopping, you forget to buy the item.

Passive-aggressive behavior is another coping style learned in childhood as a survival strategy. The passive-aggressive person wants to get her way without taking responsibility for her behavior. She is a manipulator, who blames others for anything that goes wrong. She gives double messages, induces guilt in others while making herself look good and others look bad. Her motive is revengeful, blaming and punishing. Underneath she is fearful, insecure, cowardly, and shame-based.

Just as the passive person explodes when enough frustration builds up, so the passive aggressive person can become overtly aggressive when her games don't work.

DEPRESSION

Depression is a web of negative emotions that needs to be unraveled so that each one can be dealt with. It is connected to loss, grief, and holding on to something that is over. It may occur because of the death of a loved one, the end of a relationship, children leaving home, or any number of changes involving loss, shame, guilt or an accumulation of incidents leading to powerlessness and helplessness.

Depression is the number one mental health problem in the United States, perhaps in the world, because most people don't know how to handle the inevitable losses that life involves. With every unresolved loss and forced change, we accumulate feelings of resentment, disappointment, and helplessness. When these issues pile up and are not resolved and released, energy is trapped and used in resisting buried, painful feelings of sadness , hurt, and rage.

When you don't deal with the emotions that accompany loss, physical symptoms of depression take over. If your energy level is low, you feel constantly fatigued, don't sleep well, have little interest in sex, poor concentration, memory loss, and have changed your eating habits, you are probably depressed.

The depression we all feel now and then, as a response to situations of real disappointment or sadness, is a normal emotional condition that only lasts for a short time. When depression lingers for several weeks or months, or takes extreme forms, then it becomes a problem.

Chronic depression is a long-term, ongoing situation in which a person has low energy, feels dejected, lacks motivation or enthusiasm or joy. She may feel suicidal or wish to be rescued from these feelings by fate or death. Sometimes the cause is a physiological imbalance and sometimes it is caused by not dealing with life's problems.

For example, staying in a destructive and unrewarding relationship can create a feeling of being trapped and lead to chronic depression. Someone has called this *rusting out* as opposed to *burning out*. Any time you feel trapped you also feel powerless, and depression always includes feeling powerless and helpless. It may also involve self-flagellation, feeling guilty and responsible for someone else's feelings or life. Some therapists describe depression as anger turned inwards, onto oneself instead of toward someone or something else.

Depression particularly strikes the elderly, because of the number of losses they have experienced over their lifetime, failing health, retirement, limited income which limits choices, death of peers and friends, loss of drivers license causing dependence on others, and boredom. If people weren't joiners earlier in life they are not likely to begin later in life, and these people become increasingly isolated and lonely, and having little to look forward to and little to live for.

Most of us can understand feeling down at the time of a loss such as death, divorce, illness, or separation. This is acute or situational depression. It is appropriate, normal and expected after a major change in your life. It is the part of the mourning process that gives us space between letting go of the old before we welcome the new. It gives us the time we need to gain some perspective on the loss we have suffered. Short-term depression is temporary and it gradually passes, as we get involved in new activities.

Even positive changes such as getting married or having a baby can cause you to feel sad. In order for a new phase of life to begin, the old must go. Letting go of the single life, of the independence, of sleeping through the night without a baby to feed, of the old way of being, sets the scene for a time of grief and depression.

Depression signals a change. And change is necessary for human growth. We would never grow and change without letting go of the old decayed patterns in our lives. Sometimes this can happen with sudden insight, but it usually happens with introspection and suffering over a period of time.

Grownups recognize the importance of situational depression in change. Depression is the part of this process that slows us down long enough to release the old to make room for the new. You can't fill a full cup. You have to dump out the old contents first. And to do so is sometimes sad and depressing.

HAPPINESS AND JOY

You may experience depression as a grey cloud that constantly floats overhead and follows wherever you go. You experience happiness as the elusive butterfly described in this verse:

Happiness is like a butterfly. The more you chase it, the more it will elude you. But if you turn your attention to other things, It comes and softly sits on your shoulder.   *Anonymous*

You feel happy in the present moment when you are complete, content, and fulfilled, or when there is an absence of problems and stressors that demand your time, attention, and energy. People can be happy and joyful alone or with another person. These are spontaneous feelings that come over you when you are free from the stressful debilitating emotions. Enjoyment and pleasure are so nice that you try to hold on to the experience and desire more often. You form expectations around having more and more and that it will last forever.

Unfortunately, expectations and desires are what get you into trouble. When they are not met you are cast into your own negative emotional stew. How quickly you switch into being resentful, hurt, angry, and blaming the other person for your unhappiness. The truth is that no one can make you happy and you cannot make anyone else happy, only yourself. You may feel happy when you are with another person, but whatever feelings you have are yours. If you are with someone you love or where you feel safe and secure the chances are greater to feel positive feelings.

John Powell says, "The only truly happy people are those who have found someone, some cause to love and to belong to. In union with some others we are validated, accepted, appreciated, and acknowledged".

Relationships give us the best opportunity and greatest challenges of our lives. They give us our highest highs and lowest lows.

Love and happiness are interwoven. Love is more important than any other emotion to your well-being. It is what binds people together and makes life worthwhile, and gives you a sense of worth. A love relationship also provides the potential for many moments of happiness. Special times with your spouse, lover, children, or friends, watching a good play, going to a concert, attending a wedding, the birth of a child are all happy occasions. But happiness is elusive and fleeting, like the butterfly the more you try to hold onto it the more illusive it is.

Yet you can be happy more often and more deeply when you learn to generate good feelings within yourself. In order to do this you need to become your own best friend, to become -- loving, compassionate, non-judgmental, self-forgiving. Your self-love must extend to accepting yourself just as you are -- skinny, fat, bald, spare tire, lost dreams, warts and all. You must learn to respect yourself, to forgive yourself if you make a mistake.

Learn to live in the present. Squeeze each moment for the best that you can get out of it. Treat yourself to making the quality of your life in the here and now count. Heal the past and put it behind you, wiser for your life experiences. Don't cheat yourself out of your life in the present by spending thoughts and energy worrying about the future, about security, money, job, kids, etc.

Live each moment as it presents itself to you. Concentrate your attention to enjoyment, fulfillment and contentment in the present. This is all you really have.

When you can do this you will find yourself happier much more often. With a sincere and sustained sense of self-appreciation you will feel healthier in all aspects of your life. You will feel full of joy, and you will be able to work on solutions to problems instead of getting mired in the details. You will become a full-fledged, card-carrying grownup, not a perpetual child ruled by your emotions. You will be in charge of your emotions. And you will get to know yourself in a new way.

Then and only then will you be willing and able to share your real authentic self. Then you can become vulnerable enough to achieve true intimacy with others -- which is the greatest reward of all for us social human beings. Love and sharing are crucial emotional needs.

CHAPTER NINE

TECHNIQUES FOR EMOTIONAL GROWTH

Reflection on your personal history, and therapy can help you to understand your own particular emotional history in more depth.

The first critical step in gaining emotional control is to recognize and name what you are feeling at any given moment. Look at the list below and identify what you are feeling right now. Go over your day and identify other feelings you have experienced. Refer to this list often until you can recognize and give names to your feelings.

This is not a complete list of possible feelings you may have. In the English language we have words that identify approximately 400 names for feelings. Human beings are capable of hundreds of subtle emotional states, and we often feel *mixed emotions* -- more than one feeling at a time for a situation. So there are thousands of possibilities for emotional experiences. Feel free to add to the list as you find other feelings within yourself.

NEGATIVE *DEBILITATING*	POSITIVE *ENHANCING*
humiliated	hopeful
frustrated	confident
aggressive	pleased
hassled	pleasant
afraid	accepting
discouraged	assertive
angry	proud
phobic	patient
depressed	understanding
shy	fulfilled
withdrawn	flattered
scared	accepted
ashamed	included
despairing	forceful
grieving	loving
guilty	desired
inadequate	passionate
hopeless	loyal
helpless	committed
lonely	joyful
envious	blissful
jealous	faithful
irritated	secure
worried	excited
hateful	involved
sad	content

confused	peaceful
responsible	appreciated
overwhelmed	valued
defensive	trusting
tense	generous
intimidated	determined
bored	supportive
impatient	helpful
superior	admiring
hurt	motivated
stupid	curious
sorry	eager
ignorant	honest
incapacitated	truthful
anxious	high
manipulated	capable
aggravated	purposeful
enraged	ambitious
burned out	responsible
excluded	aware
disappointed	empathetic
bitter	sympathetic
possessive	engaged
inferior	affectionate
frightened	safe
torn	playful
terrified	happy
agitated	thrilled

EMOTIONAL AWARENESS

Practice naming your feelings by imagining the following situations. As you read each of these brief descriptions, refer to the list of emotions listed above and pick out the word that best and most subtly fits your feeling. Try not to use the common emotional terms like happy, angry, and sad. Those are the names that children use for their emotions. Grownups use more specific and exact terms.

Add your own feeling word to the list if it is not found. The object of this exercise is to discover the many emotions in your repertoire and to learn to tell them apart.

Now let's practice. Fill in the first emotional response you have in the following situations:

1. You have just been told that your boss wants to talk to you in her office. *You feel* _____

   _____.

2. Your telephone rings at 3 a.m... *You fee* _____

   _____.

3. An attractive person of the opposite sex smiles at you while you are dancing. *You feel* _____

   _____.

4. You are driving behind an old man driving his pickup truck very slowly. *You feel* _____

   _____.

5. You are walking on a secluded beach watching the sunset. *You feel* _____

   _____.

6. Someone quietly walks up behind you and
   startles you. *You feel* _____
   _____.

7. Your 15-year-old daughter is two hours
   late coming home from a date. *You feel* _____
   _____.

8. You just got news that you are the new
   grandparent of a healthy baby girl. *You feel* _____
   _____.

9. You just got news that your brother or
   sister was in a fatal automobile accident.
   You feel _____.

10. You learn that the driver who killed your
    brother or sister was drunk. *You feel* _____
    _____.

11. You just watched a great movie. *You feel* _____
    _____.

12. You are making dinner for yourself. *You feel* _____
    _____.

13. You are planning your vacation. *You feel* _____
    _____.

14. A policeman stops you for speeding. *You feel* _____
    _____.

15. The officer gives you a ticket. *You feel* _____
    _____.

16. It is Saturday night and you are all alone with no
    plans. *You feel* _____

17. You just had an interview for your dream job.
    You feel _____.

18. Your graduation ceremony is tomorrow.
    You feel _____.

19. A dear old friend calls on the telephone. *You feel* __
    _____.

20. Your spouse tells you one thing, then does something
    else. *You feel* _____
    _____.

21. You hate your job, but can't quit right now. *You feel*
    _____.

22. You see someone of the opposite sex who really
    turns you on. *You feel* _____
    _____.

23. Your mother or father doesn't like the new home
    you have chosen. *You feel* _____
    _____.

There are no right or wrong answers. You are unique, and your answers are right for you. Did you respond to many situations with the same kinds of emotions? These patterns can often stand in the way of growing up if you repeatedly choose the same old familiar emotional response instead of the most appropriate one. Some of the common emotional patterns that people develop from early childhood are: fear, anxiety, guilt, shame, aggression, anger, and depression. Try the exercise again and choose different answers, more subtle and more accurate, and more creative. Try ways you would like to feel

HEALING OLD EMOTIONAL HURTS

There are two parts to becoming emotionally grown up. One is to heal from the childhood hurts that still live within you and that affect how you respond emotionally today. The other is to learn better techniques for handling the emotions that arise from events of the present.

In order to heal you must return (in your mind and heart) to the original scene of the crime--your childhood. The crimes perpetrated on you were all of the messages and punishments you got for crying, feeling sad or hurt, for being noisy, getting dirty, being tired or hungry or sick, or for normal childhood sexual curiosity or exploration. You were a victim, to some degree, of rejection, abandonment, neglect, undeserved punishment, not being protected, or of verbal, emotional, sexual, or physical abuse.

Under these conditions you developed safe strategies that helped you survive. But chances are that what worked for you at three, five, or eight years of age does not work for you now. A 42-year-old man throwing a temper tantrum in a supermarket is not a pretty picture. Nor are more subtle and sophisticated forms of control and manipulation. If you have not changed or eliminated these old emotional coping patterns, but only refined and sharpened them, you are in trouble. They will not work in mature, healthy adult relationships.

In order to grow up emotionally you need to weed your garden and get rid of your childish old ways of doing things, heal the old hurts, forgive your parents, and then try out some new, more mature behaviors.

All this hard work may not sound like fun, and it isn't. But the rewards are worth every moment of struggle, tears, and pain. You can now have loving, mutually supportive, intimate relationships with everyone in your life -- your children, parents, friends, spouse or lover, co-workers, boss, colleagues, clients, neighbors, and new acquaintances. No more controlling, hiding, lying, shaming, or blaming. Those can all become part of your past. And you will begin to attract other grown-up people to the renewed you.

The more dysfunctional your childhood, the more work you will need to do to heal your past hurts. Those with the most extreme trauma may need professional help for a period of time. Whatever it takes to heal your childhood pains so that you can understand what happened through adult eyes -- a support group, psychotherapy, reading and learning, practicing -- do what's necessary. The time to grow up is now.

A final note: please do your emotional work gently, with kindness, compassion, and love for yourself. We tend to be our own worst enemies during times of change. Learn to love yourself and to nurture the child within you. It makes the whole job of growing up much easier.

THOUGHTS AND EMOTIONS

To get your emotions back in balance, and on a more grown-up level, you can call on help from your physical, intellectual, and spiritual systems. For instance, exercise helps erase depression, getting rid of bad physical habits increases your self-esteem. Your beliefs about life's meaning can give you strength in troubled times.

Probably the most useful way to grow up emotionally is to use your mind, through self-talk, to change your feelings. Change your thinking and you can change your life. You create your own reality with the way you think about the people and events in your life. As we discovered in Chapter 8, your thoughts influence your feelings by programming truths into your subconscious. This works especially well with emotions. If you tell yourself that you are happy -- and mean it and allow it to become true --you then become happy. Most of the emotional pain you experience is self-created by your own thoughts and attitudes.

In turn, your feelings affect your thoughts, when you are feeling sad or in despair you tend to think negatively, to escape into the past or leap into the future to avoid the pain of the present. If you think your life is full of unresolved problems, then that is exactly what you experience. You have created that reality for yourself.

By changing your thoughts and thought patterns you can change your feelings about yourself and about the circumstances of your life. The process of changing a strong, possibly destructive emotion into a more manageable one requires some time and energy in the beginning. The first step is to become aware of what you are feeling. So go inside and sort it out.

When you go within, tune into what you are really experiencing emotionally, not just what is happening externally. Pay attention to your self-talk and your physical sensations.

Emotional response doesn't always occur immediately after the situation or event that produces it. Something occurs between the event and the emotion that you often don't notice -- a thought or an idea. For example, if you are late for an important meeting, or have a major misunderstanding with your spouse, or you get caught shoplifting, you'll have a strong emotional response based on your beliefs about what the event means -- perhaps anxiety, anger, or fear.

It is at this point, where you briefly register a thought about an event, that you can take mature control of your emotions. You have a wide variety of possible emotional responses to choose and use at all times. The response you choose depends solely on your thoughts at the moment.

Where do these thoughts come from? The thoughts that precede emotional response contain elements of your *values, attitudes, and beliefs* about your past, present, and future. Many of these beliefs were formed in childhood and are based on your parents teachings. Others are learned from how you interpreted events throughout your life.

For instance, if you once lost an important contract because you were late for a meeting, whenever you're running late, your subconscious thoughts may go back to that time and tell you that being late is terrible. Something bad will happen. This thought pattern translates into the emotional experience of anxiety, the feeling that arises when you're not secure about an outcome in the future. On the other hand, if you think that being a little late is good strategy that gives you an advantage with a client, then your feelings may be calm and confident. And that internal feeling will be apparent to others when you reach the meeting, and may well determine the outcome.

You create the reality in your emotional world by the choices you make in your responses to situations. You can avoid emotional traps -- anxiety that simply makes you later or that causes you to go into the meeting feeling rattled and lacking confidence -- by checking inside to see if your emotional reactions are appropriate and if not; then choosing ones that are.

When Jane came to see me she was having a serious problem with a co-worker. She complained bitterly that he singled her out to vent his frustrations about not getting an expected promotion. He embarrassed her in front of other employees, accused her of misplacing or stealing his tools, and generally behaved offensively. She tried every way of defending herself: telling him off, being assertive. Nothing worked. She was exhausted by the stress he created for her and was thinking of looking for another job.

After she explored her options in counseling, we began to examine her feelings toward the man at work and toward the conflict. She felt angry toward him, frustrated about the conflict. She realized that these feelings kept her hooked into his harassment of her. Her thoughts kept her away from her own priorities of success on the job.

Jane decided to change her thoughts. Realizing she could not change the man, Jane chose to feel compassion for him and to accept the situation. When he tried to bait her again, she smiled sympathetically and patted him on the shoulder. After a few more futile attempts to rattle her he backed off, and her problem was solved.

REFINING STRESSFUL EMOTIONS

Like Jane, you have a whole array of emotions to choose from in responding to any situation.

Try this exercise. Close your eyes and relax. Now feel regret, feel bored, feel frustrated, feel loving, feel affectionate, feel sexual. You can bring up all of these emotions because you have felt them before and you recognize them. You can think of the name of the feeling before you feel it because your thoughts and feelings are working together.

Now think of a situation in your life where you would like to change your feelings. Go inside yourself and determine what you now feel about this situation. Then choose the feeling that you prefer. Rehearse this new feeling in the same situation. Visualize or imagine this scene as if it's on a movie screen. You're the director, the writer, and the star. This is your movie and you can create it the way you like best.

Think of the wonderful freedom and control you can have over your life when you can select, use, and express positive, appropriate emotions. Choosing an appropriate emotion is critical for your well-being.

You are no longer just a helpless victim of your impulsive feelings. You can choose the best emotion for a situation beforehand through rehearsal, during by changing your thoughts, and after by reviewing the situation and deciding on another, more effective and satisfying response if a similar situation occurs in the future.

As you begin to realize you can choose your responses, you can turn your strong, negative emotions into appropriate, less powerful emotions or feelings. You will be able to change rage and anger to irritation and annoyance, hate to hurt, anxiety to a warning that something internal needs to be attended to, jealousy to disappointment and a chance to look at your fear of loss.

When you begin to recognize appropriate emotional responses you will have energy left over to face and solve your problems, both within yourself and with others. You won't be expending all your energy on holding feelings back, erecting elaborate defenses, or acting out.

Any strong emotional reaction you have is a sign that you have a problem. It may be sparked by the behavior of someone else, but your feelings are yours, and the resolution of them lies within you. Remember, you learned most of them and you can relearn a better way.

Refining strong stressful emotions to milder, appropriate ones is like refining raw ore to pure beautiful gold. You can change lust to love, passion to compassion, anger to assertiveness, depression to sadness, fear to security. You can learn to be at one with all of humanity, when you grow up enough to give up your childish pseudo-protective emotions.

FEEL THE FEELINGS

Besides recognizing and identifying your emotions, it is important to allow yourself to feel or experience your emotions. Crying if you're sad, yelling when you're angry, dancing when you're happy, removes the resistance and the powerful fear that feeling your emotions may overwhelm you. This fear of being flooded by overpowering emotions is the main reason you hesitate and resist dealing with old issues, losses, hurts, and abuses from your past.

Feelings have more power over you when you defend against them and hold them inside. John Bradshaw says you can't heal it if you don't feel it. Feel what you feel, don't hide from it. After you feel it, it will soon begin to go away, and you can move on, free and in control.

Learning to identify and to feel your emotions may take practice. If your feelings were invalidated, denied, and punished as a child you may have shut out this part of yourself. The difficulty that our culture has in allowing people to express their feelings makes growing up emotionally the most challenging part of becoming a successful and self-fulfilled adult. It is as if a part of you has been frozen, and you will need to risk melting that ice in order to grow up and reach your individual potential.

After you know what you're feeling, allow yourself to feel it. Stay in the present moment. Feel your guilt, your worry, your fear, your shame, your hurt, your joy. Experience the feeling in your body, your thoughts, your soul. Talk to it. Ask what purpose it serves in your life right now. What does it have to teach you. It is best if you work on this privately and in a quiet time at first. If you have trouble with this process, you may want to work on it with a therapist.

Often we use old familiar feelings to cover up, avoid, and/or escape deeper, more painful emotions. Try to get past the same old answers and feelings and reach the source of your feelings and see the patterns. Remember the times in your past when some event triggered the same feelings. Go back as far as you can remember. The seeds of these negative emotions were planted in childhood. Negative feelings are weeds and positive ones are flowers. Explore what is in your emotional garden. Maybe it is time to do some yard work and clean out those ugly, dried up, and useless weeds and to plant some more flowers. Flowers bring you joy and weeds bring you problems.

Sometimes this emotional yard work can be frightening or painful and can take a long time. You may avoid it for many reasons: 1. You don't know how to do it 2. You think your life is fine if you are not in crisis, or 3. You are afraid that if you unleash and drag up those powerful emotions something terrible will happen. Your worst fear is that you could go crazy, or even die.

The more childhood trauma you had, the more difficult it will be to allow those old feelings to resurface in all their power. Difficult, but not impossible. Hypnosis works well to help you remember blocked and buried events from the past.

You can find a safe and appropriate place to let yourself feel your emotions. You can cry with a friend, scream at the ocean, talk about your despair with a trusted lover or mentor, vent your frustrations in a self-help group, face your fears alone, or work with a therapist.

Once you've *identified* a feeling, *acknowledged* it, *understood* its source, *chosen* to keep or exchange the emotion you want, *felt* it, and *expressed* it appropriately, you have taken the first steps toward gaining emotional control. You'll find that the emotion is now yours. It's not controlling you, you have taken charge of it -- and taken a critical step in growing up.

Let me share with you a poem that my friend Ricardo wrote for me after a meeting of Mothers Against Drunk Drivers. The year before he was hit by a drunk driver and the crash shattered his body. He had one leg amputated, almost lost the other one, and has multiple other injuries. He came to the meeting to learn more skills to help other drunk-driving victims.

Seemed not long ago

That I didn't really know

When the tears would stop

And not so much the tears

It was the hurt.

Seemed not long gone by

That the days came and went

Came and went, and so what

It felt like there was no enjoyment

It was the hurt.

It takes so much to feel bad
To think of things gone by
Things I had, the way I was
That was the hurt.

And then comes the light
That I missed so much beauty
I forgot that I lived and loved.
My feelings were Clouded by the hurt.
It still hurts

Sometimes more than others
Yet, the beauty has come back to my sight.
I was blinded by
The hurt inside of me.

Ricardo Melendez June, 1989

Ricardo lived through his crisis and became better and stronger emotionally. He found a way to turn his tragedy into a positive event by choosing to appreciate the beauty and life around him instead of dwelling on his pain and self-pity. He now tells his story to drunk-driving offenders in a effort to help them understand how a life can be shattered by drunken driving.

When I met Ricardo, I was hurting too. A relationship I treasured had just ended. My new friend's gift was his ability to relate to the hurt inside of me. We all hurt in different ways. The sources of our pain may be different, but suffering is a common denominator among us human beings. Life is difficult. And unfelt, and unresolved emotional pain will return to haunt us over and over again, until we attend to it, until we heal it, even though it hurts.

EXPRESSING YOUR EMOTIONS

Grownups who have an emotion that is going to take some time to resolve must learn to express that feeling when and where it is safe and not harmful to do so. Expressing the emotion gets the feeling out and takes away some of its power. But expressing it at the expense of making others feel frightened, angry, embarrassed, or mistreated is childish and inappropriate.

For instance, if you feel hassled with your job situation and you don't want to take your frustrations home where they don't belong, you have some choices to make. The grown-up thing to do is to express the job frustration appropriately at the job.

If the emotions seem overpowering, one way to subdue them is to express them physically. Vigorous exercise can expel a lot of anger, depression, and guilt, and clear your head so that you can see your emotions more clearly and therefore begin to manage them, but this is only a temporary solution.

To focus on the real-life situation that's causing the problem, close your eyes for a minute and see yourself at work locked in a power struggle with your supervisor. Identify and name what you are feeling. Now rehearse some other feelings. Try feeling *frustrated ... disappointed ... curious ... sympathetic ... concerned ... calm ... accepting.* Stop reading now and do this exercise with some situation in your life today that causes emotional confusion.

See how each one feels different. Monitor the physical reactions and thoughts that come with each feeling. Notice how some seem more appropriate than others. Some give you more peace and confidence. You can choose one that will move your life forward in a productive way.

Then you can do some problem solving and let your emotions help you work toward a real resolution to the problem. We'll explore problem solving in more detail later.

Some of your emotional choices are: You can be assertive and re-negotiate the issues that have created your unhappiness, or at least ask your boss for an appointment to do so; you can choose disappointment and accept the situation by deciding it isn't that important to your well-being; or you can determine that the situation causes too much frustration and begin making plans to find a new job. Maybe you have other options I haven't thought about. Put your emotions and energy into your hopes for a better situation instead of suffering over the present one.

After you've learned to identify your emotions and refine them to manageable levels, you're ready to express them. To express your emotions you must communicate them, first to yourself, then to others, and always in a responsible manner.

Humans express emotions both verbally and nonverbally. You send messages about your emotional state by the expression on your face, the look in your eyes, your tone of voice, body position, and gestures. Sometimes the emotional message is clear, but these signals can be misread. Tiredness may look like depression, or the source of anger may be unknown to the person you're with. Usually we are not sure what another person is feeling unless he tells us verbally.

The most important thing to communicate in a relationship is how you feel. The danger in not expressing your emotions is that you will be misunderstood. Then you don't get your needs and wants met, and you deny those around you the opportunity to know and love the real you. *Others cannot read you your mind.* You must tell them how you feel.

The best way to verbalize your feelings is to use "I" statements. Say " I feel frustrated and upset by the conditions in this department" or "I feel happy when I am with you" or "I felt hurt when you said that you would call me on Saturday and you didn't call".

When you state a feeling using "I", you take responsibility for your feelings and allow the other person to hear you without being put on the defensive. This distinction in the way you communicate makes a world of difference in the response you get from others.

It is also important that your body language and other nonverbal cues match your words. If they don't, your words will not be believable.

All your behaviors have natural consequences. If you withdraw and hide your emotions you will isolate yourself and go through life feeling misunderstood and unloved.

No one can read your mind. It may feel a little risky at first to say how you feel when you fear that someone will reject you for it. But only by sharing your feelings will you find out. And only by expressing your wants and needs can you allow another person to share your hopes, your fears, and your life. It's worth the effort.

Ask for what you want. Take that responsibility! You may not always get it, but if you never ask you have much less chance of getting anything, except frustration and disappointment.

CHAPTER TEN

MORE TECHNIQUES FOR MANAGING EMOTIONS

What ever emotional pattern seems to dominate your life, the steps to getting control of your emotions are those outlined in Chapter 9 . In this chapter we're going to look at some of the most common destructive emotional patterns. Most of them are based on childhood experiences that taught you to face life from a position of fear, guilt, shame, anger, or depression.

If you recognize that one of these emotions dominates your life in a harmful way, you need to learn to control them. Right now they control you, and they prevent you from growing up.

If you have been blocked by fear or anger or some other powerful emotion running your life for a long time, learning to control it will take some work and time. But it is well worth the effort. There are several good books on each of these topics to help you but working with a therapist will get your there quicker. When you are ready to change you will make progress rather fast.

MANAGING FEAR

We cling to fear because it is a familiar companion and we have learned how to cover it up and live with it. We irrationally believe it is easier to remain afraid than to face the object of the fear.

But to outgrow your fears, you must risk facing the feared object so you can put it behind you where it will have much less power. The way to change fear to self-love and self-control involves several steps: acknowledge your fear, remember old traumatic events, lower your defenses, feel the emotions you have cut off, and let the related feelings

Franklin Roosevelt said, "The only thing we have to fear is fear itself". Don't be afraid of your fears. Fear places you in the position of having no real control. If you repress your fears, ignore them, deny them, or fight them, in time they will win and grow into phobia or anxiety. In extreme form anxiety becomes panic, the ultimate feeling of being out of control -- sometimes called a nervous breakdown. Ironically, the effort to maintain rigid, complete control eventually leads to its same, total loss of control. Your only real option is to face your fears and to deal with them.

RECOGNIZING FEAR

You may not realize how many patterns in your thinking and feeling stem from fear, because the fear is often covered up by other emotions. Remember that fear underlies many other emotions. As you learn to recognize your feelings, examine how each relates to a specific fear.

If you are not ready to face your fears you will do anything to control situations and people around you to avoid being honest with them or yourself. You will keep your feelings stuffed deep down inside you, hidden in darkness. Yet in order to be in real control, from within you, you must do the thing you fear most --

you must give up controlling and surrender.

Worry is fearing that something may happen in the future, for the most part it wastes your time and energy, because 95 percent of what you worry about will never happen. Nevertheless, pay attention to those worrying thoughts, bring them into the present, and write them down. Sort them out, discard the culls (irrational thoughts and fears), and examine what is left carefully and honestly -- for within them are the seeds of your fears.

When you get to the bottom of your fear, you will probably feel some powerful emotions like anger and unresolved grief from some incident in your past that has threads to the present. In order to heal you must grieve for the old hurt as well as the present one.

Another way we avoid facing our fears is by using defenses. Denial, rationalization, minimization, and projection are the most common ones we use to protect ourselves from others. When you use a defense mechanism to lie to yourself, you delay dealing with your real fears and consequently delay your growing up.

In order to grow up emotionally you must stop using your old ploys and defenses, and give up blaming others for the things that go wrong in your life. Take time to listen to your inner voice and begin to face your fears and heal yourself.

PHOBIAS AND ANXIETY

A phobia -- whether of flying, closed-in places, certain animals or something else -- is one of the worst problems to live with -- and one of the easiest to cure. Phobias often are based on irrational fears from some past traumatic experience. When that event happened, you were *overly* sensitized --programmed to be super-sensitive to the experiences you associate with the trauma. Short-term therapy usually can *desensitize* you (make you less sensitive and responsive) to the source of your fear.

It isn't necessary to know the underlying cause of your fear to overcome it. Sometimes phobias are born before your memory was developed well enough to relate to as an adult. You can retrain your emotions and your body to respond differently without having a complete intellectual understanding of your fearful reaction.

Systematic desensitization, conducted by a therapist, involves relaxing and then gradually approaching the feared situation in very small increments -- first practiced in the mind and then in actuality. For instance, in working with my flying phobia, I would first visualize taking a trip on an airplane. Then I would see myself buying a ticket, then packing my clothes, then driving to the airport, and so on.

You monitor your anxiety at each step. If one step really raises your anxiety level, stop and relax again, telling yourself that you can handle this. The next day you start by visualizing the step before the upsetting one, and slowly approach the anxiety-producing step again.

After you can imagine yourself successfully mastering your feared experience, you try it in real life, again step by step, reducing your anxiety as you go.

The most important thing to remember regarding phobias is not to run away from them. Stay with the feared situation until the anxiety subsides. The strength of a phobia will grow in direct proportion to the energy you give to avoiding whatever sets off the fear reaction.

OVERCOMING GUILT

Whenever you feel appropriate guilt, you have violated one of your personal values. The feeling of guilt gives you a chance to look within yourself and to evaluate the validity of that moral guideline to determine if it is viable in your life at the present. If it is, then you must stop doing what you feel guilty about, and take steps to acknowledge or make up for what harm you have caused others.

Sometimes you find that guilt is triggered by a moral guideline that you don't find valid. You may discover that you feel guilty about no longer attending church, even though you are a Christian, or about not returning someone's phone calls. When you think about it, you realize that attending church no longer meets your spiritual needs. Or you discover that you don't want to have a relationship with the caller.

If you find your guilt is triggered by values of other people that don't agree with your standards, then the guilt is inappropriate. Your moral values have changed, and you can stop feeling guilty by accepting the fact. You are the only judge of whether your behavior is right or wrong. Secure mature adults set their own moral standards.

HONESTY

If lying is a problem in your life, and you lie compulsively, as if you have no control over it, try the exercise on systematic desensitization to help overcome the obsessive behavior.

Pick several situations in which you have lied or may lie. Imagine yourself telling the truth about each one. Notice the feelings that come up. Deal with the fears or whatever feelings keep you from being truthful. Continue to rehearse being truthful until you feel right doing so, and face the consequences of your behavior without covering up.

ASSERTIVENESS

Assertiveness training is also a wonderful way to change dishonest behavior and to begin to live a more open, authentic life based on believing in and expressing your own values. Assertiveness means standing up for yourself while treating others with respect and openness.

As you assert your feelings and wishes, you allow the other person to do the same. You find that there's room for both, and that someone else's feelings need not be threatening or guilt-inducing for you. If you're true to yourself, there's no need to lie and cheat or feel guilty.

In assertiveness training you will also learn that your feelings are yours. Your anger, fear, depression, guilt, are yours, you allow yourself to feel angry, afraid, sad, or guilty. No one makes you angry, you make yourself angry, or afraid, or ashamed.

I recommend that most adults take a course or class in assertiveness. Assertiveness training is an excellent way to learn to manage all your emotions, it can help everyone, whatever your emotionally dysfunctional pattern may be. Reading about it is fine, but assertiveness is a new way to communicate. Like learning any skill it requires practice. In a class you get many chances to practice your new skills, usually in small groups in a safe environment.

One final word about becoming assertive. When you begin to change other people who are used to the "old" you may feel threatened. If you are successful they will need to change too, or your relationship with them may change. Of course it is better if you can change together. Try to encourage them to go to the classes with you and you can change together or as a family.

If others can't accept your changes, they may put a great deal of pressure on you to stay in your old dysfunctional and self-defeating behaviors. If you give in to guilt from that type of pressure you will feel even more defeated and reluctant to try new growth-producing things in the future. Remember you have choices. Your life is yours. Your decisions are yours. Growing up is for you, it is your responsibility to be true to yourself.

HEALING SHAME

To heal shame, you must re-experience the buried and hidden events that created it so you can feel the hurt, pain, anger, and grief that were pushed aside then. You must go back and do the grief work delayed for years. You can do this in a group or with a qualified therapist.

Shame-bound people -- those whose childhood experiences caused them to feel ashamed of their emotions -- suffer from delayed grief. Delayed grief is also at the core of post-traumatic stress, as we know from the experience of Vietnam War veterans who have emotional problems.

Often a shame-based person doesn't realize he has buried emotions and childhood pains for which he hasn't grieved. You can begin to recognize signs that this area needs work. Some symptoms of unresolved grief are recurring nightmares, numbed emotions, inability to become intimate, need to control, hypervigilance, little interest in everyday events, exaggerated startle responses, intrusive memories of the events, and sleeping disorders.

To overcome shame, the feelings that were shamed must be accepted and validated. You must be willing to lower your defenses, tear down your protective walls brick by brick, and reclaim your lost childhood. You can't move on to adulthood unless you bring that little child along with you in love and nurturance.

In *Healing the Shame that Binds You*, John Bradshaw says, "Perhaps the most damaging consequence of being shame based is that we don't know how depressed and angry we really are. We don't actually feel our unresolved grief. Our false self and ego defenses keep us from experiencing it. Paradoxically, the very defenses which allowed us to survive our childhood trauma have now become barriers to our growth". Fritz Perls once said, "Nothing changes 'til it becomes what it is. We must uncover our frozen grief".

In order to uncover and melt that grief you must make contact with your inner child, in some cases your inner infant. Using a guided imagery exercise, (a form of meditation) described later in this chapter, will help you do this.

Another way to reach that child and uncover your hidden pain is to buy a doll, a soft cloth or rag doll, or a teddy bear or other stuffed animal that you can hug and cuddle. This is important for both men and women, every child needs nurturing.

This doll represents you as a child. Give it your childhood name and treat it like your own offspring. Sleep with your doll, cuddle it often, love it, nurture it. Above all, listen to it. It will tell you what hurts, what needs attention.

There's another good way to contact and heal your inner child, so that you can grow up and establish a life with our own friends, values, and feelings: Write a letter to each of your parents and say good-bye. It doesn't matter if they are dead or if you are estranged from them, you won't send the letters.

This exercise is for you, to help you cut the harmful ties that bind you in emotional childhood. The positive ties will remain and help you be a better grown-up. Remember, don't mail the letter. This exercise is to help you to bring those old buried hurts and other feelings to the surface.

No one had a perfect childhood, and each of us has some unfinished emotional business with parents. Your parents are the source of your shame (as well as of many other emotional lessons).

To grow up, you must claim your emotions for yourself by asserting that your parents no longer can determine by their actions or their rules how you feel or who you are. If you had a very traumatic relationship with your parents or are still emotionally dependent on one or both of them, this may be hard to do. But do it anyway. This is not about parent-bashing it is about facilitating your liberation into full-fledged adulthood.

If your parents are still living, the letter will help you begin a new and healthier relationship with them. In the letter you will be writing as one adult to another, rather than as a dependent child to an authority figure. Age is irrelevant, I know people in their 50s and 60s who still shiver and shake at the thought of their parents disapproval.

In your letter, you can and must be honest and say whatever you want, no matter how extreme or hateful. The process of writing the letter will assist you in bringing to the surface and releasing feelings and thoughts that have inhibited your growth and kept you locked in emotional childhood.

Tell your mother or your father about the things they did or other things that happened that hurt you, made you angry, made you afraid or ashamed, things that you resent. Once you've expressed those feelings, then write a section telling them about the things you appreciate, the good memories, the useful values and lessons they taught you.

The next section should tell your parents what kind of a relationship you want with them now. Thank them if you want to. Forgive them, if you can, for their mistakes.

Then tell them good-bye. Release them with love. By saying good-bye, you are not separating yourself from your actual parents as they are today. You are giving yourself an official emotional graduation from being a child whose moods, feelings, behavior, and self-concept were determined by their reactions. You're saying good-bye to the parents of your childhood. You're a grownup now and you don't need mommy and daddy any more.

If you are in therapy, read the letter to your therapist. If not, you can read it to a trusted friend, sibling, or spouse. Be aware of passages that raise strong emotions. If they cause tears, good. Letting those tears out will help to facilitate your grieving process. They are also a clue that you need to do more work in this area.

If your childhood was filled with shame, you must begin your grief work with a person or group you trust, with whom you can build a safe relationship. You cannot be healed alone. You were shamed, neglected, and abandoned by others, you can only heal with the help of others.

ANGER AND AGGRESSION

There are two basic ways to deal with anger. One is to change your thoughts and self-talk, this is called cognitive restructuring. The other is to learn to become assertive, thereby intervening with mild emotions before they build up and get out of control. Both will take some effort, patience, practice, and commitment to be successful.

We've already looked at assertiveness. Applying these techniques in anger management means identifying the anger-related feelings before they reach the level of rage, and communicating to others in an assertive manner that you feel frustrated, resentful, irritated, impatient, or some other feeling because of a particular event.

COGNITIVE RESTRUCTURING

The second way to manage anger means changing your thoughts, especially those that provoke and accelerate your anger. To do this you need to listen to and examine your self-talk, objectively and carefully.

The best way to begin is to work with a paper and pencil. Make three headings across the top of the first page: Triggering event, Thoughts that make me angrier, Thoughts that make me calm. Now draw three vertical lines to create columns under these headings.

The next time someone does something that triggers your anger, fill in the columns. Here's an example:

Triggering Event

A driver cut me off on the way home from work today.

Thoughts that make me angrier	Thoughts that make me calm
Who does he think he is?	*I guess that guy is in a real hurry.*
Wait till I see that SOB again!	*Maybe he has an emergency. I'll get out of his way.*
I'll fix him.	*So he's a jerk, I won't let his behavior make me mad.*

Feel the difference! You will need to work with this technique a lot for a while. First, you'll notice how often you get angry at other people's behavior. In time you will notice that you are not getting hooked into wasting your energy on inconsequential events like a reckless driver.

You will learn that the anger is *yours* and you can choose other responses. Using this awareness you can break the habit of anger. Just as with quitting smoking or losing weight, you have to get started with new patterns, then stick to them.

To explore in more depth the anger that has been controlling you, keep an anger journal. Using the above exercise, faithfully record every time your anger surfaces. Also record being critical, hostile, sarcastic, calling names, and any other behaviors that express anger toward someone, usually undeserved. At the end of a month look for patterns in the issues that provoked you.

Then do two things. First, explore the underlying emotions. Ask yourself, When in the past did I feel this way? Who was involved? How many times did this type of situation happen? Was there more than one situation? Often this search will take you back to childhood when you were afraid, powerless, and misunderstood. You learned to react in ways that seemed to give you control over those situations by drawing attention to you or making you seem threatening.

But that won't work for you as an adult. When you get in touch with those old feelings you can reparent yourself, give yourself power, and choose a new way to respond to similar triggering events. You may want to describe these early events and the related feelings in letters to your parents. Any of these methods will help you see that rage isn't your only choice.

Secondly, try out new behaviors. This process is like trying on new clothes; some look good on the rack but don't fit you, some are surprisingly flattering. Ask for feedback from friends and family.

For example, next time you get angry, take a break before you react in your old way. Go for a walk and calm down. Figure out the underlying problem, see how the situation relates to your childish feelings, then go back and begin problem solving. This way you break the negative patterns, and move to resolution.

CONTROLLING DEPRESSION

By now you've noticed that the same basic process applies to dealing with any harmful emotion, whether it's anger, fear, guilt, or shame. The same is true for depression. First, you must identify the specific emotion you are feeling. It may be sadness, regret, rejection, grief, or something else. Here is an exercise to help you clarify your feelings.

Depression is an immobilizing emotion. Often people who are depressed withdraw from life, feeling that they can't do anything to change a situation or that nothing really matters. If you're depressed, you need to get past depression so you can take action and get back in the swim of life.

Get into a relaxed position, close your eyes, and

concentrate on your breathing so you can quiet your thoughts. Now focus on the situation that is depressing you. Identify your feelings (there may be several). Determine what feelings you would have to give up in order to get past the depression and to get on with your life. Now try out a few more positive emotions to replace your depressed emotions, and after you've found one that fits, make the mental change.

Let's go through this process with an example. Let's say that your brother died. You feel sad for several reasons: you have to give up a future with him; you will miss him at family events; you can't share hikes and hobbies with him; you wish you had spent more time with him. You may also feel disappointment at your loss, glad that he is out of this suffering and pain, or acceptance that you can't change the fact of his death.

When you break down your depression into several component emotions, you can work with each and determine whether it's appropriate or should be changed. You also must allow yourself time for the more painful feelings to heal. Next time you feel depressed, try this replacing of emotions. It works.

When you feel depressed, don't become afraid or worried about that feeling. Here are some positive things you can do:

♦ Allow yourself the sadness appropriate to the situation, and understand that loss is causing your grief.

♦ Accept and express your depression so you can move on out of the sadness. Fighting it only makes it stronger and gives it control over you.

♦ Talk with a good friend to help loosen the feelings you may be holding back.

♦ Use regular physical exercise to help restore your energy level and make you feel better.

♦ Have a complete physical, and be sure you follow a healthy diet.

♦ Be aware that the anniversary of a loss often brings on depression. For some people, the holidays or certain seasons trigger this feeling. You may still feel sad, but if you recognize the timing of your feelings, you'll know that they will diminish.

♦ Identify things going on in your life that really need to change. Make a realistic plan to change your depressing job, your drab home, you downer friends, the rut you're in.

♦ Discharge negative emotions in constructive ways. Let out your anger, fear, or sadness in music, art, sports, hobbies, travel, or whatever you really enjoy.

♦ Don't make major, sweeping changes in your life while you're in the midst of a depression. Don't end your marriage, quit your job, or move across the country until you've given yourself the benefit of your best thinking capacities. And you can't think well while you're overwhelmed with depression.

♦ Lean on people. Just knowing someone is listening in a caring way helps lift sadness.

If these techniques don't work, or you find your depression is chronic and not related to a specific situation, you need to seek professional help to handle old unresolved grief and anger.

The grown-up way to manage depression is to accept it when it occurs as part of change and to express the feelings it produces. If you continue to deny depression, you'll build a store of harmful emotions that will one day manifest as physical illness, explosive anger, or long-term debilitation. Don't do this to yourself. It's much harder to grow up if you're burdened down by unexpressed depression that you've carried for many years.

CREATING HAPPINESS AND LOVE

You can't be happy unless you love yourself.

You can't love another unless you love yourself.

You can't give your children unconditional love,
unless you give the same to yourself.

So that last important step in growing up emotionally -- after healing your old wounds, and learning to manage your emotions -- is learning to love yourself.

Loving yourself involves becoming a loving, nurturing parent to that scared, sad, and frightened child who lives inside of you. You need to love yourself before you can feel safe enough to expose your inner self to another. Without reversing those negative parental messages, by becoming your own parent, you remain trapped as a perpetual child, at the mercy of your emotions instead of in control of them.

Here is an exercise in guided imagery to help you to begin to give yourself whatever you need to feel secure, trusting, loving, and happy. You may even want to make a tape recording of this exercise to play for yourself regularly.

Get into a comfortable position and relax your body and mind. Loosen any tight clothing, make your shoes off, close your eyes, and focus on your breathing. Breathe from your belly as you do while sleeping. Observe any thoughts that come to mind and let them pass.

After a few minutes imagine yourself walking in a place that has special meaning to you; it may be on a beach, along a wooded country road, in the mountains, a summer meadow, or any secluded natural setting. As you get involved in the image, concentrate on the sensory experience of being in this place. See the waves, the sun, the horizon, birds flying overhead and scurrying along the shore, shells scattered here and there, the craggy mountains, the fallen leaves. Hear the roar of the waves, songs of the birds, voices in the distance, the babbling brook. Feel the warmth or coolness on your skin, the saltwater mist, the temperature of the water, the sand under your feet, the breezes. Notice the unique smells, tastes.

Allow this special place to draw you into its peacefulness and give you a sense of well-being and inner contentment. As you concentrate on every sensory detail, you will relax and soon you will really be there in spirit.

Now walk slowly along the shore or the brook, totally immersed in the experience of this place. As you look up, you see a small child walking toward you from a distance. The child is you.

As the two of you approach each other, pay close attention to the behavior of the child. What is the child's mood? Is it happy and playful, or sad and shy? Is it playing and carefree, or crying? Walk up to the child and take him or her into your arms. (You could use your doll here to make the experience more real.) What are you feeling as you hold this child?

Join the child and begin to talk to him or her. You sense that the child wants something from you. Ask what it is, listen to the answer. Take all the time you need to listen carefully to your child.

Tell the child that you love it, that you will protect it, and never leave it again. Use the words that reassure the child in the way he needs to be reassured. You will take care of him from now on. Any time he wants to signal to you, you will return to this setting to talk to and nurture this child within you. Agree on a signal for calling each other. Tell the child, "I know how afraid you are but now you are safe."

Spend as much time as you need to comfort and love this child because the child is you. When your child feels safer and more secure, walk a while hand in hand. When you are ready, tell the child that you must leave for now but you will return as often and as long as you are needed until the child is grown up and no longer needs you. Then slowly walk away and return to the room you are in and spend some time with your feelings about the experience. You may want to share this with a friend.

Stop reading and do this exercise now. When you are finished, write down your feelings and thoughts about it in a journal or notebook. Do the same whenever you repeat the exercise.

The child will need you again and call you. It will tell you different things each time -- its fears, its hopes, its disappointments, its dreams. You will respond with love, as the ideal, loving parent who wants the best for this child.

No matter how old you are, you have a need sometimes to be emotionally and physically babied, cuddled, and loved unconditionally. You can do this with the doll that represents the child within you. Hug and love that baby, rock it, talk to it, give it all the time and love it needs.

When you get in touch with the child that lives within you, and always will, you may find it a highly emotional experience, whether you're a man or a woman. Your child's hurts have been waiting for a healing kiss for a long time.

If you feel like crying, do it. Don't hold back your feelings. You are engaging in a healing process, and the tears are an important part. Love and heal that poor, deprived baby. Whenever you're feeling especially vulnerable and alone, go get your doll or object which represents your baby for you. Talk to and touch your child, touch it until your feelings begin to ease. If your childhood had a great deal of pain, you may need to set times to do this regularly. Sleep with it for a while, carry it with you around the house or in the car, just as you would with your own child. Always be reassuring, loving, and nurturing.

PART FOUR

GROWING UP PHYSICALLY

CHAPTER ELEVEN

WHAT DOES IT MEAN TO BE PHYSICALLY GROWN-UP?

Ask not what your body can do for you, but what you can do for your body.

To be grown up physically means that you accept, acknowledge, respect, listen to, and take care of your body. You don't take it for granted, paying attention to it only when it gives you pleasure or pain.

A grownup regards his or her body as an important part of the whole Self, to be cared for and given attention because of its own importance and as an integral part of one's being. Your body will serve you best, for many years, if you serve it by creating it with attention and love.

Your body is the temple of your spirit, the seat of your

emotions, and the home of your intellect. It is part of your complete Self. The body is the first early warning system that lets you know when your organism is out of balance or out of control, when one of the other aspects needs attention.

Many adults are out of touch with their bodies. So many of us fill our bodies with drugs, alcohol, sugar, preservatives, dirty air and water, we ignore its aches and pains and warning signals, hoping they'll just go away. We batter our bodies unmercifully with brutal contact sports, or bouts of strenuous exertion without first building up stamina, or by a life that ignores the body's needs for rest and exercise.

Others of us get caught up in the latest fad diet or fitness craze and abuse our bodies with steroids and round-the-clock exercise in a compulsive obsession to get in shape -- not the shape the body naturally and healthfully wants to take but a shape that meets our idea of physical and social perfection.

Over attention to the body can be as damaging as neglect of its signals and needs. We are all much more than our bodies. If only the body is developed, to the neglect of intellectual, emotional, and spiritual growth, you wind up with an empty shell, beautiful perhaps, but capable of only a Barbie and Ken existence.

By the time you reach your late teens and early twenties you've got the basic body that you're going to have to live in all the rest of your life. The first thing the grownup must do is accept the fact that some things about that body cannot be changed. Secondly, grownups learn that to feel good emotionally, spiritually, and mentally, as well as physically, they'll have to care for what they've got from now on.

TAKING CARE OF YOUR BODY

Accepting your body doesn't mean that you just dumbly say okay to whatever it does or feels, or that you give up control over your physical self. Some things about your body can't be changed, and other things can be. Growing up involves learning how to tell the difference. Then it's your responsibility --with the use of your mind, spirit, and emotions -- to make the kinds of decisions that will keep your body as healthy as possible.

First of all, you are responsible for meeting your body's basic physiological needs in order to sustain the physical part of yourself. You must have water and food to nourish the cells of your body. You need shelter to protect your body from extreme temperatures.

Clothing, too, serves the purpose of protection, but it also tells others about your social status or emotional condition. The way we adorn the body sends messages inward as well as outward. For instance, when you're depressed, you probably pay less attention to your clothing, hair care, and makeup. Those things just don't seem to matter. When the sun shines again, you buy a new outfit or wear your snappiest skirt or shirt to show the world how good you can look.

The connection between appearance and mood also works the other way around. Psychologists have discovered that clothing can actually change your mood and feelings about yourself. Remember the old cliche of a woman advising a friend who felt down in the dumps to go out a buy a new hat. That woman knew what she was talking about. Buying a new hat, putting on attractive clothes, sometimes helps people shake the blues, at least temporarily. But beware of compulsive addictive shopping to ward off the blues, it can be a quick fix, but bring financial consequences later. Better to deal with underlying causes when possible

DEVELOPMENTAL CHANGES

The physical body makes remarkable changes over a lifetime. When I look at a baby and realize that its skin will stretch into a person over five feet tall and 100 to 200 pounds or more I am amazed. Our bodies grow at a remarkable rate for the first 18 years. We develop large motor skills for walking and jumping, and fine motor control that allows us to sew and play the piano. Our internal organs grow throughout childhood, including our brains. Our bones and muscles enlarge to support a larger frame.

Throughout young adulthood, if we're fortunate, we have the energy and strength to do pretty much what we want to. Some of us stay active in athletics or learn to get great pleasure and relaxation from stress by developing new physical abilities. As young adults, if we had a few bad habits, we knew we could always change next week, quit smoking, or lose a few pounds and get back in shape.

Then, sometime in midlife, the body begins a gradual decline. This wonderful housing that has served so well for the last 40 or 50 years isn't quite so reliable. Stamina is reduced. Recovery takes longer after strenuous exercise, a broken bone or an illness. We become susceptible to the diseases of aging -- osteoporosis, cancer, strokes, heart disease, cataracts. At this point, you may wish that you hadn't taken your body for granted, that you had listened more to its messages, and abused it less with bad food, chemicals, alcohol, and tobacco.

In midlife and later, our weakest parts give way and become chronic problems. Aches and pains and cramps present themselves with increasing frequency. The immune system begins to wear down and doesn't ward off diseases with as much vigor as when we were younger.

By the age of 80 we have lost more than 60 percent of the use of our senses -- sight, hearing, smell, touch, and taste. Of course these changes don't happen evenly across the board to everyone, but these losses are inevitable if we live long enough. By the 80s we are called "frail", and must again depend on someone to take care of us, just as we did as babies.

All living tissue deteriorates over time. One gerontologist put it this way: "First we ripen, then we rot". Not a very pretty picture, but an accurate one. Just like a leaf, an apple, or a bird, each person has a physical life cycle, with a beginning, middle, and end.

The deterioration of the body that comes with growing old is something you can't avoid. But, as in many other physical aspects of life, you can accept and appreciate it. Graceful and successful physical aging involves maintaining a good self-image over the years. Loving and accepting your body as it is throughout life will make it easier to accept the gradual changes like looser skin and muscle tone, grey hair, and less stamina.

Continuing to be lovable is the test of successful aging. It is easier if you have a loving partner who reassures you. Even if you are alone, you can still give and receive love, to yourself, your family, and to friends, old and new.

Your age is a tribute to all of the lessons, experiences, and maybe a little wisdom that you have acquired. However old you are, and whatever your body has gone through, you can still look in the mirror, and smile at every wrinkle, bulge, gray hair and say "I love you, Kid."

BODY TALK

One of the fascinating things about the body is how much wisdom it has. The body carries within it messages and truths about your feelings, thoughts, and spirit. Body pains and discomforts are often physical symptoms of emotional, intellectual, or spiritual anxiety. An important key to growing up and being in balance is to learn to hear and see the body's messages.

Listen to your body Your body always knows first when something is wrong. It tries to tell you that danger is near, or that an old fear is being triggered, or that your stress level is nearing overload. Learn to pay attention.

When I am afraid of something I hyperventilate or yawn excessively and take deep breaths to try to stabilize the oxygen/ carbon dioxide ratio in my lungs. I've learned that, whenever I begin to hyperventilate, my body is trying to tell me something. I can stop and ask myself, "What is going on and what am I afraid of?" Sometimes it takes a while to figure it out. But this warning sign is consistently reliable, and it enables me to deal with the problem before the fear gets out of control.

Your body tries to talk to you too. Each person has a special signal that means "Stop! Pay attention! Take care of business!" Take a minute to think of your signal. Do you get a headache, a flushed face, tightness in your neck, shoulders, or lower back. How about your internal organs. Many people get stomach aches or need to urinate more often under stress. One client's vocal cords swell and he has a hard time talking and breathing. This is a severe physical reaction. The stronger your physical signal, the more immediately you need to give attention to something that is wrong in your life -- or else.

The "or else" means that if you continue to ignore your warning signals you will sooner or later get sick. It takes energy for the body to constantly send out alarm notices. In time your immune system wears down which results in a lowered resistance to fight off the millions of microorganisms that bombard you daily. Some get a good hold and multiply in your body and you get sick, usually in the weakest part of your body. Chronic illness is often the result.

Grief, anger, and other emotions show up vividly in the body. Our posture, facial expressions, and pains communicate to us that feelings haven't been dealt with and resolved. The nature of the physical symptom may be a clue to what's wrong emotionally. Sometimes a heart literally aches from sadness, or a back breaks from being overburdened. Some people get stiff and rigid from holding feelings in. Others build a wall of fat to protect them from what they fear.

Many of us have a genetic propensity for a particular disease. Some parts of your body are weaker than others. Under stress the weakest part of your body will become affected first. You may wind up with colitis, stomach ulcers, colds, or high blood pressure. If your lungs are the weakest part of your body and you smoke two packs of cigarettes a day, you have a very high probability of getting emphysema, lung cancer, or chronic bronchitis. If you have bowel problems, in time you could develop bowel cancer.

I get a cold which rapidly becomes bronchitis because my lungs are my weakest organ. Or my lower back goes *out*, and I have structural problems for weeks. Then my body wins and I am forced to rest, lower my stress level, and reorder my priorities.

It is so much easier just to listen to my body when it starts to signal me and to respect its natural need to protect me. I haven't been sick for several years using this method. I stop and take care of business when I need to.

CHAPTER TWELVE

ISSUES OF PHYSICAL GROWTH

Throughout adulthood, you repeatedly face issues, choices and problems involving your body. Although in one sense you become physically grownup in adolescence, you have a lifelong challenge to continue to care for your body and maintain a grownup attitude about its needs.

You may carry with you unresolved physical conflicts from childhood--issues about how you look, illness or abuse. Even if your childhood was relatively healthy, you still must make choices relating to maintaining your physical health and keeping your physical self in balance with the rest of your being. Some of the specific body issues that need responsible self-control include your attitude about your body, physical habits, healing methods, a history of abuse, and physical disability.

Most people, unfortunately, do not like or appreciate their bodies very much. Even the highest paid fashion models are critical about some parts of their bodies. They believe their breasts are too small, their nose is too big, their hair is too thin or too thick. This self-criticism comes from focusing on their physical beauty as the only measure of their worth.

Most of us don't have to look to far to find our own physical faults. We all have them, or at least we think we do. Remember though one person's "fault" may be another person's prize. If you feel that there's something wrong or imperfect about one part of your body, that part may simply be functioning as a symbol or focal point of something you don't like about your life. When you look at those big feet or that frizzy hair objectively, you may realize there's not a thing wrong with it, and others may even envy you for it.

Lisa came to my office and complained about many things in her life. Eventually her remarks focused on her hated brown eyes. As the only brown-eyed person in a blue-eyed family, she always felt "different", defective. In time she was able to resolve most of her problems, and while she couldn't change the color of her eyes, she did learn to accept and appreciate them. She realized that the color of her eyes was not so important, what really mattered was to change the things she could, and accept the things she couldn't change.

Some things in life we can control, some we cannot. Many of our physical characteristics are inherited through genetic codes and we are stuck with them, like it or not. Our stature, the color, shape and size of skin, eyes, nose, ears, hands, feet, breasts, penis, legs, hips, and bodies in general are basically determined by the genes we are given at conception. Biologists tell us that 64 ancestors contribute to the gene pool of each individual, so you may have some physical trait that isn't readily discernible in your immediate family, like Lisa's brown eyes.

Genetics also plays a role in the likelihood that one will become alcoholic, overweight, or develop heart disease, cancer, diabetes, or other diseases. In the case of serious illness, we can't change the genetic makeup, but we can use our intelligence to modify our behavior to protect ourselves and counterbalance the hereditary tendencies.

So often we become our own harshest critics, judging ourselves against media models like a cover girl on a fashion magazine, on a billboard, on TV, or someone in the movies or sports heroes. Society gives an incredible amount of attention and adulation to certain people simply because they are good looking. The rest of us try to measure ourselves against the glossy smiles and muscle tone of these idols, as if we are flawed if we are not like them.

The result is a whole generation of people with eating disorders. Anorexia nervosa and bulimia are endemic. Forty percent of young girls begin serious dieting by the sixth grade, mostly molded or encouraged by their insecure mothers and peer pressure.

It is important to remember that your body is only the outside part of you, it isn't *who you are*. Not everyone has the genetic stew to look like Jane Fonda or Robert Redford, or can sing like Barbra Streisand or play basketball like Michael Jordan. Whatever body you've got you may as well learn to like and accept it. It is the only one you have.

HARMFUL HABITS

If you smoke cigarettes, eat badly, abuse drugs or alcohol you are risking an early death. You may be in denial, but deep inside you know that bad physical habits are a form of self-abuse. It is true that habits are hard to change, but not impossible. What it takes is a real commitment to yourself to change, and getting help from professionals is a sign of strength, not weakness. Maybe therapy, a treatment program, hypnosis, or medication will give you support to follow through. It all begins with being honest with yourself. If you want your body to serve you in the best possible way then you have to take care of your body.

HEALING

Taking responsibility for your body involves learning that doctors don't heal you, your body heals itself. Physicians, like therapists can diagnosis problems, give advice, and medications, even preform surgery, but it is up to you to heal your body. Sometimes this requires taking stock and making significant life-style changes. Unfortunately, most people ignore good healthy habits until a physical catastrophe strikes.

Remember that whatever happens to one aspect of you affects the other parts and throws you off balance which leads to disharmony and eventually to *dis-ease*. Most diseases are the result of long-term neglect and abuse heaped upon the body. These include environmental effects, poor eating habits, addictions, chronic stress and out-of-control emotions.

The body is the barometer of health or problems in other aspects of you. Lasting results can only be achieved after the underlying issues are handled. If you have an ulcer because you have marital problems, then the marital problems need to be resolved before or at the same time the physical problems are treated, or healing will not take place. Even if the ulcer is temporarily cured, it will recur maybe getting worse each time.

Preventive health practitioners evaluate your risk factors for getting sick by doing some standard tests like blood pressure, stress electrocardiogram, blood work, breath measurements, taking a health history, and evaluating current life stressors. Using the results, you can make some changes to insure a better quality life with a healthier body for many years to come.

The bottom line is that your health and your healing are up to you.

CHILD ABUSE

Children can be mistreated in many ways, by blatant or subtle neglect, or by a variety of forms of abuse, physical, emotional, and sexual which damages both the body, psyche and the mind. Each episode of neglect or abuse leaves scars that have a profound impact on the developing child and on the adult. In this section on physical development we will address physical abuse and sexual abuse.

Physical abuse may be done by a pregnant woman who misuses drugs, cigarettes, alcohol or other substances that will harm her fetus. Or a father who beats his children in an out-of-control rage over little things, where the punishment does not fit the offense. Or abuse may take the form of neglecting or ignoring sickness, injury, or the child's need for food, clean clothes, medical care adequate sleep and shelter, and protection from danger.

Some parents not only are unavailable to meet the child's physical needs or emotional needs but fail to protect the child from victimization by another family member who may be abusing the child on a regular basis. Or they may join in as a co-perpetrator and hurt the child too.

All child abuse is about power. The bully syndrome, overpowering someone smaller, weaker, more vulnerable. Without regard for the damage, hurt, and long term effects on the victim. Any time an adult misuses a child by inflicting physical injury, or by ignoring the child's physical needs or feelings, by using the child for his own selfish purposes, the child will suffer for many years from feelings of inadequacy, worthlessness, shame, guilt, and confusion.

The pain of this kind of tragic childhood doesn't end by leaving home, going into military service, or getting married. The wounds are old and deep and will surface in adult relationships over and over until they are resolved and healed.

The most common way that abuse issues resurface in an abuse victim is in parenting their own children, reacting to stress or certain behaviors triggering the same familiar way they were treated. Because of this the cycle of abuse continues passed on to a new generation until someone finally stops. This usually takes psychotherapy. It is just too confusing and difficult to do alone. It takes more strength and courage to get help than to stay in denial and continue to be miserable and to keep hurting others because you hurt inside. So *GET HELP NOW*, if this is what is happening in your life.

PHYSICAL ABUSE

Physical abuse is usually the result of someone's out-of-control anger and rage, displaced and vented on a weaker person, often a woman, child or elderly parent. There are also people who use physical abuse as part of a ritual to frighten others into compliance to group rules, as in cults. Other times physical abuse is used to make an example, to observers, of what happens when rules aren't followed, such as teachers spanking children in the class room, or court martial, even death squads in the military.

Throughout known civilization we have condoned, even encouraged physical abuse as a form of social control. Only recently are we speaking about human rights and recognizing that there are other more humane ways to teach, reprimand, and control others. We humans have the unfortunate capacity to be violent with others of our own species. This makes us unique in the animal kingdom. In most species sparring, baring teeth, roaring, chest pounding, et cetera, gets the job done.

For centuries women and children were considered the personal property or "chattels" of men. Husbands and fathers kept them in bondage. Men could beat their wives and children at will and not be censored for it. In fact they were encouraged to do so. If a wife or child got out of line it reflected poorly on the man who couldn't control his property.

We are a little more enlightened now, but we still have a long way to go. In the United States we need better laws to protect victims of abuse, better rehabilitation for perpetrators, and stiffer prison sentences for the incorrigibles.

The worldwide picture is bleaker, especially in third world countries. In 1993 the United Nations met in Vienna at a Conference for Human Rights attended by 170 nations. They issued a document supporting the rights of women everywhere and called for an end to sexual harassment, exploitation and gender- based violence. They also applauded a declaration calling for the protection of children.

Abuse perpetuates abuse. You don't teach a child to be nonviolent by hitting her. Spanking a child isn't necessary. A firm **NO**, a time out, or using consequences is just as effective in punishing them.

When a child is physically abused all of the other systems are injured. The emotions, intellect, and spirit are also assaulted. In response to physical pain the emotions become distorted, all feelings are overwhelmed by betrayal, outrage, anger, and helplessness. The spirit, the joy of living, is crushed and can't provide enough internal help or support to protect the child. Then the mind learns that the only way to respond is to inflict pain. Our jails are full of living examples of the results of childhood abuse and neglect.

Violent criminals, rapists, battering parents and spouses, substance abusers, and other miserable people who inflict pain and horrors on others are frequently the products of childhood abuse. And the place where most abuse happens is right in their own homes.

Over 4,000 women are killed, murdered in the United States every year, beaten in their own homes by their husbands who vowed to love and honor them. And one woman is beaten every 14 minutes. Children are traumatized when they witness these beatings and are sometimes killed with their mothers.

Women are most likely to become victims of domestic violence if they watched it in their homes as children. Many women stay in such relationships out of fear of retaliation and death if they leave, and out of misguided love for their husbands, and denial in the form of hope that things will change. They were desensitized to family violence and abuse as children and may fatalistically believe that this is the way life is.

Without intervention, the only realistic change is that things will get worse until he kills her. There is a lot of help now for women who want to leave, every city has hidden women's shelters where a woman can go and take her children until she decides what to do next. Staying in a physically and emotionally abusive situation is dangerous and stupid. Children who witness abuse are damaged even if they are not being hit themselves. Women have a responsibility to protect their children. Sometimes leaving a bad situation is the only way to do it. If this describes your life, **get out and get help.**

The pain of physical abuse is tragic. Some people recover from abuse, some overcome, others continue to act out their pain by becoming perpetrators themselves. But all carry lifelong scars. Wounds must be healed to be able to enjoy good relationships, be creative, and find happiness.

SEXUAL ABUSE

We know that both boys and girls are sexually abused. Current statistical guesses say 75% of women and 50% of men were sexually abused or molested as children. Actual figures may be higher.

For children who were sexually misused, the onset of puberty and sexual development is a time of extreme stress and confusion. As teens drawn to explore relationships with other young people, they feel ashamed, fearful, and guilt-ridden, like they are "damaged goods".

They are confused because earlier sexual contact with an adult may have been loving and pleasurable, yet accompanied with a sense of wrong doing and threats not to tell. All these powerful feelings are difficult for a child or adolescent to handle.

There are generally two reactions to sexual abuse. One is to avoid sexual contact and to be frigidly fearful of any sexual encounter; the other is to become promiscuous, looking for love through sex.

It is hard for a child abuse victim to realize that it is possible for sexual contact to demonstrate affection, caring and pleasure when early in life he or she learned that it meant fear, pain, shame and exploitation.

The scars of sexual abuse leave one feeling unlovable as a person. The fabled nymphomaniac is not a woman who constantly seeks out sex for simple pleasure, but a pathetic woman who was eroticized too young, and is driven to use her body to try to find love, approval and acceptance. In sexual situations, she is torn by the confusion of love and guilt, pleasure and shame, the same feelings she experienced when her father, brother, uncle, step-father, mother, or other adult used her for their selfish desires.

Male children who are sexually abused growup overpowered with deep anger and rage that may manifest in rape and violence of other boys and of weaker men and of girls and women.

Not everyone can remember sexual abuse. Sometimes the memories are repressed as a protective defense for children who can't handle the pain and feelings. Disassociation is another creative defense mechanism for sexual abuse. Most cases of multiple personality disorder first began with early, severe, and ongoing sexual abuse.

Sometimes sexual abuse takes a lifetime to resolve. Alma was 73 years old when she came to see me as a client. She and her husband were still sexually active, and she said she had always had a strong sex drive. The problem was that she didn't like being touched, no foreplay, no caresses, no hugging, no holding. Her husband' wanted more touching. She froze when he touched her.

With age, sex becomes a more sensual experience involving all the senses, especially the skin which is our largest sex organ. Goal-oriented orgasm and genital-only sensation may be replaced by a long and loving process of making love and being close. As her husband's sexual expression changed to being more sensual, old disturbances were stirred up in Alma. Her uncle had molested her when she was eight years old, and since then she had felt ashamed, and guilty when anyone touched her in a sexual way. She interpreted the gentlest touch as "being pawed".

At 73, Alma had to begin learning to enjoy experiences she had associated for more than 60 years with violence and shame. It wasn't an easy task, though her willingness to heal old wounds and to deal with her feelings was the first step in helping her to grow past this long buried trauma.

If Alma did it you can too!

PHYSICAL DISABILITY

For some people life is, and will continue to be, a matter of living with severe physical limitations and pain. Life may require you to live with a physical handicap, a serious injury, a debilitating disease, or a genetic disorder. You may have been born with such a condition, and your suffering may have started early. Or you may have once been a perfect physical specimen, struck down later in life by accident or illness.

Whatever life has dealt, you must learn to accept it and live with it, as difficult and unfair as that may seem to be. It is the only way to achieve any measure of peace and happiness for you now. Sometimes in life things happen that are unchangeable. To someone with a severe disability, the person who worries over losing five pounds, or claims she "can't" stop smoking seems silly. She has no idea how difficult it is to be in a body that won't do simple things she takes for granted, like walk, talk, see, hear, or control its bowels and bladder.

People with severe physical limitations can become bitter and overwhelmed by hatred of their helpless body and the conditions that created it. They may become completely dependent on others and unable to take care of their personal needs. Their lives can be ruled by self-pity, resentment and misery.

Or they can choose to grow up and accept what they cannot change. I know that there is no easy way to accept being paralyzed or to be happy that you only have a year to live. Yet people with every imaginable kind of pain and loss have found a sense of inner peace by learning to transcend focusing on their limitations and to emphasize their strengths, and to discover all that they can be and do despite the limitations.

If you have a physical disability, you can choose to let that one fact about yourself dominate your every thought, feeling, and action, or you can choose to find fulfillment and meaning in living in spite of it. Your physical system may be damaged, but your emotions, intellect, and spirit don't have to be damaged too; they can become even stronger.

It's very hard for a person who was once strong and healthy to accept the loss of physical functioning. Blind or deaf people who were born with their disability report that it is easier for them because they have never known anything different. Those who were sighted or had hearing and then became blind or deaf have a much more difficult time adjusting.

Imagine that one day there is a car crash and suddenly you can't use part of your body. A tragedy like this can transform a life. Greg was 18 years old when I met first met him at a workshop I attended on sexuality. He was in a wheelchair, paralyzed from the waist down, bare-footed and hostile. He refused to participate in any discussion. He wouldn't even tell us his name.

Later, I found out that Greg had been the victim of a drunk driver crash two years earlier. His spinal cord was severed and he would never walk again. A very talented musician, he had played guitar with some big-name rock bands. In high school, Greg was a track star, and popular with classmates. He was a good student and planned to go to college to become a doctor.

Now he was a defeated, sullen, miserable young man, steeped in grief and self-pity. Yet the fact that he came to the workshop at all was a small positive sign.

Two years later I met Greg again. Now he was outgoing and friendly. He excitedly explained that he had become a trainer in sex education for the handicapped. He was promoting and planning a rock concert for a local charity. What a change!

Given enough time and some counseling, Greg was able

to transcend the obstacles imposed by his car crash. Despite his losses Greg was determined to make the most of his life. He turned his own misfortune into a positive effort to help others. Though not everyone makes such a remarkable adjustment everyone can learn as much as he or she is willing to learn about living a quality life, with a disability.

Any handicap forces attention to be focused on the body. Greg had to deal with his grief and anger before he could regain his old stamina and enthusiasm for doing new things in his life. You might say Greg's spirit pulled him through. After he dealt with his emotions, his intellectual ability returned and he was able to evaluate what he could realistically do with his life as it now was, and to make plans accordingly. The result was a reintegrated person, who used the best of his body, mind, and spirit to get on with the rest of his life.

CHAPTER THIRTEEN

TECHNIQUES FOR PHYSICAL GROWTH

How can you start developing the grown-up attitude about your body and learn to accept and love it as it is right now?

Try this: Stand in front of a mirror naked and look at your body. Look at its overall shape, its hair, wrinkles, flab, legs, teeth, warts, sags, blemishes, bulges, muscles, strengths and weaknesses, clumsiness and grace -- whatever is there. Accept what you see without judgment. Take an inventory of what you like and what you want to change. Make a commitment to yourself to do whatever you need to do. To take care of your physical self, you've first got to love it. Everything about it. Tell your different parts how much you appreciate the way they serve you. Praise your assets and acknowledge your shortcomings. Begin to accept your body as it really is.

Loving your body doesn't mean you can't change it. But it's easier and healthier to change it if you do so out of love. If you're looking over this body that you're not crazy about, and find yourself saying, "I'd love you more if you were 50 pounds less or had 15 pounds more or had red hair", then you can make plans to work on these changes realistically and systematically. If you decide that changes are needed, don't start by focusing on how bad things are now. First, love yourself for caring enough to take care of your body by changing it for the better.

TALKING BACK TO YOUR BODY--AFFIRMATIONS

The way you think about your body has a great effect on your feelings, mind and spirit as well as on your physical self. Every time you look in the mirror and grimace, or think a negative thought about yourself, you are programming your subconscious mind to create the message you give it. If your self-talk says, "I am so fat, no one will ever love me until I lose 50 pounds", then that is your reality. Your thoughts create and reinforce that situation, making it likely to come true.

Your thoughts have a powerful effect on your feelings and eventually on the body itself. So when you're surveying your body, stop those negative thoughts and messages with a surprise positive remark. Try saying, "Baldness is sexy", or "I look terrific, I know a lot of people who really go for big beautiful women."

These positive statements are called affirmations, and they can be used to help you like yourself as you are and to help you make changes you have decided will make you happier or healthier. Affirmations affirm or reinforce a fact about you. They reprogram your subconscious mind to gradually develop a change in attitude.

You can have better physical health, a more positive

self-image, and can accomplish the changes you want to make in your physical habits or appearance if you first understand that what you're doing doesn't just happen on the outside. It starts deep within. The subconscious mind supports you in getting what you want. If the inner mind is filled with negative programming, it stands in the way of your making progress, whether you are trying to accomplish something physical, intellectual, or emotional.

Consciously, for instance, you want to lose weight, but you deeply believe that you are fat and always will be. Your subconscious is working hard to keep you fat. To lose the weight, it's necessary to work, not only on the body through diet and exercise, but also on the subconscious mind through self-talk and changes in attitude.

When you change your beliefs, you can change your reality and your life. You can reprogram your subconscious by changing your thoughts or self-talk. The subconscious works like a computer -- garbage in, garbage out. So put in some new material. Start feeding it positive messages, and eventually your affirmations will become the reality of your subconscious -- which will then influence all your conscious thoughts and actions to do what's necessary to become the best you can.

Affirmations feed your mind positive statements about accepting or changing your body. Your affirmation is your prescription for change. You're the doctor, you're healing yourself. In formulating these statements, speak to yourself out of love and care, not from admonishment or shame, so that your mind will return that care to the body. Of course, then you have to take action to carry out this new reality, but it will be a lot easier to do the physical work if your thoughts are working with you, not against you.

To use affirmations effectively, choose a positive *specific* statement, short and to the point, tied to a date for meeting your goal. Make the statement realistic. "I will look like I'm 25 years old next year", isn't going to work if you're 42. Unrealistic affirmations guarantee failure. State the affirmation as a *fact*, not a hope. Here are some affirmations that will program your subconscious to work with you on accepting your body or reaching your physical goals:

"I now weigh 120 pounds. I feel great and look great."

"I hate cigarettes. I will never smoke them again."

"My body loves exercise. Regular swimming or running makes me feel so much better."

"I am a grown man who is five feet three inches tall. I am smart, successful, and sexy."

"By June 1, next year, I will be trim and weigh 120 pounds. I am energetic and will enjoy running five miles a day."

"My illness has made me wiser and opened new opportunities for learning and relationships and spiritual development in my life."

When you've determined the statement that you want to affirm in your subconscious mind, write it down. Write it or say it out loud, or do both, four times a day, 20 repetitions each time, every day for three weeks. That's how long it takes to reprogram your subconscious mind to help you change your beliefs and behavior.

As you say the affirmation, visualize the change. Close your eyes and vividly see the number *120* on the scale. Feel yourself slim and energetic. See yourself with clear lungs, calm, with lower blood pressure, walking and talking with others self-confidently, feeling pleasurably tired and relaxed after a workout.

You can support your affirmations by writing them out

and placing them in strategic places to remind yourself of your new reality -- on the bathroom mirror, the refrigerator door, the car dashboard, your desk, any other places where it will help to be reminded of how things are going to be from now on. Or make a tape recording in your own voice repeating your affirmation over and over, and listen to it as you fall asleep, jog, drive to work, etc.

Whenever the old negative thoughts pop into your mind, repeat the new affirmation, as many times as you need to make that old message fade. The more you bombard your subconscious mind with the new reality, the more thoroughly you will change your programming.

You can use affirmations to control physical habits, and to make other changes -- improve your self-esteem, control anger, find the love of your life, get a raise in pay, become more assertive, lose weight, or whatever would help you love and accept yourself more. Try it -- it really works!

CHANGING PHYSICAL HABITS

In order to change any harmful physical habit, you will have to call on your mental, emotional, and spiritual strengths. Following are the general steps to take. They involve using your mind to decide what you will do and follow through, using your spirit to find the will power to stick with your program, using your emotions to notice and appreciate changes in your attitudes about yourself and your life.

1. *Acknowledge the problem* to yourself. Tell the truth. Write it down.

2. *Make a commitment* to yourself to change. Practice affirmations. Write out your affirmations and say them often.

3. *Accept the fact that change will take discipline* and may not always be enjoyable. You are changing old, long-entrenched habits. This takes time and commitment.

4. *Set realistic short-term and long-term goals.* Write out goals for one-day, one-week, one-month, and one-year periods.

5. *Find sources of help*: stop-smoking clinics, Alcoholics Anonymous, weight-loss support groups, a diet partner, a rehabilitation program, other 12-Step programs.

6. *Define and imagine the good things* you will do. Focus on the change as a process of gaining something, not giving up something. Write out the positive changes you expect and have decided to achieve.

7. *Practice this new behavior* one day, one hour, at a time. When tempted to backslide, remind yourself of the new, healthier you that you are creating. Find just a little more strength and do the right thing, even if every part of your body and feelings is telling you to fail.

8. *If you do slip, forgive yourself,* and get back on track. A lapse does not mean that you have failed, nor is it an excuse to give up. It is simply a human mistake.

9. *Reward yourself for every accomplishment* -- every pound lost, every day without smoking. Reward yourself with something that's good for you, and with messages of pride and self-love.

10. When you reach your goal, *congratulate yourself on victory*. You have drawn on the best resources you have to make yourself a better, healthier person. You've learned that *you* -- not your habits and cravings -- *are in control.*

HEALING ABUSE AND SEXUAL PROBLEMS

If you are an abuse victim, or an abuser, or both, you must stop everything and make healing yourself the first priority of your life. You do not have to just react to your anger and to the frustrations of parenting by striking out at your child. You don't have to continue the cycle into another generation. You can't change what happened to you as a child, but you can learn better ways to live with it than simply to continue inflicting pain and hating yourself more for doing so.

The process of healing from physical abuse involves learning that you have worth as a human being. It also includes crying and giving voice to your pain, perhaps forgiving those who abused you. It's the act of the frustrated, helpless, overwhelmingly bitter victim to make someone else a victim too. But the most important step is learning to manage your anger.

One of the breakthroughs in psychotherapy is anger management. We have some very good counseling strategies to control anger now. The most successful one is called cognitive restructuring, which simply means analyzing the trigger events and learning to rethink the event over in a new way. After a while, with practice, a person can learn appropriate emotional responses, instead of inappropriate overreactions.

The interaction of mind, body, spirit, and emotions is the key to breaking the cycle of abuse. Through cognitive restructuring, you can learn to think about what happened, allowing yourself to feel more appropriate responses and to nurture yourself spiritually. Then you can change the physical behavior by learning to act in a more constructive, positive way.

If you were a victim of physical, sexual or emotional abuse as a child, it is imperative that you find help for any unresolved feelings about what happened to you. Self-help groups exist, like Parents Anonymous, for abusing parents, and

Parents United for sexually abused children and adults. Other help comes from seeking individual therapy to work out and resolve your old traumas. You must grieve for what happened to you and for the things that you didn't get, like love, validation and acceptance.

If you know or suspect that you were sexually abused as a child, you must deal now with how that experience affected you or it will continue to overshadow your sense of yourself as an adult. It's never too late to heal the healthy feelings that early abuse deprived you of. You're entitled to all that adult life has to offer, you don't have to remain an abused kid forever. You can unload this burden, with time, help, patience, and willingness.

If you're a sexual abuse victim, you have complex emotional and physical conflicts about your present sexuality. It's not necessary to go through the rest of your adult life filled with sexual guilt, self-consciousness, and inhibition. You can face these issues now, and put them behind you. If you are stuck on the thought that there's something wrong with some part or function of your body, put some effort into changing what you can and accepting the rest. There is no need or benefit in continuing to harass yourself.

You can use affirmations to help you accept your body and your sexuality as they are. Perhaps you can work out some of your feelings through honest talk and patience with your mate.

The time is now to forgive yourself for errors of the past and to forgive those who have damaged you. Read any of the numerous books on healthy sexuality. Decide for yourself what behavior you consider responsible and don't let yourself be talked into anything different. If you feel you don't know enough about sex or if you have specific problems with sexual functioning, look into some short-term sex therapy.

Of course, the experience won't disappear. You won't forget it, and the memory will still hurt. But you have a choice, now, to take away some of its power, to say, "Yes, that happened, and it was terrible, but I am something more than a victim. I am going to cry and grieve for my stolen innocence. I'm going to express my anger and then put this problem away. Then I'm going on with the rest of my life."

There arc many sources of help for putting sexual abuse behind you. Go to a therapist who is experienced with these issues, often short-term therapy may be all that is needed. You can join a group of other sexual abuse victims, a national network called Daughters United has groups for children, adults, and families in many cities. Rape crisis centers also offer programs. New Anonymous groups based on the A.A. model are springing up weekly such as Incest Survivors Anon, Sex and Love Addicts Anon, etc. Check to see what is available in your community.

Every adult has rights in sexual relationships. Here's a good guideline:

SEXUAL BILL OF RIGHTS

1. *That we will make love to each other as persons, not as objects.*

2. *That we will be considerate, sensitive, and aware of each other's sexual responses.*

3. *That we share equally in stimulating each other.*

4. *That we openly communicate our sexual preferences and needs to each other.*

5. *That we can enjoy spontaneity.*

6. *That we look and see, listen and hear, feel and touch, smell and taste together in a fully sensual sharing experience*

7. *That we each agree not to use our sexual interaction to exploit or manipulate the other.*

8. *That we both can risk vulnerability and reject pretensions.*

9. *That we are not performing for each other, but are joining together to express mutual trust, respect, esteem and satisfaction.*

10. *That we remain separate but equal human beings.*

TRANSCENDING DISABILITY

It's easy to get stuck if you have a disability, to refuse to grow past your sorrow and pain. You have suffered a big loss in one of life's gambles, so you're not anxious to risk anything else.

But does spending the rest of your life in the safety of self-pity make sense? Do you want to continue to be a victim or do you want to become a survivor and a liver of life? You already know how miserable you are and what you don't have. Why not take one more risk and see how much you can do with what you do have?

One transcendent way to make something positive, even joyful, out of your own misfortune is to use your firsthand knowledge of the problems of ill or handicapped people to make life easier for others. Join a group of other handicapped people.

Get Political! You are in an ideal position to provide public education about your particular illness or disability. Draw on your anger and turn its energy toward making good changes for others, rather than making yourself more bitter. Reach deep into your spirit and find how much you really have to give when you care. Use your intellect to understand and deliver information that nobody knows better than you.

Your body may be weakened, but as long as your mind is strong, there is no end to the ways you can get your message out in this information-hungry age. Discover computer-based methods of educating the disabled, lobby for your public schools and libraries to buy this equipment, or develop teaching programs to be used with it. You can make it possible for children who experience disability to avoid some of the obstacles that you had to face.

Educate yourself about the causes and cures for your disability. Organize events such as fairs to demonstrate the talents of the disabled, raise funds, and create publicity. Bring in disabled role models to inspire young people and the entire community. Lobby for changes in public policy, safety, job training, an end to discrimination.

You can notify the news media about people who achieve despite disabilities, about the facts versus the myths of an illness. You can write or talk to governmental bodies about the need for better access to public buildings, parking facilities, and public transportation.

Life may have left you a lesser person physically than others around you, but you can leave this world a better place for others who will suffer the same way you have.

If you've lived in anger and bitterness for some time, it may seem impossible to find the energy to transform your pain into a drive for a better world. But it doesn't take any more energy to do something constructive than to keep yourself bound by old fears and angers.

How do you find the energy, the will? By acceptance of what can't be changed, by support that comes from associating with others in the same situation, by educating yourself, by refusing to accept limitations that only exist in your imagination. Instead of focusing on "why not?" Ask yourself, *why not!*

PART FIVE

GROWING UP
INTELLECTUALLY

CHAPTER FOURTEEN

WHAT DOES IT MEAN TO BE INTELLECTUALLY GROWN UP?

"I think therefore I am. But what then am I? A thing that thinks? It is a thing which doubts, understands, affirms, denies, wills, refuses, which also imagines and feels."

Rene Descartes

Intelligence -- the ability to formulate thoughts, acquire knowledge, solve problems, and convey information to others -- sets human beings apart from all the other species that share this planet with us.

Your big human brain is both an asset and a liability. It's an asset because it lets you communicate more effectively with other members of your species. By using your intelligence, you can alter your own behavior by self observation and changing the way you interpret your actions, attitudes, and beliefs. You can also use your brain to understand and make changes in the spiritual, emotional, and physical aspects of yourself. Intelligence can help you grow up; you can change yourself by changing your thoughts, because indeed you are what you think.

This powerful brain is a liability because it is difficult to stop your thoughts. Our minds are very busy and chatty, always turned on when we are awake. Most of our thoughts are undirected nonsense. Growing up intellectually means learning how to channel and direct the energy of your thinking processes to serve your needs, and goals more effectively.

It is also a liability when you allow it to judge and evaluate the behavior of yourself and others. More often than not, we judge harshly rather than compassionately, creating negativity rather than growth.

Growing up intellectually, or learning, is not just something you do in school. As a youngster, you went to school, learned to read, memorized the multiplication tables, took tests, got promoted, and graduated. The purpose of education is, or should be, to teach people to think. But as part of the usual educational process in this society, you and your parents and teachers may have often lost sight of that goal and acted as if the purpose of school was to do well in school -- to learn the material, pass tests, get a good report card, get promoted, graduate, and get admitted to college.

Growing up intellectually means really appreciating what the brain can do, and using it for your benefit, not just to get through school. Even when you're not part of the formal educational system, you still need to be able to *think, learn, decide, and evaluate* before you act. Whatever your school history, whether you were a good student or a poor one, when you're grown up, every day presents you with the need to learn -- deciding whom to vote for, learning new skills to advance in your career, figuring out a budget or an itinerary for a vacation.

The reason to grow up intellectually is no longer to be the best in the class or to pass the course; it's to be able to become informed, think clearly, reflect, solve problems, continue to learn, and make decisions for the benefit of every aspect of your life. It's your grown-up responsibility to use your intelligence to do these things as well as you can.

In spite of the failings of the educational system, you did acquire along the way some learning and thinking skills that you can apply. And you add new intellectual skills all your life. Along with learning your lessons, you may also have learned some things that have stayed as part of your self-concept ever since. Did your teachers and parents give you an intellectual label, "not college material"..."a dummy"..."book smart but no practical sense"... "a slow learner"? If so, you may have learned that lesson so well that you still believe it. These labels form obstacles to your growing up intellectually. If you believe you can't learn, or that you learn in only a certain way, then you'll limit your learning as an adult.

Some children have real learning problems that haunt them throughout life. Many students finish high school without ever really learning to read. Others, who learn quickly by doing things with their hands, struggle with information on the printed page. Did you have to drop out of school to support your family? What have you done to make up for that gap in your education? Do you believe that, after you've finished high school or college, you don't need to study any more? As an adult, do you think you're too old to learn? Do you watch too much TV, and never read? Are you afraid to go back to school?

The time has arrived to throw away all those misconceptions about your intellectual capacities and try something new. Your brain is trainable and strong, just as your spirit and your body and your emotional self are. There's no need to go through the rest of your life with a label someone gave you in first grade or junior high. Learning takes place all your life, whether you realize it or not. You can learn to learn better by becoming aware of how you perceive and take in information and what you do with it. When you're grown up, you can learn what really interests you; many adults who disliked school as kids have a wonderful time returning to the classroom in later years because they are motivated by real interest and desire to learn.

You're grown up now and the secret is out. Teachers and parents didn't know it all. But you do. You know yourself; you know what you're capable of, what you're curious about. You have inner wisdom that you may not yet have put to use. There is no end to the opportunities you have to learn and develop intellectually, all your life.

INFORMATION, KNOWLEDGE, UNDERSTANDING, AND WISDOM

Real learning eventually leads to wisdom, the kind of knowing that adds to the value and meaning of your life. But before we acquire wisdom, we must start learning by gathering information. The information we gather must go through several steps, involving different parts of our intelligence, before it becomes wisdom.

You are constantly acquiring information as you read, go to school, memorize facts, listen to the radio, watch television, and talk with people. With that information as a starting point, you then apply your mind to solve problems, make decisions, form judgments, and add to your understanding. This process is so automatic that you do it without conscious effort.

Information is what you acquire as you learn specific facts and skills, like operating a computer, auto mechanics, bookkeeping, the state capitals, a foreign language, the names of your new neighbors. You have to learn some of these skills in order to perform the job you want to get or to pass an exam in school or to drive to work. When you grasp the principles behind the facts, you have knowledge -- you know the way an automobile or computer operates and why a breakdown in one part will affect the working of another part. Knowledge is the ability to grasp the underlying structure and significance of the facts.

The other aspects of learning involve more complex forms of intelligence like thinking, memory, intuition, and decision-making. Understanding means grasping the meaning of the way things are related, being able to recall, reflect, analyze, synthesize, and evaluate the facts and information you have learned. Wisdom is the ability to call on and apply your knowledge and understanding in a similar situation. Without understanding and wisdom, learning is rather useless. It may help you pass a test, but it doesn't help you live better.

The lifelong learning process starts with acquiring facts and information from infancy on. As children, we begin putting facts together and accumulating knowledge. As our formal education is completed, and throughout our lives, we add to that store of knowledge and develop increasing amounts of understanding and wisdom.

Consider the child who is fascinated by a hot stove. Her mother tells her a fact --"Don't touch the stove because it is hot and will burn you. "The child hears her mother, but has no knowledge or understanding of the concepts "hot" or "burn," so the warning doesn't make much of an impression.

When the mother turns her back, the child, still curious, touches the hot burner. Then she acquires for herself the knowledge of what "hot" is about. She screams as she understands that "burn" is connected with pain. In the future, the child demonstrates wisdom because she never touches a hot stove again, and she tells her little brother not to do it. Of course, he will have to learn for himself just as she did.

We get wisdom by making mistakes. It is never a mistake to make a mistake. We learn, not by translating our mistakes into bundles of guilt, self-reproach, and self-hate, but by using information and mistakes to create knowledge, understanding, and new and better ways to be.

Wisdom also involves developing a positive attitude toward learning and intellectual development. It means being receptive to the evidence that experience presents, to the information that others convey, and to hunches and guesses.

When you are open to learning, you have so many more options to explore and a much better understanding of how each fact can or cannot solve your problems and answer your questions. Sometimes we are "slow learners" and continue to repeat the same errors over and over until we finally, painfully learn the lessons.

LEARNING

Learning is a fundamental process in which behavior changes over time as information is gathered and assimilated into knowledge. You can learn from books and lectures, but unless you apply your knowledge to real life, that learning may never become understanding. Learning from experience, on the other hand, has an effect, either direct or indirect, on future behavior.

You learn in different ways, not just through the brain. Your body learns to depend on substances or to get hungry at certain times of day; your emotions learn what to fear; your spirit learns what to believe in. All of your learning is supervised intellectually by the brain. Your responsibility as an adult is to pay attention to the information you gather, to examine it and learn from it, turning it into knowledge, understanding, and wisdom.

One simple way we learn is by conditioning; Pavlov's famous dog salivated at the sound of a bell that announced its dinner was soon to follow. Human beings also learn by conditioning, and we call it learning by trial and error.

HABITS

We can condition ourselves into habits -- responses that become automatic through repeated trials. Habits do not require thinking either for their formation or in carrying them out; in fact sometimes thinking interjects new information and interferes with their smooth performance. Habits are learned easily when they are associated with pleasant or rewarding feelings, like having a cup of coffee after a meal, or smoking a cigarette. Habits can be extinguished or unlearned when they are associated with punishment or withdrawal of pleasant stimuli.

Eliminating bad habits is the most difficult in changing any behavior. It takes will power, commitment, determination and hard work to change.

DISCOVERY

The best way to learn is through discovery. Discovery is an attitude of excitement about what you've learned -- results from a genuine quest for knowledge and a real desire to grasp the underlying significance of and connections among facts. Discovery doesn't mean just learning facts or fundamental ideas; it is the magic thing that happens when you really want to know and when learning becomes personal.

Educators and psychologists have known for a long time that what we learn best are things connected to personal experience.

We learn certain things best by doing. Creative teachers now teach traditional subjects like math by methods that permit students to find out the real-world answers through experience, then to discover the more intellectual generalization that underlies a particular mathematical operation.

For instance, a high school science teacher had his class build boats out of cardboard and waterproof glue. When the students put their boats in a pool, the boats sank, some sooner than others. The students, having vividly seen the results of their actions, became curious and ready to discover basic principles about water displacement, boat construction, and related topics. They had fun, and they will remember this lesson much better than a lecture or textbook chapter.

This method of learning is a little more time-consuming in the beginning, but it lasts so much longer. The student learns to recognize the similarities among ideas (knowledge), participates in group problem-solving, creates excitement about learning, and improves self-confidence about his or her abilities.

Discovery is also important for learning outside of school. You can be told it is dangerous to drive too fast but you don't really learn how dangerous it is until the day you miss a curve and discover the terrible fear of losing control of the car and facing death. In individual and group therapy, when a person discovers the underlying reason for and the effects of self-defeating behavior, real change can take place.

THINKING

Thinking involves the formation and retention of meaning in what you have learned and experienced; it is a crucial part of the process that changes knowledge into understanding. In your thoughts you develop a set of images, symbols, and concepts that become inner representations of the things, events, and relationships in your life. By adding new information you create a new level of understanding. You grasp the meaning of how facts relate together and then you can use information and knowledge in more expansive ways.

Though we all have thoughts, not everyone thinks. The thoughts that run through your head can be pretty meaningless -- fleeting fragments of a past conversation, a line from a song, a fact seemingly unrelated to what's going on at present, a partly formulated plan for a weekend outing, or other irrelevant debris. To think well, you must learn to harness your thinking ability so you can focus it on a specific task or problem.

Thinking means using your intelligence to create meaning out of what you experience and know. Fruitful thinking employs reasoning and analysis to deduce solutions to problems and to transform knowledge into understanding. For instance, you may know how the internal combustion engine works and be able to describe it. But if you work as an auto mechanic, you have to be able to sort through that knowledge and find the right part or parts of it to repair the malfunction of the car you're working on. Then you need to be able to generalize your knowledge to another situation. If you learned by practicing on a Chevrolet, you must understand how to apply your knowledge to a Ford.

Reasoning is a form of thinking that uses a combination of symbols and language to reach a conclusion. When you think about how to solve a problem, your brain combines existing knowledge, symbols, and language in a new way to generate a new image, concept, or idea. If you want to change a behavior, you can help yourself do so by thinking of all the reasons to quit a bad habit or to begin a good one. Writing down the reasons helps to reinforce your resolve by working on both your conscious and subconscious minds.

Use your thinking to help you make the changes that will add a positive quality to your life. Nothing new or different will happen in your life unless you first think about it, and have an idea or concept of something new. For example, if you want to move to Hawaii, you cannot move unless you first think about moving. Then you must formulate plans to follow through on the idea and carry out your move.

The process of thinking is also called *self-talk*, which we explored earlier. Generally we can think faster than we can talk, but thinking is a verbal process. To convert knowledge into understanding, we use words; thinking is communicating with yourself. That's why talking out loud, taking notes, or making lists or diagrams often helps you think.

ANALYTICAL AND INTUITIVE THINKING

Analytical thinking is logical and systematic. When we analyze we go step by step through the available information like a scientist, using deductive or inductive logic to prove or disprove a theory or hypothesis. Most schools ask students to learn various subject matters analytically. Computer development is based on this logical, step by step, quality of human thinking.

To think well, you must learn to harness your thinking ability so you can focus it on a specific task or problem. Setting goals, using time-frames, making plans all help to structure your thoughts. This uses your left brain functions and is tied to analytical thinking.

Learning through discovery, on the other hand, taps into *intuitive thinking,* and is more closely related to the right side of your brain.

Intuitive thinking is the ability to apprehend or *know* immediately a solution, structure, significance, or meaning of a problem or situation without using analysis. Intuition sees the whole picture at once, not just pieces one at a time. Sometimes, if there's a gap in the knowledge base on which you are trying to figure something out analytically, your intuition will fill in the missing piece. At the same time, intuition isn't concerned with accuracy, so you often must validate its message by analysis. Sometimes an idea will just seem to pop into your mind. That's intuition.

It is common knowledge that Albert Einstein got the theory of relativity, the scientific breakthrough that led to the development of nuclear energy, in a flash of intuitive thinking. Of course, Einstein wouldn't have been able to achieve this insight without a solid basis of knowledge of physics. His conscious knowledge paved the way for his intuition to supply the theory that tied certain facts together; then he and other scientists were able to test the premises and conclusions of his theory and verify it's validity. Creative and novel solutions and ideas often result when knowledge and analysis meet intuition.

Intuitive and analytical thinking complement and need each other. Both types of thinking are necessary to develop understanding and wisdom. Intuition makes it possible to find shortcuts and leap ahead to creative solutions to issues and problems. Analysis is needed to create the basis of knowledge and information in which intuition can blossom, and to check out the correctness or feasibility of the intuitive solutions.

MIND AND BRAIN

As highly developed and remarkable as the human brain is, intelligence involves something more. The mind is also a part of the intellect; it's a part that begins in the brain but is much more than the brain. It is the connection between logical understanding and the subconscious and superconscious. While we don't have any concrete proof of this, it is widely accepted in modern psychological theory. Just as we don't have a logical explanation for the way intuition works, we can't see, touch, or hear the mind, yet we know it exists and what it does.

The mind is where we get meaning from what we learn. The brain is the physical component where learning and thinking take place, while the mind is the active, dynamic processor of the truths that we know in different ways. The mind puts together what we know physically, emotionally, intellectually, and spiritually. It brings experience together with the spiritual wisdom of the superconscious.

The brain itself is a complex organ. Most forms of thinking take place in the cerebral cortex. Other parts of the brain serve specific functions like speech, hearing, motor skills, balance, pain, and impulse control.

In recent years much research has been done to identify more specifically the functions of the two hemispheres of the brain. The left side of the brain relates to concrete forms of thinking. It is verbal, linear, analytical, rational, mechanical, calculating, practical, and predictable. It takes its information from sensory experiences, and focuses on limits. This is the part of the brain that most of us learned to use in school, the part that memorizes, comprehends, learns how to do algebra or read a map or spell big words. The left side of the brain also translates what we know and understand into symbols that communicate messages to others -- words or numbers or musical notes.

We use the right side of the brain to visualize, grasp the bigger picture, imagine the possible, dream up new ways, fantasize, create, gain insights, and intuitively confirm our choices. The left brain bases its information on responses of the senses; the right brain on creativity and intuition. The right side of the brain carries out the more symbolic, artistic, creative, relational, and intuitive parts of our thinking, knowing, and imagining. It's more closely related to the spirit and the emotions than to the body or to straight verbal learning.

The right side of the brain is the home of powers and insights that we call *psychic* because the left side can't explain them. Your right brain *knows* when something is right or wrong, even when your left brain can't explain why. The right brain has a line on universal knowledge -- the things we know just because we're alive, the things we don't know we know, yet are available to us when we need it.

The right brain is the part we use to integrate our left-brain, physical, spiritual, and emotional knowledge. It is the part of the brain that makes it possible to turn understanding into wisdom.

Psychologists measure left-brain intelligence with I.Q.(intelligence quotient) tests, and they examine the right brain through tests like Rorschach ink-blots, the Thematic Apperception Test or other projective tests. In these tests, the individual's subconscious projects attitudes, present concerns, or past experiences.

INTELLIGENCE

We all differ in our intelligence -- the ability to learn and solve problems. About fifty years ago psychologists started to measure intelligence in children. I.Q. Tests compare one person's mental ability to that of others of the same age throughout the population. They measure primarily left-brain functions like verbal and mathematical skills.

I.Q. tests are controversial because they fail to measure right-brain activity or to allow for cultural differences among children from different backgrounds; for instance, children from poor or minority families may have fewer opportunities to learn in their preschool years. They may never have had a coloring book or seen pictures in a magazine. Children from abusive and dysfunctional families have similar problems. Such deprivation doesn't mean a child can't learn or isn't intelligent. Low I.Q. Scores may just mean the child hasn't learned. Yet instead of concentrating on helping deprived children overcome their late start in learning, I.Q. scores and other forms of evaluation are often used to classify children by ability and to label them as learning disabled.

Children who are labeled early as having low I.Q.'s or learning disabilities may never reach their full potential. They are in danger of being victims of a self-fulfilling prophecy. If everyone says you're stupid or slow, then you believe it's true and act as if this is true.

One of my favorite true stories is about the new teacher whose classroom contained all the difficult and low-achieving fourth-graders in the school. She was told that they were the brightest and most creative children in the school. The teacher treated them as if this were true, and they all excelled by the end of the semester. They responded to her expectations and began to believe in themselves, fulfilling a different prophecy.

Raw intelligence is generally attributed to heredity. But environment plays an important role too. Environmental factors are often played down, however, because they are harder to measure scientifically. There are also different kinds of intelligence. Most school tests are geared in favor of students who are highly verbal, memorize easily, and can report back what the teacher has taught.

Perhaps you learned better by hearing than by reading; or you have mechanical skills and your hands can learn to do things that verbal people never master. There is also no correlation between talent in art, music, drama, or other creative fields and measurable intelligence.

While some people demonstrate their intelligence by obtaining a formal education, others are streetwise. This kind of intelligence includes a natural understanding of what motivates people's behavior. Streetwise people know how to manipulate other people and systems to get what they want; those with a little bit of larceny often become good salesmen or con artists.

Common sense is another form of intelligence that you can't learn from books. It's a wonderful gift to be able to see through a situation to what is really important, without letting analysis or textbook learning get in the way.

Perhaps you're creative with crafts or storytelling or music or imaginative play activities for kids. Creative people are interested in complexity and novelty. They are intrigued by situations that require some resolution, instead of cut and dried solutions. In some research, highly intelligent subjects were found to be low in creativity. In general, highly creative people use their intuition as well as their intelligence; they use both sides of their brains effectively.

We are not all created equal. Some of us are born with a tendency to be very smart, and others are less intellectual. Some of us use our intuition in problem-solving, communicating with others, and getting information about people and the world. Others ignore or distrust intuition and militantly rely on analysis, concrete facts, visible evidence, and a rational scientific approach before they accept any truth.

To be grown up intellectually means recognizing your abilities, strengths, and talents and using these resources to reach your full potential. It means using your thoughts to enrich your life, not to beat yourself up. Intellectual grownups accept their shortcomings graciously, and with kindness for themselves, not in a self-condemning or self-critical way.

You   are what you think. If you keep your thoughts positive you will   reap   the   harvest of positive results. If you think negatively you will   always fall   short, and   will be disappointed with yourself. Figure out who you are and what you want, then march to the beat of your own drummer.

CHAPTER FIFTEEN

ISSUES OF INTELLECTUAL GROWTH

What you think about yourself is ultimately what you become. Your thoughts are so powerfully connected with your belief system that you create your own reality by the way that you think. Your emotions then respond to your thoughts. The process becomes automatic after a while.

Because it all happens so subtly it is very difficult to determine which comes first, as with the chicken and the egg. Behavior fits in here too. It is the outward manifestation of your thoughts and feelings. If you think you are stupid (because someone once told you that you were) you probably still believe that you are stupid (thought), feel bad, depressed, defeated, maybe angry (emotions), and you will quit trying to do difficult or different things because you will be afraid to reinforce your stupidity (behavior).

Now you are set up and when you make a mistake you are your own worst enemy. As soon as you notice the mistake, you call yourself stupid, and reinforce the entire cycle.

With such a setup, you could go through life avoiding interesting people and not taking risks because of your fear and shame, worrying that the whole world will find out how stupid you really are. When all the time it was a not true, you were not stupid only a victim of someone's abuse or personal projection.

What is probably true is that you are not stupid at all. Someone told you that you were stupid and you believed it. This is perfectly natural to do, especially if you were a little kid, and if you heard the message over and over. The person who told you this was really talking about himself, not you. He was projecting his feelings of being stupid onto you. This is one way that our thoughts get you into trouble by running old mental tapes in your head.

What a shame to live life, your life, according to someone else's misbelief about himself. Recording this kind of harmful and inaccurate information is one of the problems that comes with having a big human brain.

There are *benefits* and *problems* associated with our ability to think, plan, analyze, ponder, worry, and use other brain functions. One benefit is that we have survived and developed far beyond other predatory carnivorous species. For the individual, the advantages of a developed brain includes the ability to acquire and apply huge amounts of knowledge to make life more comfortable and to communicate both verbally and nonverbally with other members of our species.

The negative side is that we have developed bad habits

in connection with our big brains, like worry, ruminating, obsessing, and often reaching the wrong conclusions, especially when we ignore spiritual, physical, or emotional knowledge. As a species, this advanced brain has created technology beyond our ability to control primitive emotions so that we live in constant fear that some angry or fearful leader will push a button and blow all of us to kingdom come.

One of the most important tasks that we currently face, as a species and as individuals trying to grow up, is to balance our intellects and our emotions so we can use our rational capacities to make decisions, solve problems, and resolve conflicts. To do this effectively we must use both sides of our brains. We need to gather facts and information, and to apply intuition and creativity, in order to explore choices and options that enable us to reach the best, not necessarily the most obvious, solutions.

BALANCING THOUGHTS AND EMOTION

It is true that we are not all alike or equally endowed with brilliance. Someone may be very bright but also be emotionally immature or morally bankrupt or in poor physical shape.

Another person who has a very low I.Q. or is even retarded in terms of intelligence may be kind, thoughtful, sincere, and compassionate. This person may have more peace of mind than a renowned political leader, minister, concert pianist, or college professor, because the intelligence is in balance with the other aspects of the self.

When imbalance continues for a long time you develop *dis-ease*, which may manifest in your body, mind, emotions, and within your spirit. Until balance is restored you become more dysfunctional -- unable to function as a competent adult -- by being emotionally disturbed and agitated, mentally confused with faulty thinking, physically sick, and spiritually disconnected.

When this goes on for years, as it frequently does for those who experienced childhood abuse, neglect, and trauma, it may take a lifetime to recover. Recovery requires dealing with the issues that created the imbalance in the first place, and the difficulty of doing so depends on the severity and duration of the abuse.

You weren't born to be out of harmony within yourself. If you are living in a state of dis-ease, get help. The twelve-step programs offer almost-free support groups for many problems, or you can go to a therapist who has experience working in the area of your need.

Once you heal your dysfunctional emotions, you can begin to repair your confused thinking, heal your headaches or low back pain or other physical problems, and reconnect with your spirit. When balance is restored, or established for the first time, you will begin to experience the lightness of heart, happiness, joy, and feelings of contentment that you deserve.

SELF-CONCEPT

The way you treat yourself is deeply rooted in the way you think about yourself. These ideas about who you are, what you can do, and what you are worth began very early in your development and, unless changed, they stay with you throughout your life. They depend on how you were treated and what you were told about yourself when you were an infant, a toddler, a child, and an adolescent.

The basis of your self-concept, what you believe are the fundamental truths about yourself, was formed by the way your parents responded to you. You integrated that knowledge and formed an image of yourself. If you were neglected as an infant you will have trust issues as an adult, if you were shamed you will be secretive and easily embarrassed or shamed as an adult, if you were raised with rigid values and rules you will have guilt problems as an adult. These beliefs and behaviors learned in childhood can become irrational responses in adulthood and interfere with your ability to have open, loving, secure relationships.

As you continued to grow, your innate personality traits were overlaid with the effects of your environment to form the structure and processes that you have used to grow, learn, change, and restructure your beliefs, values, and attitudes about yourself, others, and events throughout your life.

If your parents reflected back to you an image of a lovable, valuable being who was worth all of the trouble and patience needed to raise a child, then you probably have little trouble believing in your own worth and value. If, on the other hand, you were neglected, overprotected, or given inconsistent or double messages about your worth, you may have grown up with confusion and doubts, feeling untrusting, shamed, guilty, and worthless, and even self-hate.

Most people move through life seeking and setting up confirmation of their basic self-concepts. Such confirmations have deepened and reinforced original patterns of primitive, prelogical, and immature thinking. It's important for you to remember as a grownup that the self-concept that your parents helped to create grew out of their problems and insecurities -- their failure to be grown up -- but now these dysfunctions have become yours in the distorted self-image that our parents unknowingly passed on.

Even if a cycle of abuse or fear of exposure and shame have been perpetuated and passed on through many generations in your family, you can use your intellect to stop this destructive process and to change the messages. You can reparent yourself with love and bring up your children to accept and love themselves.

If a child is given the messages and love necessary to develop a positive self-concept, then growing up to be responsible and loving will be part of the natural life process. But the child whose self-concept was damaged will have to overcome problems as life unfolds.

Some of the consequences of a faulty self-concept are distorted and erroneous beliefs regarding basic aspects of identity such as lovableness, self-worth, competence, incongruence between self-impressions and feedback from others, and a rigid and defensive attitude toward oneself. This person is his own worst enemy, because he is constantly judgmental and self-critical. Growing up is difficult for such people because they are locked into pre-verbal and prelogical infantile thinking patterns and emotions. (However, as we will see, by using your intelligence, you can reprogram this early thinking.)

Probably most of the people on earth today have suffered some damage to their self-concept. Very few of us were fortunate enough to have completely secure and enlightened parents who were emotionally available to us. It is only within the past 15 years that this culture has developed parenting classes and considered children assets instead of chattel or property, only good for working on the family farm or for taking care of their parents in old age.

Other factors besides interaction with parents contribute to the formation of your self-concept. One is the influence of the family structure. For instance, in a family with lots of children, an individual's needs are almost impossible to meet.

Secondly, if a large extended family lives nearby, different members may reflect information to the child that either reinforces or contrasts with parental messages. Sometimes a child raised by dysfunctional parents will be able to find loving support from a grandparent or an aunt or uncle or even neighbors, teachers, and family friends.

Finally, life events contribute to the self-identification process. These include: illnesses; bereavements for the death, loss, or abandonment of a parent, sibling, friend, grandparent, or significant other; moving frequently, as children in military families do; interrupted relationships with parents; adoption; and abuse or neglect of any kind.

DEFENSES

To compensate for a poor self-concept, most people construct defenses during childhood. They continue to use these defenses throughout adulthood to hide and protect the fragile, frightened child living inside a grown-up body. When children or adults feel fundamentally worthless, shameful, or unlovable, they will develop defenses to cover up these bad feelings from themselves and from others.

Some of these defenses are:

◆ *Denial:* This is a way to pretend that nothing is wrong and nothing bad has ever happened. A lifelong pattern of denial is seen when an adult refuses to take responsibility for hurting others or letting them down.

◆ *Minimization:* This is a way to play down the significance of painful experiences from the past, or to blame oneself for what happened. The adult who recalls, "Sure, I got spanked sometimes, but I always deserved it", may be minimizing a childhood filled with repeated beatings.

◆ *Repression* : This is a method of burying an old or recent trauma deep inside so one doesn't remember the painful events. This adult hopes that repressing the pain will make it disappear, but usually the pain and anger are expressed in some other inappropriate way.

◆   ***Rationalization***: This is a way to make excuses for the perpetrator of abuse or dysfunction. Rationalizing tries to find a comfortable answer for an uncomfortable situation. This again denies the personal pain involved but doesn't erase it.

◆   ***Projection***: This defense is really an offense. It puts the feelings and blame on others or ascribes attributes to others that are really true of oneself. Saying, "I hate the way John always criticizes and finds fault with everyone", may say more about the speaker than about John. People often project when they don't want to acknowledge some fault in themselves.

◆   ***Identification***: We sometimes identify with the person who has inflicted some pain upon us. It is common in cases of abuse to identify with the perpetrator or to make excuses for the abuser. The person with this defense often later becomes an abuser.

Defenses are ways that you use to protect yourself. They may be necessary to your survival when you are vulnerable, as in childhood. But for adults, they are psychological devices that render you emotionally distanced from the pain, trauma, and reality of your life experiences. They delay your healing.

Defenses don't serve you well as a maturing adult because they interfere with your ability to be close or intimate with another or honest with all those around you. If you are numb and out of touch with what you are feeling, you cannot open yourself to true compassion, intimacy, and love. *When you defend against the pain you also defend against the love, and you live your life as an emotional cripple.*

THINKING CLEARLY

A poor self-concept often interferes with clear thinking because we start with a distorted view of ourselves, other people, and events. The human mind can twist the meanings of what it knows or remembers or experiences in harmful ways.

Thinking isn't always clear and perfect. Sometimes it's incomplete, rationalizing, prejudiced, defensive, or inaccurate. If you allow yourself to hear all your thoughts about a subject, you can gather the information you need to make a good decision or understand an event. But if you hide from some of your thoughts, or don't recognize that you don't have all the facts, your thinking may become faulty.

This irrational self-talk can lead to deviant behavior or unreasonable responses. You can tell yourself things that aren't true and don't make sense, or leave out important considerations. If your thinking is confused and cloudy, you may need to talk to someone who can help you sort things out.

COMMUNICATION SKILLS

In this sophisticated age of high-technology methods of communications -- computers, facsimile machines, modems, car telephones, and all the rest -- we are still poor communicators in our personal relationships and in one-to-one situations. Yet communication with other human beings is the most important ongoing event of our lives. We can, however, learn simple communication techniques like paraphrasing, clarifying, behavior description, feeling description, using "I" statements, feedback, active listening, and being assertive.

Most of us learned how to talk with other people by picking up the way our parents or peers conversed with family and friends. Speaking their language got approval responses from those around you, so that manner of speaking became second nature. Now you probably fall into that same habitual style of talking when you're in conversation with others at home, at work, or at a social occasion.

But your conversational or communication style may not work in every situation. Sam was a good storyteller and people liked to hear him talk. He enjoyed the attention he got when he talked, and over the years he had developed a habit of interrupting people while they were talking, it was an unconscious habit, something he did without thinking. After about five years of marriage, Sam's wife, Maureen, was frustrated because she felt that he never really listened to anything she said; she got the feeling he was just waiting for her to finish so he could speak. Both were aware that they did not feel as close to each other as they had in the early days of their relationship.

The reward for Sam's habitual conversational style had diminished, especially with Maureen, and it no longer served the purpose of communication or approval. It was time to get rid of his old pattern and learn skills for better, more attentive communication.

Since talking to him wasn't effective, Maureen wrote Sam a letter explaining that they needed to learn better ways to communicate or their marriage might be in real trouble. This unusual approach got his attention and reminded Sam that his marriage was more important than his need for approval for his verbal skills. For the first time in years, he listened carefully to what Maureen said.

Sam learned that his habit of interrupting was irritating and a sign of poor listening. He thought he was moving the conversation along by breaking in to tell of an experience he was reminded of. But butting in is a self-occupied, inconsiderate habit. The interruptions left Maureen feeling discounted because she never got a chance to finish her story or make her point.

Sam's eagerness to respond caused him to miss half of what the other person was saying.

Sam began to learn to listen actively; to focus on the other person's words, then wait a moment to make sure he had heard and understood them. When he began to practice this, he didn't forget what he wanted to say or miss opportunities to contribute; in fact, sometimes he found he was going to respond inappropriately because he had only picked up on part of the speaker's message.

Grownups can benefit from reviewing their own communication style, examining how it affects their relationships with others, and learning better methods of speaking and listening.

MEMORY

Another tool that the brain uses for learning and thinking is memory. Memory links what we have already learned with the present. It is the storage chamber of experiences from the past. Physically, learning is a biochemical process in which information is etched into cells in our brains. The more intense the material stored, the stronger the impression and the easier it is to recall at a later time.

Memory has both left-brain and right-brain elements. It stores mental facts, especially those we deliberately commit to memory. It also recalls the emotional and physical feeling or meaning of a significant experience -- the fears and excitement, the smell and sounds, the sense of connection with the flow of life. These right-brain aspects of memory account for phobias, deeply felt emotions, or nostalgic experiences of sadness, regret, and longing for the past. For example, a child bitten by a dog will carry *fear-of-dog* messages in his or her memory for many years. The memory of the earlier experience will trigger fear every time a dog barks, snarls, or gets too close, although the person can learn to decrease the severity of the emotional response.

Memory is the inner representation of the past. It is what we build on when we learn new things. You remember much more than you think you do. Over time, specific details fade from the conscious mind, but many facts can be recalled under hypnotic regression, which indicates that we have an unlimited capacity to recall events thought to be forgotten.

As you get older your long-term memory actually improves, you recall events in the distant past in great detail, with varying degrees of accuracy. At the same time, short-term memory --"Did I pay the light bill?" or " Where are my keys?" -- declines because of the reduced chemical impression made on the brain for registering an event, especially one that seems unimportant at the time.

There is evidence that we remember important things better than unimportant ones. We recall things that are pleasant to remember better than unpleasant things. Threatening and unpleasant events are repressed and buried in the subconscious. And meaningless or irrelevant material is barely remembered.

The emotional aspect of memory serves the function of protecting us from bad experiences and reminding us of good ones. Children or young people who have shocking, traumatic experiences sometimes forget them by burying them so deeply in the memory that they can only be recalled consciously by another shock or by intensive therapy. Yet the unconscious memory still affects our emotional responses to certain events or people. You may feel uncomfortable around some type of environment or person or thing, but you just can't remember why.

Laura told me this story. One day when she was 13 her uncle was visiting from out of town. Both her parents were at work, and her mother telephoned and asked Laura to entertain her uncle until they got home. She agreed, but felt a little uncomfortable though she couldn't figure out why. As she anticipated her uncle's arrival, her discomfort grew into panic.

Thinking that it was an irrational fear, Laura tried to talk herself out of it. Suddenly, in a vivid flash, she remembered that when she was 3 years old, this uncle had molested her sexually. She had forgotten it happened but now she remembered the incident in great detail. When she called her mother to tell her what she had remembered, her mother suggested that she stay at a friend's home until later that evening. In this instance, the fear and shock of having to be alone with this man released Laura's old forgotten memory to her conscious mind in order to help her escape another possible molestation.

Some memories are so traumatic that they keep resurfacing uninvited and interfering with normal life. War veterans who have seen battle are often so traumatized with shock to all their senses that painful memories recur to be relived again and again until the feelings of rage, grief and fear are dealt with and resolved.

Those who experience frightening flashbacks of post-traumatic stress know it is a living hell. When your defenses are down, while you are relaxed or asleep, your subconscious mind brings the dreaded images and sounds and feelings to conscious awareness through dreams or sudden images. This kind of memory presents you with another opportunity to deal with the emotional pain of the past. You may have to go through that hell again to exorcise all of it, but if you do it right, with a support group or a therapist, you can heal those memories.

Memory is important because it gives us access to what we already know. The information is stored and accessible to us when we need it. Without this storage system we would have to relearn from the beginning every time we needed information. In every aspect of growing up, we learn from our mistakes, from our problems, from our pain and suffering. If we couldn't remember we would continue to make the same mistakes over and over, like rats running in a maze. Memory is one of the tools that the intellect uses to help us grow up and achieve wisdom.

IMPROVING LEARNING SKILLS: FACING LEARNING DISABILITIES

Problems with learning can be physiological like visual or auditory dysfunctions, or being crippled and unable to use limbs for writing. These problems are not necessarily related to low intellectual capacity, as the wonderful book and film *My Left Foot* demonstrated in conveying the life of Irish author and artist Christy Brown, who was afflicted with cerebral palsy all his life.

Some learning problems stem from emotional problems. It is impossible for a child to concentrate on school work if she is being sexually violated on a daily basis by her father, or if either parent is actively abusing drugs or alcohol. Occasionally a child from a dysfunctional family will become a super-achiever at school, but be an emotional mess inside. Eventually, such performance will take its toll when emotional issues surface, as they always will.

Other learning problems are due to low-functioning intellectual capacities. In these cases it is important to help the person to reach his or her highest level of life skills, which may be learning personal self-care like bathing, hair washing, and dressing, and independent-living skills including shopping, cooking, washing clothes, and house cleaning.

Learning is a lifelong process. We are constantly presented with new information and situations that we must integrate into our lives in a way that makes sense to us. Our brains are always working to create new categories and procedures to assist us in managing our lives. For instance, every few weeks you may have to learn something brand new: like how to set the clock on your VCR, how to record a television show being aired when you aren't at home, how to use your new electronic microwave oven, how to program your telephone to dial numbers automatically, to use a new telephone system at work, and so on.

It is important to stay in control of your time, energy, and what you want to learn. Even though we are constantly bombarded by more and more things, we still have choices. A exercise these choices wisely, and don't take on more than is reasonable. You can use your skills, talents, and areas of interest to help you choose what you want to learn, how, and when, and where. Enjoy learning your entire life, it keeps you young.

CREATIVITY: USING YOUR WHOLE BRAIN

The reward for dealing with the problems in your life is that you can become creative and balanced by using your whole brain. You can use your right brain to visualize new and creative images, styles, or patterns to solve the everyday or long-term problems in your life. Or you can use your senses and special talents and imagination to create new music, poems, films, dances, sculptures, or stories, or to devise creative solutions to problems.

Then you can use your left brain to evaluate the work produced by your intuitive creative side. You can use your left brain to negotiate a sale, or to market your new idea or product., invest in the stock market, fix your car, do brain surgery, become a rocket scientist.

We always are happier when we are in harmony with all parts of ourselves. We cannot separate body, mind, emotions, and spirit. All of your parts contribute something special to make you uniquely *you*.

CHAPTER SIXTEEN

TECHNIQUES FOR INTELLECTUAL GROWTH

Some people believe that the highest part of human evolution to date is our big brain and the capacity to use it. Scientifically and technologically speaking we have demonstrated capacities in these areas superior to those of other species with whom we share this planet. But in the areas of human relations -- both in our interrelationships with others and our *intra* relationships with ourselves -- we lag behind.

In some ways we are still very close to our primitive ancestors when it comes to resolving power struggle issues, like border disputes between nations and neighbors, religious differences, taking down the walls of cultural distinction. We are still a long way from global compassion, being nonjudgmental about the affairs of others, and loving unconditionally.

Yet we *are* making progress. As individuals we can use our intelligence to grow up and be responsible to ourselves and to others within our families, our country and for the planet.

EMOTIONAL AND INTELLECTUAL BALANCE

If you learn easily and use your intelligence effectively, you have a great advantage. People who develop a habit of curiosity and love of reading early in life usually go on through life acquiring facts and assimilating new information easily. It's wonderful to have developed your intellect to serve you in many ways, but if you rely too much on intellect to determine everything, you may be ignoring your emotional responses, discounting the importance of physical well-being, and rationalizing away your spiritual needs.

Another problem for the intellectual is the sheer amount of information that's available today. Sometimes it is overwhelming. Schools and the business world encourage people to specialize early in life and to become experts in some small aspect of a subject area. In a sense, this helps protect you from the information overload we live in, but it can also lead to imbalance if you understand little about other aspects of life.

Voracious readers, busy professionals, and students who mastered all subjects equally well in high school and college may discover as they get older that they just can't keep up. At some point, you have to accept the fact that you can't know it all in the late 20th century. You may have to choose some things to keep up with in detail, and settle for a superficial knowledge of other subject matter. Our century has seen incredible advances in the conveyance of information, and for many people, the challenge today is not to learn everything but to choose what to learn.

The intellectual can use that agile mind in several ways to

restore balance. *First,* remain curious about other things, not just your specialty. An electronics engineer can take a real vacation in an art museum. A politician may experiment in a greenhouse as a hobby. Balance your intellect with creativity.

Second, learn to use your mind not to shut out the other aspects of your being but to open them up. Your brain knows that you need to get more exercise so let that brain figure out the ideal exercise program for your life-style and preferences. Your studies may lead you to disagree with certain religious doctrines.

Don't deny your awareness of life's mysteries; use your knowledge in your quest for something spiritual to believe in. Your mind knows that you've never resolved certain emotional conflicts with your parents, so assign it the job of planning a scenario for discussing some long-time problems with them, so you can get that business finished. Realize that you will feel pain and fear and probably relief, and let yourself feel them.

Finally, don't use your intellect to hide from your feelings; use it instead to understand and perhaps change them to know that to be well-balanced, your emotional, physical, and spiritual sides need validation and expression.

IMPROVING YOUR SELF-CONCEPT

If you were fortunate enough to receive unconditional love, respect, warmth, and sense of safety and protection as a child, then you are most likely an adult who can accept your strengths and shortcomings with equal ease. You have self-respect, self-confidence, and a sense of independence and responsibility. You're well on the way to being a well rounded honest-to-God grownup!

If, as a child, you were criticized and given negative labels that had an adverse effect on your self-concept, your little inner child needs nurturing to heal from the pain the labels caused. You can now complete the process of growing up intellectually, first by believing in your own intelligence, then by learning how to put it to use.

To heal the old wounds and learn to believe in yourself, give yourself messages about the things that you're good at learning. Think about all the things you've accomplished by using your mind -- on your job, with your family, the life decisions you've had to make. Whatever test was applied to you in school only measured a small part of your intelligence and learning ability. What you've done with your knowledge about life is a much better measure of how intellectually grown up you are.

In terms of growing up, using the intelligence you have is what really matters to keep you in balance. Whatever approach you use is right for you as long as it works to help you accomplish your goals and live comfortably with others.

To counteract that negative self-concept, you can reprogram and change those old messages to positive self-nurturing and self-loving and self-accepting ones.

You also need to work on healing that little hurt kid that still lives inside of you and sometimes surfaces as a spoiled brat when threatened, and sometimes acts as prosecutor, judge, jury, and your own worst enemy, falsely confirming what a worthless and useless person you fear you are.

Here are some specific steps that you can take, using your mental skills, to start believing what a terrific person you really are. Most of these are ways of changing the self-talk that shapes your inner beliefs about yourself throughout the day. First you must become aware and recognize what you are doing to yourself.

1. Start a thought journal. You can't change your thoughts if you don't know what they are. You may be shocked to realize how critical you are of yourself. **DON'T JUDGE!** Just honestly record your self-talk for one week. Take a notebook along with you and use shorthand phrases to jot down all the messages you are aware of verbalizing to yourself. At the end of the week group together criticisms, compliments, plans, and other types of messages, so you can see what your patterns are.

Another thing you can do is to keep a ***Put Down Bank.*** Get a roll of pennies and a little jar or empty medicine holder, to carry with you all day and night. Every time you put yourself down, or have a negative thought about yourself, put a penny in the jar. Tally them up at the end of the day and record it. Keep track for one week. You will be surprised at how often you "beat yourself up" mentally.

The next few steps will help you change those patterns.

   2.   Start to make friends with yourself. True friendship is one of the most treasured of human relationships. It takes time, energy, love, patience, and sometimes sacrifice to " be there" for someone. How much of this do you do for yourself? Do you like your own company? Are you interesting to be with? Or do you avoid self-intimacy, call yourself names, like "stupid" when you make a mistake or "fatty" when you look in a mirror. Think about it and make an effort to be nicer to yourself. Now start the most important friendship of your life -- with you!

   3.   Support yourself with affirmations. Begin by looking in a mirror and saying your name, followed by " I love you", *"John, I love you!"* Say it over at least ten times a day, morning and evening. You may feel uncomfortable at first, or shy or sad; you may even cry. But, believe me, it works. If you don't love yourself how can you expect others to love you?

Also compliment yourself on everything you do well. Start to notice how many things you do that are praiseworthy and heap on the good words (thoughts). Write them down in your journal to reinforce and confirm them. Friends notice and praise good things about each other, so be a friend.

4. Change the things about yourself that you don't like. You have the power to do this. Change is often slow and always difficult. The familiar is more comfortable, even when it is outrageously dysfunctional and causes you pain. You can change if you want to.

Decide how you want to become, and put your brain in charge of becoming just that. Investigate and decide on taking the necessary steps to do what you want. Be patient; you may slip back into your old ways when you try to change patterns and habits. Don't give up, just start again. Pretty soon you will have it mastered.

5. Don't expect others to change for you. The only person you can really control is yourself. Trying to control others or to get them to change will only turn you into a manipulating shrew. If you are in a situation that you don't like, look at your options and the pros and cons of each, then make a choice and follow through. One of the negative payoffs in having a poor self-concept is that you believe that you don't deserve to be happy, or to be treated well, or you believe that you can't take care of yourself. Baloney! What advice would you give to a good friend in a similar situation? Okay now, listen to your best friend -- you!

LOWERING DEFENSES

Defenses are ways that we use to protect ourselves. They may be necessary to your survival when you are vulnerable, such as when you were a child. But for adults, they are psychological devices that render you emotionally distanced from the pain, trauma, and reality of your life experiences. Defenses don't serve you well as a maturing adult because they interfere with your ability to be close or intimate with another or honest with all those around you.

If you are numb and out of touch with what you are feeling, you cannot open yourself to true compassion, intimacy, and love. When you defend against the pain you also defend against the love, and you live your life as an emotional cripple.

In order to allow yourself to really feel, you must be willing to feel the pain as well as the joy. If you have shut off your feelings during one or continual childhood traumas, you must go back and open yourself to experiencing the feelings you shut off then. Then and only then can you heal.

Defenses are like bricks in a wall that separate you from other people. If they have been there for a long time, they are hard to take down. They become so habituated and comfortable that they are hard to remove, even when they may cost you the loss of a loving relationship, friends, or trouble at work. They are even difficult to recognize by yourself.

The best way to heal and to stop defending the hurt child within you is in therapy or in a trusting relationship with another person. You need to tell the stories of your pain and feel the shut-off feelings. Opening these wounds may involve anger work, crying, feeling sadness and loss, and other grief reactions to what you lost or had taken away from you. I don't recommend that you do this work with a spouse, child, parent, or other person to whom you have an emotional bond. It isn't fair to them nor is it fair to you.

Dropping your defenses may seem frightening or overwhelming at first. But you do it gradually, brick by brick. With each one gone you feel lighter, freer, more like the person you were meant to be. The rewards are great. You have the capacity to become more loving, more creative, more self-confident, and more compassionate.

POLISHING COMMUNICATION SKILLS

Grownup communication skills reflect responsibility, for saying what you think and feel, and for listening to what others want you to hear. These skills include active listening, using **"I"** statements to own or take responsibility for your own feelings, giving feedback, and being assertive.

Active listening means really paying attention to what the other is saying, not just waiting without listening until it's your turn to talk. You can assure the other that you are listening -- and that you care what he or she has to say -- by giving various types of feedback, and clarifying what you heard by repeating what was said in your own words.

If you want to develop active-listening habits, practice paraphrasing *"So what I heard you say was that you like the cat but it makes you sneeze; is that right?"*; behavior description *"You seem to be playing with your food; is something wrong?"*; feeling description *"You seem to be angry, are you?"*; and feedback *"When you slam the door like that, I feel frustrated with you"*.

It's important to be sure that you really understood what was communicated, not just to assume that you do. Then you'll be able to make a much more meaningful response in conversation, because it shows your family, business associates, friends, or even strangers that you really care what they say.

Another important communication technique is always to use *"I"* statements followed by naming a feeling when talking about personal matters or opinions, such as *"I feel rejected when you decide to work on weekends without asking me if I've made any plans."* With this strategy the person speaking takes responsibility for what she feels or thinks. The other person need not feel defensive, but can join you in solving your problem, even if his behavior was involved.

When you say, *"You make me mad"* or *"You always*

ignore my needs," the other person rightfully feels attacked because *"you"* statements are blaming statements. Because of this the other person reflexively responds in a defensive way by denying or attacking back -- and the communication gets nowhere.

Blame is always about making someone else wrong or at fault because you are not getting what you want. It is childish, irresponsible, and leads to increased conflict, which is really the opposite of what you want, and the opposite of problem solving.

People must give listeners a chance to process and understand what has been said before demanding an answer. This is a good time to clarify and be sure you are on track.

Conversational style is one of the things we humans learn through practice, just as we learn to type and drive; by memorizing reciting, remembering, and ultimately by combining different pieces of information, we achieve understanding that we can then use to solve problems. Effective communication takes effort and practice but it is essential to be able to understand others and to be understood.

IMPROVING MEMORY

Sometimes memory loss is related to old deep emotional pain that has been repressed. Other times it is connected with aging and physical degeneration. Everyone loses the capacity for efficient short-term memory as we age. Learning is said to be slowed down for things like mathematical formulas too.

There are many techniques for improving the memory. The left brain latches on to mnemonic devices, like key words in which each letter stands for an item or other association that you train your mind to make. Using the memory takes concentration -- a conscious effort to store what you want to remember, and time and attention to search through the storehouse when you want to recall something. There are lots of books and programs on improving the memory, and if memory is a problem to you, they would be worth looking into.

Memory is affected when you are grieving, overwhelmed, tired, or responding to an illness. Don't expect your memory to function the same all of the time. Concentration is affected by these same issues that seem to throw you off balance temporarily. Don't despair, they will return in time, as other healing takes place.

IMPROVING LEARNING SKILLS

Each of us has a preferred learning style. Some people learn best by reading, some by listening, others by doing or watching. You may rely on books and courses for much of what you know, or you may consider yourself a graduate of the school of life. Or you may choose to base your understanding in a spiritual, religious, or ethical system.

Keep in mind that an intellectual grownup is not close-minded to the other styles or foundations of learning. Be tolerant of other approaches to learning, knowledge, and wisdom, and give them a try yourself sometime.

Open-mindedness is a characteristic of the person who is always willing to learn, from any possible source; that's a wise, intellectually mature attitude, no matter what the I.Q. tests say about you. Even if your curiosity and open-mindedness do not lead you to go back to school and finish your formal education or get an additional degree, they certainly will lead you to ask questions, read, and seek answers.

This open-to-learning approach to life will have positive effects in your physical, emotional, and spiritual life, by opening your conscious and subconscious minds to possible paths to change, growth, and understanding.

Learning is growing, wherever you find your answers and information. In conversation, others' will respect your intelligence more when you listen to their ideas, and then contribute opinions or information that add to others' understanding. This shows that you care more about learning than about being right. Being open to learning enables you to transcend any defects in your education and the early messages about your intellectual ability.

We all have so much to learn from and to teach each other. Don't let short sighted thinking stop you from being open to other ways of perceiving ways of learning and knowing. Ultimately we are all trying to get to the same place. Wisdom doesn't care what path we take.

CREATIVE PROBLEM SOLVING

Everyone has problems of all kinds. One of the unavoidable parts of being grown up is that you have to solve your own problems and make your own decisions. As with many other living skills, you may be good at problem solving, or not so good. You can always become better at it by learning how to use your intelligence to solve problems; you can learn techniques that you can apply to any problem, whether it is grounded in the intellectual, emotional, physical, or spiritual aspect of your life.

When you are confronted with a situation that requires a change in behavior or a new or different approach, you have to know how to find that solution. If familiar solutions and the things you already know how to do will not work, then a creative approach is necessary.

Most people see and meet the world as they expect it to be, based on their previous experiences. If there's a problem, they use familiar methods to solve it. Try exploring new ways of thinking or of solving problems. Changing and doing something new is foreign and risky. But if you never tried anything new, how would you ever learn anything new?

Ken Keyes's little book, *The Hundredth Monkey,* tells a story about how a species learns by creating novel ways to solve a problem. The food didn't seem to taste very good, so one day a young female monkey tried something new; she washed a potato before she ate it. It tasted better and soon all of the other monkeys were washing their potatoes before eating them. Researchers found the same new behavior had evolved in a distant monkey troop at the same time that had no contact with the first troop.

This is how we advance and evolve as a species. Someone dares to try a new way to solve a problem, and the word spreads because others are ready for a solution. We also learn this way as individuals, by being open to new ideas, wherever they come from.

There are ten possible solutions to every problem. They may not all be obvious at first, but with some brainstorming and digging deeper into yourself you will find them. The usual approach to solving a complex problem or making a decision is to identify your options, consider the pros and cons of each option, eliminate the unacceptable ones, and decide on the one that will work best for you now. The most creative solutions may require you to make some drastic changes or to reorganize your life. Give each option careful consideration before you discard it.

Sometimes the best opportunities in life come to us disguised as problems. The rational problem-solving method allows you to structure your thinking, reduce your confusion, and discover what further information you need. Then you can make a decision without guessing on the basis of irrational emotions and incomplete information. As you allow your real feelings, your intuition, and your clear rational understanding to take balanced roles in solving your problem, you are taking charge of your life with real, grown-up wisdom.

The hard part about making a decision sometimes is that there isn't a right or wrong answer. Probably any decision you make, any solution you choose, will work, if you're willing to put the commitment and energy into it. But you must choose the option that has the best chance of success so you can attain the happiness you want or security for your family. You must listen to both your analytical and your intuitive minds. It's not a time to let your emotions rule completely, but to temper your feelings with knowledge and reason.

DEVELOPING INTUITION

Some researchers believe intuition is a special gift that some people are born with; others think it is a function of brain chemistry. I believe everyone has the capacity to develop his or her intuitive nature; it is simply a matter of learning to listen to your hunches, then checking them out through more logical means to see how accurate they are. A long time ago, I created a motto for myself, *When in doubt, don't!* I found that when I went against my inner knowing, my intuition, I often got into trouble. Now I listen to that interior voice and save myself delays, frustrations, and heartaches.

It's important to distinguish between true intuition and messages produced by irrational fears. Practice examining the sources of your thoughts and feelings and you will begin to appreciate the difference.

THOUGHT STOPPING

To be able to hear your intuition or to put both sides of your mind to work to solve a particular problem, you have to be able to focus on one thing and to clear away the busy, confused, and irrelevant thoughts from your conscious awareness. Try this:

Sit back, close your eyes, and clear your mind for 60 seconds. Don't think of anything.

If you are surprised at the results you are in for an interesting adventure. Most people cannot stop their thoughts even for five seconds. Our minds are busy all of the time both when we are awake, and even when we're asleep.

To focus on one problem or creative activity, you must be able to rid yourself of much of the distracting, annoying interference of trivial everyday thoughts. You must be able to relax your mind as well as your body.

The best way to clear your mind is to learn a relaxation technique such as meditation, prayer, self-hypnosis, and auto suggestion. There are many excellent cassette tapes and videotapes on the market that talk you through a variety of ways to relax. Some are structured; others recreate environmental sounds like ocean waves, forest sounds, or a thunderstorm. Others have the soothing music of a flute or harp.

REDUCING BODILY STRESS

Essentially all relaxation methods enhance the same thing, relaxing your body allows your brain waves to slow down and you enter a slightly altered state of consciousness. Your mind starts to slow down along with your body. Like anything worthwhile it takes practice. Don't get discouraged and give up. At first you will have many intrusive thoughts tumbling into your mind. The trick is not to hold onto or get involved in any of them, just notice them and let them go. After a little while the thoughts will stop. It may seem like taming a wild tiger at first.

You can use progressive relaxation, such as lying still and telling each part of your body, starting at your feet, to relax, then visualizing the tension slide away from each part. Or make up a visual image that works ,such as seeing yourself floating down a stream. Each of your cares, and each of your physically tense feelings, falls into the water, one at a time, as you float away from all worry.

Another method is to tense each muscle group in your body, holding the tension to the count of 10, then suddenly releasing and relaxing . Try it now with your right arm. Good! Now do your whole body. Start at your head and face, next neck and shoulders, each arm individually, chest, abdomen and lower back, legs and feet. Now your entire body. Notice the difference between tension and relaxation. Strive to keep relaxed!

Or, you can follow the instructions on deep breathing and meditation given earlier. If you follow this method, you'll be relaxed, and in a slight euphoric trance. Nothing dangerous, just a new place. As you begin to breathe normally with your belly like you do when you are sleeping you will notice how comfortable your body feels, and you will experience an overall sense of well-being.

MANTRAS

Another good focusing technique is to choose one word that you repeat over and over. When you focus on that word, your mind empties faster. Some people visualize the word *"RELAX"* as if it were written on the inside of their foreheads, and repeat the word over and over, rhythmically with their breathing. Others use a religious word like *"JESUS."* The word should have two syllables that are soothing to you. I use *"RAMA"*, which is one of the Hindu Gods. It resonates and I can say it very slowly to force me to concentrate and slow down my overactive brain and thoughts.

Once you learn to quiet your mind of its usual trivial

chatter, you will notice many benefits. One is that you can induce this form of relaxation anywhere you choose -- sitting at a stoplight, before an examination or job interview, at work, in the middle of an argument, at church, before falling asleep, and many other times. You have just learned how to reduce your stress and to return your entire being to a state of wellness. This ability is free. Add it to your wellness toolbox and use it.

PART SIX

GETTING IT ALL TOGETHER

CHAPTER SEVENTEEN

UNIVERSAL TRUTHS: VALUES, ATTITUDES, AND BELIEFS

Life is like a school in which we are constantly presented with chances to learn the necessary lessons in living. Life is a never-ending parade of challenges and opportunities to grow. Growth is often difficult, especially if we resist and only do it when forced to, kicking and screaming.

Some of us meet these challenges with openness and a willingness to learn. Others resist, rebel against, escape from, and deny these opportunities, and try not to grow. But growth is part of the human process; we are always moving to a higher state of awareness, of compassion, of wisdom, and of other positive qualities. If we resist growing we remain mired in suffering, hurt, pain, confusion, and we try to blame others for our problems. These forms of resistance don't stop growth from occurring, they only delay it and make it more difficult.

The things that make this school of life and growth difficult are that teachers are hard to recognize, the rules are never clearly stated, the lessons are fuzzy, and the process of learning seems more often chaotic than orderly. As in the schools of your formal education, this school of life has a system of rewards for lessons learned well and punishments for lessons not learned. The reward for a lesson learned is that you are allowed to move on to the next lesson, and the next, until they have all been mastered.

We all have the same lessons to learn. With each lesson learned we awaken a little more, become more aware, less resistant, more trusting, more loving, more giving, more joyful. We are more enlightened and more grown up.

The punishment for resisting a lesson is that you must keep doing it over and over until you get it right. You will continue to be presented with that same difficult lesson until you learn, understand, and integrate that lesson into your grown-up life, then move on. This may sound like a drag but the process can be challenging, exciting, and fun. It depends on your attitude and your receptivity to these opportunities for growing.

Growth is the real purpose of your life and of mine. We are not here to gather material goods or status or to get Ph.D.'s or to impress our neighbors and friends. We are here to learn the necessary lessons to advance our souls, to serve each other, and to live in love and peace and harmony.

During this learning process, which is the pathway to growing up, many teachers give us guidelines to help us. There have been great teachers in every age and every culture on the planet. Some renowned examples are religious leaders: like Jesus Christ; Mohammed, Buddha; Lao-Tse; philosophers like Socrates; Plato; Gurdjieff; Alan Watts; and Krishnamurti. Political reformers like Gandhi and Martin Luther King, and countless forgotten people who sacrificed their lives for a cause, like writers and poets Emerson, Thoreau, and Whitman. Some of us are moved by music, art, theater, and acts of heroism.

We also learn from people and places and simple acts of

kindness in everyday life. Not just from those who have offered their wisdom to the world, but ordinary people. Opportunities to learn abound in unexpected events and from other people.

Our best teachers are those who are in relationships with us. They often hold up mirrors in which we can see ourselves reflected back to us. They give us feedback, or tell us things about ourselves that we don't know, or support us when we are in pain or in grief, or refuse to let us get away with dysfunctional behaviors.

Teachers are there for us to listen to, and their messages are simple. All the great teachers, all those who know the keys to true growth and wisdom, say the same things over and over throughout all of recorded time and in every culture. These sayings are *Universal Truths.*

These are truths that are recognized in some place deep within each human soul who is passing through this school called *life*. A universal truth is a concept that holds true for all of mankind. It transcends race, color, creed, gender, national borders, time, politics. It crosses all cultures. It is a positive idea that is expressed in many ways, passed on from generation to generation in the religions and/or folklore of all countries, tribes, and groups.

These truths are simply stated but are often difficult to grasp totally, to internalize and to live by. All your life you have heard people say these truths, but have you really learned them, deep within? Learning them in the depths of your intellectual, emotional, physical, and spiritual self is the challenging path to real growth. They are the ultimate lessons on everyone's journey.

Most of us live our lives superficially. We put our time and energy into petty skirmishes, defensiveness, protecting our insecurities, and avoiding vulnerability. Consequently, we avoid or miss out on intimacy, honesty, and true connections with other human beings and, most important of all, with ourselves.

The *secrets* of being able to attain these things are not secrets at all. The answers are as present today as they have been for centuries. They *are within you,* and the universal truths are your guides on the royal road to living your life in peace, harmony, balance, and in *Love.*

The guideline lessons focus around five basic universal truths that are the keys to personal growth. As individuals learn and practice living life from a deeper inner place connected with universal wisdom on a world-wide scale, then and only then can all of us together transform our planet into a place of justice and peace.

We all want to live a life that works, one that allows us to give and receive love and support, to live in peace, to be free, to develop and use the best of our talents, to be happy. We can be guided on the way to achieving balance, responsibility, and selfhood by living these universal truths. While there are other truths that are equally profound, I have chosen to focus upon these five:

♦ *Love your neighbor as yourself.*

♦ *To thine own self be true.*

♦ *There is no freedom without self- responsibility.*

♦ *Do unto others as you would have them do unto you.*

♦ *Love conquers all.*

LOVE YOUR NEIGHBOR AS YOURSELF

Before you can live a life of love, or truly love even one other person, you must learn to love yourself. Not an easy task, you vacillate from self-love when things or relationships are good, to self-doubt and feeling insecure when your situation is shaky, to self-hate when you have committed an offense, used poor judgment, or been shamed.

To love your neighbor as yourself, it is obvious that the ability to love begins within you. Your neighbor is, of course, everyone else in the world, everyone who is not you. A neighbor may be a blood relative, someone who lives in your neighborhood, your town or city, your country, on the planet earth, or perhaps beyond.

Love to me *means* being healthy physically, feeling good emotionally, thinking positively, and spiritually being willing to go the extra mile to help or serve someone else without expecting to be paid back.

Love does not mean getting something better from another -- a better deal, a better price, a better opportunity. It means instead giving a little bit more than is asked or expected. It means coming from a place of psychological abundance, not from scarcity. If you believe that you have plenty of love, plenty of money (even though you may be living from paycheck to paycheck), plenty of food, extra room, extra time, et cetera, then you will have enough to give some away, no strings attached.

This feeling of having enough for yourself comes from self-love, from being grown up enough to believe in yourself, that you can provide for your own needs and still have love to give away.

We all have good intentions, and good within us that we know we could share. When you know that you always have enough, you carry your goodness and love around with you all of the time. The grownup has integrated that love into everything in his life. The grownup makes it a priority to make the time to create win-win situations. This willingness to give will make you and others you deal with feel good about your transactions.

This process sounds simple, but it may be difficult to do. If you need to make some personal changes in order to grow up enough to give love, be patient with yourself. Change takes time, awareness, practice, and some mistakes. To integrate unselfish love and service into your life, you may have to give up some deeply entrenched familiar patterns.

Not everyone will return your neighborly gestures of love with equal consideration for you. If you are taken advantage of, don't let those experiences tempt you to withdraw and become bitter. Just because someone else isn't grown up doesn't mean you have to drop to that level of immaturity. This is only a test. Don't give up. We are still evolving as individuals and as a species, and not everyone has the desire or the capacity to love himself, let alone his neighbor.

I am not suggesting that you allow yourself to be hurt repeatedly or used or exploited. You need to protect yourself by setting limits, even conditions, on how giving you choose to be in each particular relationship. But the grownup doesn't let hurts make her hard-boiled like an egg, hard and rigid inside. Instead, she stays soft and flexible like a boiled potato.

Remember, your neighbor is every person on earth. As human beings we are all connected. The love within you recognizes that all humans, all living things, are worthy of the same love you give yourself. While you may feel that you have frustratingly little impact on the major problems of the planet like environmental destruction, threat of war, overpopulation, hunger, crime, or injustice, you can have a positive impact on everyone you meet.

Something as easy to give as a smile or a kind word can make a difference in the life of a friend or a stranger. We get opportunities to help others often in our daily lives. Sometimes your neighbor needs something practical, like a ride or a meal or a place to sleep or help changing a tire. Sometimes loving your neighbor means giving money, or sharing information that will help someone solve a problem, or forgiving him for a mistake, or listening when someone is confused or hurt, or needs a sympathetic ear. Be receptive! Opportunities abound to serve and help. Sometimes a simple smile is enough!

Loving one's neighbor means opening the door to those with whom you share the planet, and not restricting your concept of who that neighbor is. Then it means considering that person's needs as being as important as your own. When a gift is given, or help is offered, or love is expressed with no thought of payment, you are reaching out and spreading kindness and love. Like a pebble dropped into a pond, love has a ripple effect, it spreads far beyond the simple gesture that starts it.

TO THINE OWN SELF BE TRUE

One reason it's hard to love ourselves is that most of us don't know who we really are. We create an idealized image in our minds of who we think we are. But this image is only a composite picture made up of caricatures of what we thought our parents, friends, and various teachers wanted us to be. Your immature ego, which wanted to please and to avoid displeasure and punishment, set you up with this ideal image, which may confuse you throughout your life.

As an adult, you may still believe in and protect this image formed when you were a child. You continue to present yourself to the world as if this were really you. Being true to your own self means that you must peel away the false images and establish your own values, attitudes, and beliefs about who you are and how you fit into this world.

In times of crisis, meditation, and reverie, when you ask yourself, "Who am I?" and "What is the purpose of my life?", you are approaching the reality of this universal truth. But the answer is elusive. First you must peel off the layers to get to the core.

If I asked you to write 25 responses to the question, "Who am I?" I'll bet most of your answers would describe your social roles -- i.e., "I am a mother", "I am a wife", "I am a son", or they would be behavioral traits such as "I am a hard worker" or "I am a dreamer", or they would be facts like "I am Margie O'Brian" or "I am 27 years old". Yet none of these descriptions tells me about your *Self*, about who you really are inside beyond roles and facts and behaviors. So how can you be true to yourself, if you don't know who you really are beneath these layers of social and superficial characteristics?

I know who you are. You are a creative, loving, open, belonging, healthy, happy person buried under your false personality -- the ego created by the immature child you once were. Your ego works hard to keep you childish, vengeful, and afraid. It tenaciously keeps control and puts you in a struggle with the true open self that lives within you. When a more highly evolved or more grown-up part of yourself surfaces, your ego moves to squelch the intruder.

The oracle at Delphi gave us this mandate, *"Know Thyself"*, and we spend most of our lives searching for the answer. We spend our adult years relearning, working through, releasing, overcoming, understanding, and forgiving what we learned and experienced in childhood.

This *process of becoming* is common to all mankind, though the specific issues are exquisitely unique to you. For many of us, the struggle goes on with no progress. But the sooner you begin the work and the more techniques you know for liberating the inner you, the sooner your joyful spirit will be free to allow you to become all that you can be, to reach the potential that you were born with.

LET YOUR CONSCIENCE BE YOUR GUIDE

We all have an inner monitoring system called our conscience. Your conscience tells you what is right and what is wrong for you. It judges and gives you feedback on your functioning as a human being. It is an inner knowing beyond intellectual knowledge, that includes total personality response and a feeling state.

A part of your conscience tells you about rules, laws, duty, and self-sacrifice. Another more humanistic part deals with values, attitudes, beliefs, and whether your behavior matches these deeply known truths. It is the guardian of your integrity and self-respect, and it validates you as a loving human being. When you violate a personal value, attitude, or belief you suffer a *guilty conscience*, your signal that something is wrong.

Conscience represents your true self, the moral essence of your being. It is the gatekeeper of the human principles that you have learned from various sources and have integrated as your own as you have made progress in growing up. It serves the important role of keeping you in balance and harmony. When in doubt about a decision, action, or a desire for retaliation, do as Jimminy Cricket said, "Let your conscience be your guide."

THERE IS NO FREEDOM WITHOUT RESPONSIBILITY

One of the signposts of being grown up is taking responsibility for every part of your life. Is this a frightening prospect for you? The infant within you wants life on a silver platter. It wants what it wants, *how* it wants it, and *when* it wants it, *where* it wants it. It doesn't want to be bothered with training, hard work, mistakes, learning, understanding, pain, and accountability. The infant says," Give it all to me, NOW." This reflects our instant gratification mentality.

This is how many people envision God, as a benevolent, pampering parent who gives and indulges your slightest whim with graciousness and good will. But just let something go wrong and God catches Hell. Listen to yourself pray. What do you say? What do you ask for? Help? Changes in your favor? Do you want Utopia -- the best of all worlds? Rather than forever wishing that this rosy, but naive childish fantasy would come true, you'd be better off praying for opportunities to learn and grow, or asking God for the ability to recognize the wisdom and lessons in your experiences.

The childish ego in you wants the freedom to make independent choices and decisions and to take credit for them when they are successful, yet the kid doesn't want to accept the responsibility for his own mistakes. The fact is, there is no such thing as a free lunch. You have to pay the bill. You have to take responsibility for your actions, right or wrong.

When you refuse to accept responsibility for your part in every event in your life, you keep yourself in bondage, embroiled in superficial childish skirmishes. When something goes wrong and your automatic response is to blame someone else for it, remember that blaming is the infantile way to shift the responsibility to another. When you do this, you are denying a part of yourself and admitting your dependence on other people and on events.

Remaining dependent has a price. You delay and block your own growth. You also put yourself in slavery to someone else. You're not a grownup until you pay the bill -- i.e., take the responsibility, pay the price, forgive, ask for forgiveness, make amends, make decisions, protect those in your charge or do whatever it takes to free yourself.

Some of us try to have it both ways -- a medium-size helping of independence with a side dish of escape from responsibility, topped with denial. Perhaps you take responsibility in some parts of your life, but not in others, usually those in which you feel helpless, frustrated, or confused.

Look   inside yourself. Learn from your mistakes.

Mistakes really don't have to be so frightening. All human beings make mistakes -- that is how we learn best. While you may fail at a specific task or relationship, but *you* are not a failure. You are simply an ordinary, fallible person who made a mistake, nothing more. No big deal. Pick yourself up, dust yourself off, and try again. When you take responsibility for your mistakes, you can use them as ways to learn to avoid the same pitfalls later. This kind of learning is what life is all about.

Once you realize that freedom and responsibility go hand in hand, you will also realize that nothing anyone else does can harm you. You cannot control an event or someone else's behavior or attitude, but you are free to choose your response to the actions of others. It is also your responsibility to protect yourself from being used or abused by other people.

If someone wants to use, exploit, or otherwise harm you, you have options for how you will respond. One is to say **no**, loud and clear. Other options may be painful, such as ending a destructive relationship, quitting a job, or joining a program to get support in dealing with a troubled adolescent. It is responsible to put yourself and your growth first. It is irresponsible to stay in relationships and places that drag you down.

As a responsible grownup you know that you can handle any situation that comes up in your life. You are truly in control of your life and of your choices from within. Grownups must take this control, and they know that their choices are all they can control.

This is where free will comes into the picture. *You have choice in every part of your life.* All you need to do is exercise it. The opportunities you choose to take are the paths for learning your lessons in this lifetime. Not to choose also can be a responsible choice. Whichever way you go you will learn, although if you always take the safe, known path, you probably will learn more slowly.

Life is an ever changing, dynamic process. If you approach the freedom that your choices give you with a sense of adventure and an eagerness to learn, without fear of the work or pain involved, you will free your spirit and liberate the love you were born to share.

While you seek and treasure your personal freedom you must not hold others in bondage. You do not own another human being -- not your spouse, your children, your students, your employees -- nor does anyone else own you-- not your spouse, your parents, your teachers, your boss. You must liberate those close to you to carry out their inner tasks without shackles or locks that squelch their growth. Honor their freedom and they will honor yours. You cannot have freedom unless you are willing to give freedom.

As you recognize and exercise your personal, internal freedom, you know that you are free to choose your opportunities, and the lessons that you will learn from them.

DO UNTO OTHERS AS YOU WOULD HAVE THEM
DO UNTO YOU

We are interdependent beings. We all have needs and wants from other people. We are born alone and die alone, but during the time we spend on earth we are involved in a myriad of relationships with others. The New Testament's Golden Rule-- *Do unto others as you would have them do unto you* -- is another spiritual guideline that can make your path smoother. The first step is to decide how you want to be treated. Most of us want to be taken seriously, to be treated gently and with respect. To be able to ask for and to give help to others when the need arises. Not to suffer from intolerance and prejudice just because the color of our skin is different, or we wear different clothes, or have a handicap, or because of any perception of who we are.

How do you want to be treated? What do you want in your relationships with others? Do you want fairness? Love? Freedom? Do you want others to be responsible in their dealings with you? How honest and responsible are you with them? If you think you have been wronged, do you try to get even or do you state your needs and forgive?

Before you can live the Golden Rule, you must define it for yourself. You must decide what your response will be if others do something to you that you consider wrong, hurtful, bad, or malicious. Do you *do unto them* the same way? Or can you turn the other cheek and forgive?

No one is perfect, you will make mistakes and consequently hurt others. If you want to ask "forgive us our trespasses, as we forgive those who trespass against us" in your prayers, you must put forgiveness into practice in your everyday life. And sometimes this is very difficult. It requires all your grown-up knowledge and control. Yet when you carry around vengeance and hate, you harm yourself more than you realize.

Grown-ups let go of resentment, and replace it with love and positive energy. Remember forgiveness is for you. To release you of resentment and other negative feelings that impede your growth.

Every college of business in the country teaches the doctrine of *caveat emptor,* "Let the buyer beware." The responsibility is placed on the buyer to see that he is treated fairly, not on the provider of the goods and services. The implication is that it is all right to cheat, steal, and lie, but be careful not to get caught. If you do get caught it is the fault of the purchaser who was naive enough to trust you.

It's time that we transcend this narrow and selfish way of living in our relationships, both business and personal. Erich Fromm in *The Art of Loving* equates the Golden Rule in Western society with the Fairness Doctrine in social and economic relationships. Fairness means not using trickery, deceit, or fraud in exchange for goods or services. Maybe it is time to take a good look at the way you conduct your business and social lives with others, as well as your personal relationships .

Maybe it is time to stop looking over your shoulder, expecting to get kicked. If you want to be treated with fairness, respect, sensitivity, responsibility, and love, then you must manifest these qualities and live this way, ignoring society's sanctions. It's impossible to be loving at home and self-serving in business, you can't apply the Golden Rule selectively.

Grownups respect all relationships. You must create a new way to be in the world. This way will bring you peace and growth, even if others are still living by the law of the playground. In order to bring peace to this planet, we first must find peace within ourselves. Gandhi said, "The only devils there are, are the ones running around in our own hearts." The devils that interfere with individual growing up, as well as with mankind's ability to coexist peacefully, are our negative emotions running rampant.

Hatred, racism, bigotry, and anger are the big dividing devils that lead countries and groups into power struggles, violence, and war. When these negative emotions are transformed to positive feelings we become more sensitive to the cruelty and injustices that surround us. As individuals, and as groups and nations, we can change defensiveness to compassion, fear to love, rage to engagement, and fairness to justice.

Then and only then does the Golden Rule become more than another trite edict of a religion. It becomes a commitment to yourself and to each other to live in love. When we *do love unto each other*, everything becomes golden.

LOVE CONQUERS ALL

Love is the strongest force in the universe. It is the force of unification. It brings us together, it bonds us, it teaches us, it nurtures us, it lives and loves through us. Love is endless and bottomless, eternal. It is the kingdom of God within you. Once you tap into the love within you, you can constantly give it away and never run out.

Unfortunately very few people feel, understand, or allow themselves to experience mature love. There is a direct connection between the unfulfilled love needs of the child and the adult's problems. But if you allow love in, if you will love yourself and your neighbor, if you will be true to yourself, if you will take responsibility for your actions, and you will do unto others as you want them to do unto you, you will tap into the bottomless well of love within you.

Childish love is needy, dependent, possessive, and demanding. Immature love is based on fear, insecurity, and lack of trust. The child's fear of losing the loved one leads to jealousy and domination. Childish love is selfish, conditional, addictive, and leads to separateness. Mature love is just the opposite. It is nonconditional, nonaddictive, not dominating or possessive. Based on wisdom, it cherishes the individuality, growth, and development of the other person. There is always enough mature love. It is nondependent and nonexclusive. It brings people together. It encourages and enhances growth in oneself and everyone else.

LOVE RELATIONSHIPS

Adults who are emotionally immature look for love partners to give them the love they didn't get from their parents. They are attracted to someone who has some of the traits of the parent who deprived them most, and they continue to play out the scenario of parent and child with this new "parent". Or they may choose someone who has aspects of the parent who came closer to meeting their needs so they can try to get more.

You can never win in such a situation because you expect

your lover to treat you as your parent did. You project onto him or her your old unmet needs. The child in you is trying to master the situation once again, but inevitably the child must lose because your expectations can't be met by someone outside yourself. In losing again, the child feels once more the devastation of failing to get his needs met.

This subtle and destructive process must be recognized and stopped. Until this cycle is broken you will never be able to give or receive mature love -- to be loved for yourself and to love another as he is and not as you want him to be. True love is the ability to reveal yourself without reserve to your loved one, and in turn to be receptive to knowing her or him. This kind of love happens when there are no defenses, no withholding, no games. Love occurs in a spirit of adventure, acceptance, and trust that creates constant discovery of new heights and depths in yourself and in your partner.

Love with a special partner is one of the most precious gifts life offers. It is childish to take it lightly or to fail to cultivate it. A grownup appreciates, nurtures, and treasures this kind of love.

If you have a life partner, you must continue to rekindle the sparks of love that brought you together. If you are unattached, you can be open to finding a partner who is willing to share with you at the most intimate levels. Risk vulnerability and be yourself. You are perfectly loving and lovable to the right person. Draw this person to you. Grow together -- accepting, giving, trading times to be strong, to be weak, supporting, loving physically, mentally, emotionally, and spiritually.

Love is expressed through intimacy. As trust builds you can lower your defenses and allow yourself to become vulnerable and to open yourself to another person. Intimacy is validation and recognition of each other at your deepest levels.

Sexual contact is often mistaken for love or intimacy, but

relationships rooted in lust are no more love than is tying your shoelaces. Sex can be the physical expression of love that involves the emotions and spirit as well as the body, it also can be no more than the animal act of copulation. Some people misuse their sexuality to search for love, but are unable or unwilling to create true intimacy in their relationships. Often these people have been hurt in the past and have a hard time trusting others or believing in their own lovableness.

No matter how many times we have been hurt in relationships we are still drawn to contact with others. We are all looking for recognition and validation with another. The fear of giving and feeling love is tied to the fear of losing the person you love and of the suffering that goes with loss. Grownups know they could lose in love, but they love anyway. There is only one guarantee if you take the risk to abandon fear for love, you will know yourself better and feel more deeply than you ever have.

LOVE AS TEACHER

Love is the access point to the God within you. It is the highest human emotion, the one that can bring incredible joy and happiness. And, when misused or misunderstood, it can bring incredible pain. Love is the universal teacher. We learn from those we love, and from the experience of loving them and receiving their love. There are at least ten types of love relationships that we experience in a lifetime.

1. Teacher/student or employer/employee

2. Friendship

3. Parent/child or child/parent love

4. Love between spouses or committed partners

5. Romantic love

6. Love of self, called self-regard or self-esteem

7. Abstract love of truth, justice, beauty, the
    arts, or other concepts

8. Unconditional love, agape

9. Love of God or a higher power

10. Love of family, extended to the family of all
    mankind.

Mother Theresa said, "We must step forward and share love in the world." But we can't share what we don't have. Just feeling love or having the desire to share it isn't enough. You must have the wisdom to disperse your love in a way that enhances yourself and others.

You can heal yourself with love, then join others in a life filled with service and healing. Go inside yourself and connect with the powerful love force. Rest, nurture yourself, regenerate in this special place. If it is hard to touch at first, don't give up. You may have built up an insulation that needs to be penetrated before you can reconnect with your heart/love center.

When you are full of your love/life force, let it flow and pour out to your friends and enemies. Focus and direct your attention to people and priorities that are important to you. Send love and light to all of the leaders of all nations. Remember people who are homeless or in hospitals, nursing homes, jails, prisons, and other institutions. Send your love to children who are being abused at this very moment. Let it flow out to the saints to support their activities, to the terrorists and tyrants to soften their hearts. Remember everyone on this planet is your neighbor, and we all are caught in the web of human suffering. We are all connected by the God force within us. When others suffer so do you, when others are peaceful and happy so are you. Love plays an important role in spiritual development. Any work you do in helping yourself grow up will raise you to a higher level of loving. Using positive affirmations and meditation are some ways to become more enlightened.

Here are some affirmative statements to use to increase your ability to love:

I live, thrive, and expand myself in love.

Love lives in me and through me.

I choose to love and to create miracles in my life.

I offer unconditional love to everyone I meet today.

All that I have to give is given in love.

Select one or more of these statements and say them twenty times twice a day -- and miracles will happen. Or make up one of your own. This is how love conquers all -- by being allowed to blossom and to express itself throughout your life. There is no stronger force. Tap into it and experience the natural bliss and joy you were born to know. The stakes are high, but the rewards are higher. Let love set you free!

Finally, the Dalai Lama, winner of the 1989 Nobel Prize for Peace, says, "Compassion and love are the key things. On a family level, on a national level, on an international level. They are the keys to success and happiness." Love and compassion are the keys to sanity and peace at all levels. Love is the prize that is worth the effort of your life to strive for and achieve.

CHAPTER EIGHTEEN

WHOLISTIC LIVING

> "Hell is watching movies of what you could
> have done with your life, and didn't."
> Anon.

After you've lived thirty or forty years, you begin to realize that life is very short and full of distractions. If you waste your time, you waste your life and you may discover on your deathbed that it's too late to make the most of what you were given.

To become everything that you can be, you have to use all of the resources of your body, emotions, intellect, and intuition, and your time, and put them to work with will power and determination. After you make the commitment to yourself to grow, you can stand back and watch the opportunities come. You may not like all of them, but if you work them through you will benefit in the long run.

When you commit to live wholly and to put your life in balance -- to grow up -- you will do things you haven't done before. You will take a few risks, then more risks, you will stretch beyond your level of complacency and comfort to try something new. You will face your problems and solve them instead of avoiding them. With every risk, every stretch, every solution, comes more growth. With growth comes change. True change involves patience, time, energy, courage, and honest self-observation. You'll need to draw on every bit of these qualities that you have.

At the end of Chapter 2, you evaluated yourself on your development in the four aspects of your life. Now is the time to do it again, to discover where you are after reading this far. Stop and do this now before you read on. Before you answer, search your heart and be as honest as possible with yourself. No one knows you like you do. This is not the time to deny or to hide behind defenses or to impress someone else. So rate yourself, with complete honesty, now.

PLACE AN X ON THE LINE CLOSEST TO YOUR LEVEL
OF DEVELOPMENT

1 2 3 4 5 6 7 8 9 10

PHYSICAL   1------------------------10 Score _____

INTELLECTUAL   1------------------------10 Score _____

EMOTIONAL   1------------------------10 Score _____

SPIRITUAL   1------------------------10 Score _____

I hope you didn't get a 10 on any of these aspects, because then there is no room for growth. Ten would be perfection, but perfection is rarely reached in the human condition. And trying for it puts you in the difficult position of constantly judging yourself and never measuring up to some elusive goal.

No one is perfect, and striving for perfection is not the goal or the reward of growing up. You'll find more happiness and fulfillment in the process of continuing to try to become the best that you can. Then you will appreciate new opportunities to learn, even when they are challenging and difficult. If you gave yourself a score between 1 and 4 in any area, then that gives you a clue to the area(s) that need your immediate attention. The healthiest profile is a score of 7 to 9 in all the areas. This indicates balance, and still allows room for growth. Though the highest score you can get is 40, the total is not as important as the distribution. For instance, if your total is 28, and it's made up of 7 in each aspect, this shows good balance. If your 28 consists of two 9's and two 5's, then there's work to do to get back in balance.

This simple self-evaluation device is one you can use often to check up on yourself and to see what progress you're making. You're the best judge of that. When you feel mature and in balance, then you are. When you feel, know in your heart, intuitively or from your own experience , that something is out of balance, then you're the wise one advising yourself it's time for a correction.

We are always changing so you can use this self-evaluation to check up on yourself often. Do it mentally before you go to sleep at night, or after an argument with someone, or after going to a ball game.

You can also check on your growth progress by reviewing your responses to the ten questions in the Grown-Up Questionnaire in Chapter 2. What patterns do you see? Do your answers show patterns of concern with money, with physical appearance, do they show fear or anger? Do they show respect only for intellectual values? Do they show that you don't love yourself, or that you are overly concerned with others to your own detriment?

What strengths do they show? That you care about others as well as yourself? That you have curiosity, imagination? That you have a grasp on the spiritual significance of life? That you trust your intuition? Do they show a personality in balance? Examine these answers to see what patterns appear. They will give you a key to the areas in which you may want to work on growing up.

THE WHOLE YOU

You are always at the same time a biological organism; a unique feeling, reacting personality; a social being; a creative person; a thinking, remembering, reasoning person; and a spiritual entity.

You have your own private image or self-concept of yourself, which consists of a collection of beliefs about who you are, what you like, and what you are capable of doing. This self-image varies from situation to situation. You may believe that you are a good father, but may lose your self-confidence when you want to ask your boss for a raise.

The key to being as grown up as possible in all situations is to live wholistically, and see yourself as a whole being made up of the four aspects described in this book and their interactions. In everything you do, each of those parts of yourself is affected and each plays a role in shaping how you will respond, how you will take responsibility. Grownups know how to use the strengths in some areas to help out in the other areas and to bring the whole self into balance.

Living wholistically means staying centered, on track. It means being balanced and peaceful within yourself. It means feeling contented, happy, and joyful most of the time. If you get thrown off balance, you know what to do and you can follow through with behavior that will get you back in balance. It means setting realistic goals, then staying focused enough to follow through with what it takes to reach them. It means being able to look at the big picture, like rising above the ground skirmishes in a helicopter to get a better perspective. It means feeling secure that whatever comes along, you can and will handle it.

You have choice over the direction of your life. The only limits you have are the ones you create yourself. You are the creator of your destiny. By believing in yourself you can go beyond your old boundaries and change the world. Then you can experience the joy of knowing that you have the power to make things in your life be as wonderful and beautiful as you want them to be.

Growing up may not sound like much fun. But it really is. The feelings of accomplishing a goal, creating a new product or idea, contributing to the welfare of one human being or the whole planet, can give you a thrill beyond description. The sense of personal mastery, of achievement, of giving can become addictive. Once you begin to recognize the personal satisfaction of bringing joy into another life you will want to continue the practice.

Don't waste your life. Examine your strengths, look at your talents, make a list of your interests, set some priorities, and then see how creatively you can use all of the above to change the world. Start with a positive attitude. Look beyond the obvious. Walk down a different path. Be receptive. Be flexible so you can learn and grow.

GROW UP NOW

Deciding to grow up now includes three steps: cleaning up old business, setting new goals, and monitoring your progress. Cleaning up old business means setting yourself free once and for all from those destructive patterns learned in childhood that hold you back as an adult. It means taking responsibility for who you are now, and no longer using an imperfect childhood as an excuse for dysfunctional behaviors.

Cleaning up old business is an important part of growing

up emotionally. It is necessary to do this before you can grow up in the other aspects because the emotions are the strongest forces shaping how we see, think, believe, and feel physically. You can use the self-evaluation scale to take an inventory and identify what old business needs to be cleaned up. To see how this old behavior or self-talk is interfering with your joy in living, cultivate the ability of self-observation. To review the situation, stand back and be an observer, take yourself out of the picture. Replay the scenes of your recent life in which you were not the person you would like to be.

In observing yourself, be gentle and loving. No judgments, no beating yourself up. That will only make you feel like a child being punished, and punishment doesn't lead to improvement. This is a time to learn, not to feel bad. Sort out what part of you is defensive, frightened, hurt. If it is the hurt, abandoned child within you, nurture the child and negotiate taking a risk to try again. Find ways to build in self-protection, and practice ways to nurture yourself emotionally.

Find the part of you that is out of balance. Is it irrational thoughts? Are memories of deception and betrayal in another situation surfacing again now? Do you have a physical reaction? Are you being pressured to make a decision when you're tired, unprepared, or need more time or information? Do you see yourself having the same strong reaction every time a similar situation occurs? These patterns are the key to the old business that's holding you back.

Focus on one piece of business at a time, and make a commitment to change it. When you've accomplished control in one area, you can come back and do it more easily in the next area. Still being the objective observer, try out several scenarios as possible alternatives to the first area in which you would like to rid yourself of old baggage.

Imagine how you would like to be when one of these

specific situations arises. Imagine several choices, no matter how *far out* they seem at first. Run each of them through your body, feelings, mind, and spirit internal systems. When you find the right answer you will know it. Then you can follow through by practicing this behavior when the situation arises again.

Other important steps in cleaning up old business are forgiveness and acceptance. You can't change the past or relive your childhood with kinder parents or better schools or more money or better health. But if you are carrying around resentment and anger over the things you didn't have as a child, you are refusing to grow up, and you are staying stuck in childish pouting.

If forgiving and making amends for what you have done to harm others seem like vague suggestions or too hard to do alone, you can get help at a community mental health center, with a private therapist, or with a self-help group. There are many *Anonymous* groups now based on the Alcoholics Anonymous model, focusing on specific issues, but they often overlap. There is Emotions Anonymous, CODA (for codependents), ACOA (Adult Children of Alcoholics), AL-ANON (for families of alcoholics), groups for sexual-abuse victims, Overeaters Anonymous, SLAA (Sex and Love Addicts Anon) and new ones are starting every day. Participation is free of cost, except for voluntary donations. They have helped millions of people get a grip on their lives. If you have some dysfunctional behavior in your past you could benefit greatly. When you risk opening yourself up you can make enormous gains.

If you like the twelve-step system that most of these groups follow, get a sponsor and work the steps. You will really help yourself on the road to recovery. Self-help groups are a good adjunct to therapy, but not a subsitiute for professional help.

SETTING GOALS

Hand in hand with cleaning up old business, and saying good-bye to destructive elements from the past, comes the opportunity to set some new goals and make positive changes. You can re-create yourself. No longer slave to your childishness, you have the freedom to be the best you that you can imagine.

If your self-evaluation shows that you're out of balance and you feel your life is not working the way you want it to be, there is a basic set of steps to follow to open the way for growth.

1. **Identify the area that you would like to change**: physical, emotional, intellectual, or spiritual.

2. **Choose specifically what behavior or attitude you want to change**, then write down your goal, i.e., I want to quit smoking, or I want to control my anger, or I want to improve communication in my marriage, or I want to be less critical of people. The more specific you are, the better your chances.

3. **Set a time frame** and then write out a specific goal for the thing you want to change i.e., By September 1, I will stop smoking.

4. Next, **make a list** of what you are going to do to achieve your goal. Include all resources, people, places, and things that will be involved, and how they are going to help you. For the smoking example, your plan may be to enroll in a stop-smoking class and attend all of the sessions, or to go to a hypnotist, read a book on the subject, or whatever else you will commit to doing.

5. Now **write out an affirmation,** a positive statement that you can say over and over to yourself to reprogram your subconscious to support you in making the change. Remember that these statements must include many messages of self-love. I no longer smoke. I care about myself and I will not harm my body in this way. I am going to stop smelling of cigarettes. I hate them and

their smell. I no longer offend the people that I love. I'm going to save the money I spend on cigarettes and take a nice trip. Add your own decisions and reasons. Keep them in positive terms, not as self-criticisms.

6. Finally, you need to **let go of the old behavior.** One way to do this is to visualize yourself in the old situation, then see yourself making the change. Close your eyes and watch yourself throw the pack of cigarettes away. After a meal, instead of lighting up, see yourself going for a walk or brushing your teeth or eating a hard candy. It is a good idea to use both the visualization and the affirmation techniques for a few weeks before you actually schedule the change because then your inner resources will be enlisted to help your efforts.

It is important to write the goals, how to's, and affirmations because the writing helps you to clarify, structure, and make your plan more concrete. Don't try too many major changes at once, or you may feel overwhelmed and give up in defeat. Start with a small change that you will follow through on, then move on to more difficult ones as you master the steps.

Following these steps brings all the powers of your emotional, spiritual, physical, and intellectual self to work to help realize your goal. Your plan will include nurturing yourself emotionally, reprogramming your subconscious, building in good physical habits, and rational decision making.

Changes involving your emotions may take a little more work and time. If you get stuck go to a therapist for some short-term counseling. It can really accelerate your process to have someone to talk to while you are making difficult changes. A nonjudgmental friend can fill this role for you, but a professional can get you back on track when you waiver or take the wrong path and a therapist is trained to separate the wheat from the chaff to facilitate clarity, and give suggestions that can save you a lot of time and heartache.

It is very important to acknowledge your victories and compliment yourself for accomplishing your goals. Get into the habit of being positive and praising yourself. We are all experts in putting ourselves down. Often we are our own worst enemies without realizing it. What we don't do enough is build ourselves up. Start your own cheering section today with you as the charter member.

If you know you are unhappy but you don't know where to start in changing your behavior, here are a few questions to ask yourself. Do I enjoy pain? Am I for or against myself? What is the payoff for continuing to be miserable? Do I enjoy controlling others? Do I have all of the love that I want in my life? What am I afraid of? What do I have to lose by changing? What do I have to gain? What can I change in myself? Am I willing to do it? Remember, wishing for other people to change or to treat you differently is futile. The only person you can control is yourself. Be realistic in your expectations of others, and of others, and of yourself.

OBSTACLES TO GROWING UP

There are several things that will interfere with your growing up, no matter how good your intentions. These include your lifelong programming, expectations, and attitudes. With awareness, you can stop these from thwarting you before they stop you.

EXPECTATIONS are one of the major causes of self-imposed human suffering, especially when they have an element of fantasy and illusion attached. When your focus is on future possibilities, it robs you of living in the present.

Wishes, fantasies and unclear expectations can lead to disappointments and even to grief. You may grieve for the loss of your dream or hope or for a person or situation that was never yours. To avoid getting trapped in expectations, communicate your wants as clearly as possible and get answers when they are available to assist you in realistically evaluating the situation. Unrealistic expectations are not the same as goals for growth. You need to keep your expectations flexible so that if they are not met the way you had hoped, you can give them up or revise them. Sometimes unfulfilled expectations force us to face reality like a cold shower on a winter day. If your self-evaluation scores reveal an area of your life that needs attention, formulate some specific things that you can do to make the changes that you want for yourself.

ATTITUDE is the way you look at a situation. It is the driving force within that triggers a positive or negative reaction to a person or an event. Your attitude is based on your past experiences, beliefs, and values. A person with a positive attitude believes everything is possible and doesn't create false barriers. He or she says, "Why not, let's give it a try."

On the other hand, a person with a negative attitude says, why not, and follows up with a million reasons not to try. Of course she believes that all the pitfalls really exist and stops herself with her self-imposed limitations. A positive attitude is tied closely to hope.

Hope is the internal belief that helps pull us through our darkest hours. I remember when my baby daughter was born prematurely, and the doctors told me that she had only a 2 percent chance out of 100 to live. I desperately held on to the hope of the 2 percent possibility, until she died two days later. My hope didn't save her life, but it kept me going during the crisis.

Hope keeps people going and enables them to overcome tremendous odds. There are many stories of people who survived incredible odds because they kept their hope. When you lose sight of hope you give in to worry and fear and lose sight of the true goal for your life. Without hope you give up.

We have all experienced hurt, betrayal, public embarrassment, heartbreak, pain, and humiliation. Yet some of us pick ourselves up, dust ourselves off and go on, hoping that the future will be better. Others give up hope, and use their hurts as excuses to stop themselves from taking any more risks. They continue to go through the motions of life without really living.

MONITORING YOUR BALANCE

Backsliding happens. You never just get grown up and stay there. Life's road has turns and circles and zigzags. After you get it all together sometimes you forget where you put it. Before you slide too far back, listen to the early warning signs. Use the self-evaluation to see where you are from time to time.

You can learn to recognize the early warning signs of getting out of balance. Your body will warn you by showing illness in its weakest part. Your emotions warn you by becoming extreme and taking control of you instead of you controlling them. Your mind will warn you by being confused and having trouble making decisions or thinking clearly.

Your spirit will warn you by giving you signals that your morals or conscience are being violated. When you slip, go back and review the techniques. Put wholistic techniques to work. Use your mind to observe and analyze, listen to your self-talk. Then make changes in the body through healthier habits. Adjust your emotions by identifying your feelings and choosing to control them. Reprogram your subconscious for what you really want.

Other ways to be sure you are growing in a positive direction involve keeping in touch with your inner self and cultivating your inner wisdom. Review the methods described earlier in this book: listen to your intuition and inner voice, use daily meditation, keep a dream log, become more inner-directed.

Spend some time with yourself regularly, and get to know yourself. When push comes to shove you are all you really have. Become your own best friend. Tell yourself, "No matter what, I will never abandon you....I love you....I think you are terrific....Boy, you did that well....Congratulations!" Acknowledge and appreciate your personal victories.

THE JOY OF GROWING UP

Joy is the signal and the reward of being grown up and in balance, healthy in all four aspects. One of the signposts that tell you that you are on the right road is pervasive positive feelings, and maximum positive regard. You will experience more happiness and joy, an increase in creativity, and find yourself by being more open and vulnerable with others, more trusting, more intimate. You will be a better friend, to yourself and others, be more tolerant, less judgmental, and be able to project loving acceptance to everyone in your life. People will be attracted to you and will feel good in your presence. You will find yourself laughing more, enjoying humor, and having fun.

You will live in the here and now, instead of worrying about the past or waiting for things to get better tomorrow. You'll enjoy today for its own sake. You'll find that you rise above pettiness and have the courage to follow your convictions. Your bad times will be less intense and farther apart.

This growing-up business may sound like a lot of work and no play, but it really isn't. Children in adult bodies don't really have much fun. They are often irresponsible and frequently find themselves in trouble of one kind or another, depressed, lonely, isolated and friendless.

It is a natural human drive to continually push and be pushed to a greater state of growth, like it or not. It is only resisting this growth that gets us into trouble. You have much more to lose by not growing than by facing the truth and going forward, even when you don't know for sure what is on the horizon. Grownups do have a lot of fun, because they are flexible, spontaneous, secure, and creative. You can be too. *Go for it.* You have little to lose and everything to gain.

CHAPTER NINETEEN

A GROWN-UP WORLD

"Even in religious fervor there is a touch of animal heat."
Walt Whitman, *Democratic Vistas*

The world will be grown up when the individuals who inhabit it are grown up. Life is a dynamic, ever-changing process, always in motion, like every cell of all matter. We are moved toward a more complex state of organization. We are always in a process of evolving, maturing, growing.

Consider the current state of post-industrial technology and how it builds upon itself to create newer, more complex forms of communications with computers, fax machines, cellular telephones, automatic cameras, and so forth. The list goes on and on. By the time you read this book the list will be updated by more advanced gadgets.

As the world of technology advances so do human beings evolve, although sometimes the majority of us seem to lag behind the geometric proliferation of technology. We now have machines making machines, but we don't know how to stop rampant starvation, apartheid, drug and alcohol abuse, violent crime, or shameful child abuse that leaves lifetime scars.

We don't know how to make it rain in drought-parched deserts, or to create social programs to take care of basic human needs without creating generations of dependent people. We have walked on the moon, but we aren't very effective in solving international boundary disputes. We try but haven't quite made it yet. What a paradox!

Clearly, we are more comfortable and successful at solving the problems posed by machines than with those that challenge us in the human arena.

Physically we are born the most underdeveloped and dependent new newborns of all species. Birth casts us into an environment that is hostile at the worst, indifferent, and occasionally nurturing at best. We are raised by parents who don't have a clue about modeling and teaching skills in agape, being nonjudgmental, flexible, noncompetitive, and receptive.

The impact of early experiences sets up the patterns of behavior in each individual that will be dealt with or ignored for most of that person's life. The norm for most souls living on the earth today is internal doubt, chaos, confusion, and sometimes terrorism.

This life is often called *the hard path.* Some people believe it is Hell, the embodiment of biblical descriptions of separation and suffering. At birth we are separated from our spiritual family, our entity (soul) mates, our God-oneness, and cast into a hostile place without rule books or memory of our former lessons learned, connections, nurturing support, or encouragement to advance our souls. But we are pushed in the direction of growth by some invisible force.

GROWTH AND EVOLUTION

Like it or not we are all driven, urged, and moved toward a higher level of development and organization in all areas of our experience. Like a newly hatched salmon that instinctively goes to the ocean to live its life, then is driven to return to the exact spot of its birth to spawn, lay eggs, and die, we too are driven to leave our spiritual home, live our lives, and eventually return to be reunited with our spiritual God- self. The drive is called evolution, the process is called growth. In each stage of growth we must master the lessons, challenges, and tasks before we are ready to move on to the next stage or level. We master and transcend that level, take with us the former awareness, and begin to learn the lessons of the next stage.

Ken Wilber, in *Up From Eden,* traces the evolution of the human race and equates it with spiritual evolution. Using his time frames let's look at the processes of evolutionary development in each of our four dimensions, body, emotions, mind, and soul.

Wilber says that the human race emerged between six and three million years ago when pre-humanlike creatures began to emerge. He calls this stage of evolution the archaic stage.

INFANT SOULS

The next stage or the rational stage from 3,000,000 B.C. to about 200,000 B.C. equates with physical and spiritual infancy. The human infant has no language, no sense of body awareness, no emotions, no mental capacity or perceptions. It cannot distinguish itself from the material environment. It has no spiritual consciousness. Imagine life at this time. Cave tribes living an animal-like existence, traveling, hunting and gathering together for warmth, safety, security and protection. Evolved to the point of recognizing that there is safety in numbers, and that together they could slay big game for food and hides, which they could not do alone. Living basically on innate animal instincts. Learning to distinguish themselves from another. Concerned primarily with physical survival and basic physical needs like food, shelter, weather conditions, etc. A good fictional account of life during this stage of human evolution is given in *The Clan of the Cave Bear* by Jean Auel.

In the physical realm the journey of the soul begins here, virtually as an infant, unable to differentiate between itself and it's material environment. It equates to a child between birth and two years.

The psychological or emotional developmental task during this time is to develop basic trust or mistrust. The newborn cannot tell the difference between itself and its caretaker. As it matures it is able to distinguish a mother or primary caretaker. Trust is based on the response to its discomfort of being hungry, wet, soiled, or sick. It increasingly responds to attention and inattention as it masters physical tasks of sitting, crawling, standing, walking, and some primitive language skills. There is no distinctive mental cognition yet, and little memory storage. There is no awareness of its own soul.

BABY SOULS

The next level of development may be called the baby soul level. It equates to a child from ages two to five. Wilber calls this the magical stage. Anthropologically it started around 200,000 B.C. and lasted to 100,000 B.C.

The human race slowly emerged as if from a deep sleep. Language began to develop. More controls were put on personal behaviors, a primitive system of social controls and sanctions started. Medicine began in the form of healing herbs and plants, the dead were buried instead of left to be devoured by predators. The idea of a force greater than man emerged and evolved into worship of animals and objects like the sun, rain, scarabs, and cats who were assigned mystical, magical powers.

Beginning about age two the child can distinguish between the material environment and its body. It lives essentially as a body until about seven years old. Part of the body awareness is testing emotional limits.

The psychological task of this stage is to begin to learn control of bodily functions, specifically of bowels and bladder, and to assert individuality. If the developmental goal of autonomy is not met, shame and doubt surface which must be resolved before moving on to higher forms. It is also the time when urges must be controlled and channeled into socially accepted behaviors. Internalized values can lead to guilt later in life. This is the time when the seeds of shame and guilt are planted to be harvested over and over in adulthood.

From ages four to about seven children develop mental capacities. Piaget calls it the preoperational thinking in which the child masters language skills, insight, and deferred imitation, and representational thinking, meaning that he can think about an object or event even when it is absent. The child is egocentric in that he doesn't know that his viewpoint is only one view among many. He thinks that his viewpoint is the only and correct one.

Children at this age also have what is called magical thinking. They believe that they have special powers and that they can will some thing to happen and it does. It is a dangerous time if a parent leaves or dies. The child in a rebellious rage may have wished the parent dead, and if the parent does die the child writhes in guilt for believing he caused the death.

Baby soul religious beliefs and practices are demonstrated in magical thinking also. For centuries polytheistic beliefs, the worship of many gods with each believed to be in charge of various aspects of human behavior or events in nature, was the preference to cover every possible inevitability. Magical beliefs are still practiced in some places in the world today.

YOUNG SOULS

The next level of development begins at about age seven and goes through puberty, about twelve years of age. Wilber equates it with human development from 100,000 B.C. to around 10,000 B.C. He calls it the mythical period. It is equated with young soul development.

Historically, this was the time when tribes changed from hunting and gathering nomads to settling down in one place and the beginning of farming. Specialization of labor allowed artisans and priests to be supported in their pursuits and the great civilizations of ancient Egypt, China, India, and Africa emerged.

Developmentally, the tasks during these childhood years are to master learning and competence skills, or if not mastered to experience feelings of failure and inferiority. It is also the time to identify with the role of the same-sex parent.

Learning is called concrete operational and includes the ability to classify, multiply, predict, and understand relationships within systems. The child is less egocentric and becomes aware that her point of view is only one among many. She can now understand and follow rules of games. However, she can only deal with concrete objects and events, she cannot yet deal with all of the possible combinations of characteristics, or coordinate systems to form a higher-order system.

Spiritually, the young soul is less concerned with eternal salvation, and more with impressing other members of the congregation with a new dress or suit. They tend to have a yuppie mentality, and are more concerned with impression management of their external persona than with transcendent spiritual values. They are moving more toward a mental perspective, but still engulfed in ego needs, in receiving recognition, applause, and external validation of their worth.

MATURE SOULS

Beginning adolescence heralds the period that Wilber calls the rational period, starting about 10,000 B.C., and lasting about 1,000 B.C. What distinguishes this period is the beginning of philosophy and theology. Until now thinking had been based mostly on mythology or magic. This great change marked the beginning of the modern age and parallels a child's mental development from ages nine through adolescence.

Around the sixth century B.C. the Golden Age of Greece dawned, and Socrates, Plato, and Aristotle emerged to influence thought for coming centuries in the Western World. Life was more settled and civilized. Of course we still had wars, and killed millions in the name of God as we still do. Only now it is a little scarier because we have such a tremendous capacity to destroy the entire planet with a single switch.

The psychological developmental tasks of adolescence are to deal with issues of sexual and personality identity. It is the time to decide who he is, sort out values, choose an occupation, and make plans for his life as an adult. The developmental crisis is between intimacy and isolation. Once he can be intimate then he can relate in a positive, loving, emotionally available way to a mate.

By the end of adolescence a maturely grown-up person is capable of trusting, autonomous, can take appropriate initiative, is competent, and can be intimate. On the other hand, a person could be mistrustful, full of shame and doubt, guilt ridden, with feelings of failure and isolation. Most people have a combination of these issues to work on. Remember you must work through issues at the earliest levels of development before you can move on to the next level. So if you can determine where you're stuck, you know where you need to begin to work and catch-up.

Piaget calls intellectual development in adolescence the formal operational period. The child now can think hypothetically and carry out systematic tests of the various possible explanations of specific events, ruling out possible causes until he finds the correct cause. The formal operational period continues to develop into adulthood. Spiritually a mature soul is involved with sorting out material and ego connected values with the work of the soul. Identity issues involve seeking balance, transcending the ordinary, and beginning to explore higher inner states like the superconscious.

OLD SOULS

The majority of souls on the planet now are young souls and mature souls. The time frame is from 1,000 B.C. to the present time. We are collectively evolving toward a higher level of development. Time is accelerating and evolution seems to be moving at a faster pace. As we evolve to higher levels we will have more interaction with older souls. Older souls transcend the mind and reach out for higher levels of inner awareness.

There are old souls among us now. The lives of older souls are spent in service and as teachers for younger souls. They have resolved the problems of the earlier levels of development. They are not concerned with impressing or approval from other people. Their values include freedom to use their time as they see as most effective. They like to be in a natural setting as much as possible. Their physical systems are often sensitive and they are rarely substance abusers.

They have a charisma that attracts people and animals to them. They radiate a sense of inner peace and tranquility that rises above the usual day-to-day frustrations of most people. They have an innate kindness and flexibility that helps set a positive example for others.

There is no evolutionary time frame because they are ahead of their time. They are parallel to mature adulthood. The developmental tasks are being productive and having internal integrity. The conflict is to fall into stagnation and/or despair. They have a tendency to become depressed.

Their intelligence is in the form of wisdom, an internal knowing that includes all systems. They are highly intuitive with their intuition based on the wisdom of the ages. They can tap into this wisdom at will through meditation and prayer. They are often psychic and have extrasensory capacities which they may or may not use to heal and help others.

Spiritually, when they awaken they are attracted to the inner life and find peace, joy, harmony and a sense of universal connectedness within. They know they are not alone only temporarily separated from the path but still supported, and surrounded by other loving spirits.

WHERE DO WE GO FROM HERE?

There are souls now living on this planet who are at every level of personal evolution. They can evolve in a state of harmony and balance if they flow with their growth and don't resist. Some salmon fight swimming upstream every inch of the way, others take it in stride and enjoy the trip.

We are each a combination of the animal and the divine. It isn't what is handed to us in life that counts, it's what we do with it. Eleanor Roosevelt said, "It is always better to light a candle than to curse the darkness."

We are internally motivated to move toward union, reunion, and wholeness. It is our inner spiritual mandate. We seek atonement (at-one-ment) with the positive forces in the universe. As you strive for wholeness you will realize that your journey upstream is a solitary one: there may be other fish in the same water, but the swim you swim you do on your own. How long it takes and how gracefully you do it is entirely up to you.

You can empower yourself to look for and exercise choices and options that will enhance your growth. Your possibilities are limitless. We human beings rarely reach our potential. We get scared or set limits that may outwardly feel safe, but in fact constrict and restrain, even trap us. Set yourself free, stretch a little further, try new and different things, broaden your horizons, accelerate your evolution.

Finally, the boundaries between countries on this fragile planet are shrinking. We share finite natural resources. We also share air, the ozone layer that protects from cancer causing ultraviolet rays, and the oceans and seas that flow between us. When the rain forests are cut down in Brazil the entire world is affected. We need to work together to achieve balance between countries, just as we do within us. When one child dies of disease or starvation anywhere on the planet, it is my child that dies, it is me that dies, it is your child that dies, it is you that dies. We are all connected by bonds that are invisible to the naked eye, but exist as surely as the wind exists, or a spot over the horizon.

Our archaic shortsighted vision that allows petty cultural differences to separate us must be reduced and eliminated. All human beings share human emotions of hurt, pain, suffering, happiness, and joy. We all are bound by the physical demands of our bodies for food, shelter, elimination, health. We all have the capacity to learn and to develop our minds. We all have souls. We must respect the differences, and celebrate the similarities that we share with all other human beings on the planet. We need each other, we are each other.

We are all evolving together. As you seek wholeness, balance, harmony and peace within yourself, expand that loving light from your heart outward to every other soul in the world.

Peace.

Index

Order Form

La Mariposa Press
P.O. Box 13221
Tucson, Arizona 85732-3221 USA

(602) 326-9292
Fax: (602) 326-3305

Date_____ Purchase order number_____

Customer name _____

Address_____

City_____ State_____ Zip_____

Telephone_____ Fax _____

Ship to: Name_____

         Address_____

         City_____ State_____ Zip_____

Quantity	Title	Each	Total
	How To Grow Up When You're Grown Up (Paperback)	$14.95	
	How To Grow Up When You're Grown Up (Hardback)	$24.95	
	Letting Go With Love: The Grieving Process (Paperback)	$12.95	
	Letting Go With Love: The Grieving Process (Hardback)	$22.95	
	Letting Go With Love: The Grieving Process (Spanish, Paperback)	$15.95	
	Letting Go With Love: The Grieving Process (Audio Cassettes)	$15.95	
	The Legacy of Suicide (Video Cassette, VHS -- 55 Minutes)	$59.95	
		Subtotal	
	Please add $3.00 shipping and handling per book		
	Arizona sales tax (7.2%) *Arizona residents only*		
		Total	

Payment: ☐ Check enclosed Amount _____
Credit card: ☐ VISA ☐ MasterCard ☐ American Express

Credit card number_____

Signature_____ Exp. date_____